The trespass of the sign

Ann Ferguson

The trespass of the sign

Deconstruction, theology and philosophy

KEVIN HART

Lecturer in Literary Studies
Deakin University

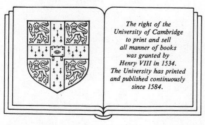

CAMBRIDGE UNIVERSITY PRESS

Cambridge

New York   Port Chester   Melbourne   Sydney

Published by the Press Syndicate of the University of Cambridge
The Pitt Building, Trumpington Street, Cambridge CB2 1RP
40 West 20th Street, New York, NY 10011-4211, USA
10 Stamford Road, Oakleigh, Melbourne 3166, Australia

First published 1989
First paperback edition 1991

Printed in Great Britain at the University Press, Cambridge

British Library cataloguing in publication data

Hart, Kevin
The trespass of the sign.
1. Christian theology. Deconstruction
I. Title
230'.01

Library of Congress cataloguing in publication data

Hart, Kevin, 1954–
The trespass of the sign: deconstruction, theology and philosophy /
Kevin Hart.
    p.   cm.
Bibliography.
Includes indexes.
ISBN 0-521-35481-1
1. Theology. 2. Deconstruction. 3. Metaphysics. I. Title.
BT83.8.H37   1989
230'.01–dc 19   88–29237 CIP

National Library of Australia cataloguing in publication data

Hart, Kevin, 1954–
The trespass of the sign: deconstruction, theology and philosophy
Bibliography.
Includes index.
ISBN 0-521-35481-1.
1. Theology. 2. Deconstruction. 3. Metaphysics. I. Title.
230'.01

ISBN 0 521 35481 1 hardback
ISBN 0 521 42382 1 paperback

CE

ad maiorem Dei gloriam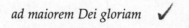

Contents

Contents

Preface

This study poses two questions, seeks to demonstrate that they are intimately related, then examines several aspects of this relationship. One question – What is deconstruction? – is very new, while the other – What is the relationship between metaphysics and theology? – is very old indeed. Upon my reading, however, some of the earliest answers to the second question also partially answer the first. If this is so, metaphysics, theology and deconstruction have always existed in a covert economy; and in realising this, we can come to a better understanding of all three.

There is little doubt that 'deconstruction' is the most illusive of these three words. It has been endlessly quoted out of context, grafted onto various critical and political projects, become the butt of parodies, and been pronounced in so many tones, from contempt to reverence, that it cannot be formally defined without some remainder, however small. In fact the fate of the word 'deconstruction' offers one of the best indications of what deconstruction is: the demonstration that no text can be totalised without a supplement of signification. That this definition gives no hint of the wider institutional and cultural import of deconstruction points to its own need for supplementation. Yet the difficulty of pinning down 'deconstruction' is not only a consequence of the state of affairs the word describes but also a matter of polemics, politics and influence.

Over the last twenty years or so the writings of Jacques Derrida have acted like an intellectual yeast. Very few people have actually read such large, imposing tomes as *Of grammatology*, *Dissemination* and *Glas* from beginning to end, yet everyone, it seems, has been influenced by what they say. After all, reading Derrida is nothing if not arduous: without a detailed knowledge of a certain philosophical tradition – one that includes Kant, Hegel, Nietzsche, Husserl and Heidegger – and a close familiarity with writers such as Blanchot, Jabès, Mallarmé, Ponge and Sollers, one has small hope of following Derrida's essays in the kind of detail which they require. For Derrida is preeminently a 'slow reader', someone who, as Nietzsche put it, reads 'slowly, deeply, looking cautiously before and aft, with reservations, with doors left open, with delicate eyes and fingers',[1] and not to know *what* he is reading is often to miss the points he develops *by* that reading. Even so, Derrida's influence has not so much been by way of slow reading as through digests and popularising commentaries, through discipleship and antagonism, journalism and polemics. Little wonder, then, that Derrida's name has been linked with views he does not hold and with positions he has been at pains to criticise.

Although much of this study takes its bearings from specific texts by Derrida, and while I argue for a particular reading of his work, I should make it clear that my abiding interest is in bringing deconstruction into conversation with Christian theology rather than confirming Derrida's individual programme. True, Derrida is aware of the *'religious* aspects' of deconstruction;[2] but Christian theology does not form a distinctive part of his intellectual itinerary. A number of thematic links between Derrida's writings and Judaism are unmistakable, yet it is easy enough to uncover similar connections between Derrida and many cultural and political movements. What is remarkable in Derrida's work is his persistent translation of local thematic concerns into structural questions, and these inevitably touch on Christianity. That this translation will always leave behind a supplement is one reason why much of this book is taken up with reading Derrida's exemplary writers as well as the mystics and theologians he does not discuss.

There are two common ways in which deconstruction has been framed: as a refinement of the Nietzschean doctrine that God is dead, and as a displaced negative theology. Upon my reading neither view is correct, for deconstruction's target is metaphysics, not theology as such. A difficulty immediately arises, though, concerning the scope of metaphysics. On the one

---

1 Friedrich Nietzsche, *Daybreak*, trans. R. J. Hollingdale (Cambridge: Cambridge University Press, 1982), p. 5.
2 Jacques Derrida, *Mémoires*, trans. Cecile Lindsay, Jonathan Culler and Eduardo Cadava (New York: Columbia University Press, 1986), p. 16.

hand, Derrida contends that metaphysics has a far greater extension than has ever been acknowledged. And on the other hand, he develops a transcendental argument that any discourse will contain the means to call its metaphysical claims into question. What Derrida offers us, in short, is a way to trace and circumscribe the metaphysics within theology. So deconstruction is not an attack against theology but an answer to the theological demand for a 'non-metaphysical theology'. ?

This answer is far from final, however. For Derrida argues that any attempt simply to pass beyond metaphysics remains entangled in that metaphysics. 'Non-metaphysical theology' may mark the closure of some philosophical and theological traditions yet it can never entirely escape their determinations. It comes as no surprise, then, to discover that most attempts to develop a non-metaphysical theology are destined to fail before they begin. In my view the strongest attempts are made by the mystics, especially those who develop negative theologies, such as Pseudo-Dionysius. Contrary to the Thomist tradition, I argue that negative theology does not merely correct positive (or metaphysical) theology but supplements it at its ground and origin. Deconstruction may not be a negative theology, as Derrida repeatedly and rightly insists, but negative theology may deconstruct positive theology. In general terms, deconstruction helps to clarify the concept 'non-metaphysical theology', while its strategy of using language 'under erasure' illuminates particular moves and attitudes in mystical texts.

From Descartes to Russell, mysticism has often been represented as philosophy's 'other', as that which must at all costs be excluded from philosophical discourse. Deconstruction enables us to trace the effects within a discourse of precisely this kind of exclusion; and to do so gives us a greater understanding of both 'philosophy' and 'mysticism'. But this situation also has consequences for deconstruction; and in my final chapters I explore the troubled connections between deconstruction and mysticism in the work of two philosophers whose work has greatly influenced Derrida: Immanuel Kant and Martin Heidegger.

Many colleagues and friends have discussed with me the themes and arguments developed here. For intellectual stimulation and encouragement, my warm thanks go to Damien Byers, Richard Campbell, Max Charlesworth, Simon During, Howard Felperin, Paul Kane, Henry Krips, Philip and Jenna

Mead, and Brian Scarlett. My thanks are also due to Bernard Bartl for a partial translation of Kant's *Der Streit der Philosophischen Fakultät mit der Theologischen* and a complete translation of his *Vom einem neuerdings erhobenen vornehmen Ton in der Philosophie*. I am grateful to Robin Derricourt for all his help in overseeing the book's progress, and to Trudi Tate for her meticulous care in copy editing the typescript. It is a pleasure to offer particular thanks to Kevin Presa for sustained help with this project over a number of years. Finally, my greatest debt is to Stephanie Trigg whose advice and encouragement mark every page of the book.

I | Confrontation

I will not bring you into a strange country; but I will perhaps
teach you that you are a stranger in your own country.

Nicholas Malebranche

1 | Interpretation, signs and God

1 Philosophy and the Fall

Upon meeting Adam in the eighth heaven of Paradise, Dante
has no need to voice his questions, for, as Adam explains, the
poet's intentions are already perfectly reflected in the 'veracious
Mirror' of God.[1] A redeemed soul, entirely consonant with
God's will, Adam knows Dante's thoughts with far more certainty than Dante can know the most elementary truth; his
perception of the poet's mind is immediate, unhindered by
language; and when he begins to answer, explaining the true
cause of the Fall, Adam's hermeneutic mastery is no less complete. He deftly distinguishes between *signum* and *res significata*,
informing us that the eating of the fruit merely indicated what
was at issue, namely 'the trespass of the sign', a failure to
observe the proper limits assigned to man by God. In short,
Adam offers us a model of perfect understanding, one in which
language can be mastered and in which intentions can easily be
recovered, whether human or divine. How ironic, then, that the
ideal Adam represents is withheld from us precisely because of
Adam's sin. For as the canto explains, although Adam's trespass
was chiefly moral in character it was also a trespass of the
linguistic sign – a desire for unmediated knowledge – and the
sign of this disobedience is none other than the mutability of all
signs. In Paradise, wholly one with God who stands above
language as the 'Alpha and Omega of all scripture', Adam now
enjoys immediate knowledge in the manner approved by God,
and for him interpretation poses no problem. On earth,
however, the consequences of the Fall are still felt: man is no
longer the master of signs but is frequently mastered by them,

1 Dante, *Paradiso*. The Temple Classics (1899; rpt. London: J. M. Dent and Sons,
1965), Canto XXVI, line 106.

3

and the *Commedia* shows us many who have been damned precisely because they allowed themselves to be mastered by signs. One of these is Master Adam, the Florentine counterfeiter, whose very art is a trespass of the sign, the effacing of the difference between a sign and the sign of a sign. Dante's point in the *Commedia* is unmistakable: the proliferation of signs caused by Adam and increased by those such as Master Adam can be arrested only by a belief that Christ, the New Adam, is the faithful sign of God. Without the presence of God, in Paradise or on earth, there can be no hope of understanding oneself, others, or texts. One would be lost in a maze of signs, with no possibility of distinguishing true from false.

We see here, in miniature, a very familiar picture of the relations between interpretation, signs and God. Dante's account is broadly Thomist in its emphases, but its roots can easily be traced back to Augustine, Paul, and ultimately to Greek metaphysics. Certain details, such as the view that language fell with man, are elaborations upon a far more persistent theme – that God guarantees the possibility of determinate meaning. The Fall may establish the human need to interpret yet it simultaneously sets firm limits to interpretation. No longer in harmony with God, this world becomes a chiaroscuro of presence and absence; everywhere one looks, there are signs of a divine presence that has withdrawn and that reveals itself only in those signs. Whether in nature or scripture, these signs must be interpreted, yet only in ways which acknowledge that timeless truths wait behind them and can be separated from them. Seen in this way, the sign is always a representation of a presence which precedes it, a passage from one presence to another, from infinite to finite mind. More generally, we can also see here the rudiments of a common theory of communication, equally applicable to discourse between humans as between God and humans: a presence represents itself by means of signs which are then recovered by another presence. Within this system, remarks Jacques Derrida, 'The sign is always a sign of the Fall';[2] and from this curious observation we can begin to draw out the problem which will interest us, in various ways, throughout this study.

2 Jacques Derrida, *Of grammatology*, trans. and preface Gayatri Chakravorty Spivak (Baltimore: Johns Hopkins University Press, 1976), p. 283.

Before anything else, though, we need to define some of Derrida's key terms. Quite clearly, the concept 'sign' presupposes a concept of presence: a sign is always a *sign of* something present or presentable. Following Heidegger, Derrida grants 'presence' a very wide extension, ranging from its ontological sense (an object's temporal status and the determination of Being as presence) to its epistemological sense (a subject's presence to another subject and to itself). He then defines 'metaphysics' as any science of presence. Specific problems arising from the enormous reach that Derrida attributes to metaphysics will concern us later, but we need to be sure now, in general terms, what is claimed here and what is not. True, Derrida wants to argue that *all* metaphysics is the 'metaphysics of presence'; but he does not contend that metaphysics forms a homogeneous *unity*. On the contrary, he argues that there is no neat boundary which surrounds metaphysics, and much of his time is spent in showing the various ways in which that boundary is divided. If this is so, the question arises as to the relations between metaphysics and other discourses – art, history, literature, politics, and so on – and the discourse of immediate concern here is theology. Hence our guiding question: how are metaphysics and theology related?

Let us approach the question, first of all, from the side of theology. However it is read, the Adamic myth is a story of proliferating dualisms or, more precisely, proliferating hierarchies. The Fall from innocence to experience not only divides the world but also introduces a definite structure of value: we fall from an undifferentiated knowledge of good to a differentiated and fatal knowledge of good and evil. From God's presence we pass to His absence; from immediacy to mediation; from the perfect congruence of sign and referent to the gap between word and object; from fullness of being to a lack of being; from ease and play to strain and labour; from purity to impurity; and from life to death. The list could be extended indefinitely, but instead we shall try to understand something of the consequences of the Fall, and for this we turn to Augustine, the very theologian to whom we owe the concept 'original sin'. After a long discussion of the sin in Eden, Augustine turns to consider its radical import, and does so by way of endorsing the ascetic rigours of the *via negativa*: 'Accordingly, two cities have been formed by two loves: the earthly by the love of self, even to the contempt of God; the

5

heavenly by the love of God, even to the contempt of self'.[3] After the Fall, Augustine says, we are creatures of pathos, living in exile, in what he calls a *regio dissimilitudinis*, a land of unlikeness.[4] This figure repeats the first – the earthly city is *unlike* the heavenly city – yet, when placed in context, it also opens out in another direction, depicting human language as a region of unlikeness.[5] Language, too, has fallen – from the proper to the figural – with the consequence that intention and interpretation will often fail to connect. Our difficulties controlling tropes, their tendency to trespass over *our* signs, is a sign of our trespass of *God's* sign: even the scriptures can merely point to the truth and never incarnate it.

If the first figure tells us something about the psychological burdens of the *via negativa*, that one must deny the self in order to draw close to God, the second leads to the epistemological problem of negative theology: how to talk properly of God when language can only improperly signify Him. 'Have we spoken or announced anything worthy of God?', Augustine asks, 'Rather I feel that I have done nothing but wish to speak: if I have spoken, I have not said what I wished to say'.[6] It is only after the Fall that a theology is needed. We need an account of what God is, and of the differences between God and us, so that we can try to do what God would have us do: we need, in short, to develop a positive theology. Yet developing an explanation of God's actions in the world is only one part of the task; we need to ponder what it is to speak of this God whose ways are not our ways, we need to analyse our talk of God, and this involves us in negative theology. Augustine is quick to reassure us that God accepts our praise, imperfectly expressed though it be; but his conception of language as fallen leads us to see that positive theology requires a supplement of negative theology in order to check that our discourse about God is, in fact, about *God* and not just about human images of God.

3 Augustine, *The city of God*, trans. Marcus Dods and introd. Thomas Merton (New York: The Modern Library, 1950), p. 477.
4 Augustine, *Confessions*, trans. R. S. Pine-Coffin (Harmondsworth: Penguin, 1961), Book VII, Chapter 10, pp. 146–47.
5 This point is taken up in more detail in Margaret W. Ferguson's challenging article, 'Saint Augustine's region of unlikeness: the crossing of exile and language', *Georgia Review*, 29 (1975), pp. 842–64.
6 Augustine, *On Christian doctrine*, trans. D. W. Robertson Jr. (New York: Library of Liberal Arts, 1958), Book I, vi (pp. 10–11).

The relations between positive and negative theology, between the *via negativa* and negative theology, between negative theology and Derrida's theory of supplementation – all these will concern us in due course, as will the status of our guiding concept, 'fall'. But we do not need to invoke negations of any kind to recognise that Christian theology is, on one level at least, a semiology. I do not mean this in the sense whereby Nietzsche dismissed moral judgement as nonsense yet allowed that 'as *semeiotics* it remains of incalculable value'.[7] I mean, rather, that because it regards God as a presence who, after the Fall, represents Himself and is in turn represented by signs, Christian theology is always a study of signs. If we picture God according to His attributes – as omnipotent, omniscient and omnipresent – we are plainly imagining Him as a plenitude of presence, both ontologically and epistemologically. By dint of Adam's sin, though, God is for us an *absent* presence, and so any theology, whatever else it is, must also be a semiology. In natural theology God is approached through the natural signs of His absent presence, and signs are equally crucial in revealed theology.[8] '*Videmus nunc per speculum in ænigmate, tunc autem facie ad faciem*', wrote Paul in what is, perhaps, the single most influential remark on signs and faith. 'In this life we can comprehend God only in the mirror of faith', as one common gloss puts it; but another, just as common, places the accent elsewhere: 'we can know God only imperfectly, reflected in the mirror of language'. And for this reason theology must always be, in the precise etymological sense of the word, a *speculative* discourse.

If the Fall introduced a gap between man and God, words and objects, thereby making signs the indispensable and imperfect vehicle for any knowledge, religious or otherwise, the economy of salvation was also worked out according to signs, specifically verbal signs. Thus Christ was held to be the Word of God, the mediator between man and God, the one perfect Sign in an

---

7 Friedrich Nietzsche, *Twilight of the idols and the anti-Christ*, trans. and ed. R. J. Hollingdale (Harmondsworth: Penguin, 1968), p. 55.
8 Thus Karl Barth: 'He unveils Himself as the One He is by veiling Himself in a form which He Himself is not. He uses this form distinct from Himself, He uses its work and sign, in order to be objective in, with and under this form, and therefore to give Himself to us to be known. Revelation means the giving of signs.' *Church dogmatics*, ed. G. W. Bromiley and T. F. Torrance (Edinburgh: T. and T. Clark, 1957), Vol. II, i, p. 52.

imperfect world of signs. Like other signs, Christ is both signifier and signified, body and soul. But Christ is also unlike other signs, for here the signified – God – is perfectly expressed in the signifier. He is at once inside and outside the sign system; since Christ *is* God, what He signifies is signified in and of itself: He is what Derrida calls a 'transcendental signified'.[9] Yet Christ is also a transcendental signifier. Miraculously formed, His body is uncontaminated by the very Fall which required the proliferation of signs and the distinction between presence and the sign of a presence.

The story of the Fall has been used to illuminate all manner of topics which have attracted philosophers. Questions concerning the nature of choice, obedience, guilt, the will, man's natural state, not to mention the origin of language, have often dilated around Adam and Eve. But arguably Derrida is one of only two philosophers who have taken the Adamic myth as providing some sort of explanation as to the genesis of philosophy as such. The other is Hegel, and a comparison and contrast between them is instructive. Both agree that the story illustrates that natural unity is disturbed from within rather than from without, and both agree that this is the condition of possibility for philosophy. For the moment, we shall remain with Hegel. 'The serpent was the tempter', he remarks, 'but the truth is, that the step into opposition, the awakening of consciousness, follows from the very nature of man; and the same history repeats itself in every son of Adam'.[10] Here, as elsewhere, Hegel affirms that what the story of the Fall represents figuratively as a contingent

9 Upon Derrida's understanding, the 'transcendental signified' is an imagined fixed point outside the system of signification. Derrida makes it quite clear that God (in the Hegelian sense as pure thought thinking pure thought) is a paradigm of the transcendental signified: see *Positions*, trans. Alan Bass (Chicago: University of Chicago Press, 1981), pp. 19–20. For further discussion of the transcendental signified see *Of grammatology*, pp. 49–50 and *Writing and difference*, trans. and introd. Alan Bass (London: Routledge and Kegan Paul, 1978), p. 136.

10 G. W. F. Hegel, *Logic* (1830), trans. William Wallace with foreword by J. N. Findlay (Oxford: Clarendon Press, 1975), p. 43. The Hegelian removal of the Fall from history to a realm of transcendental truth is anticipated by Kant in his *Religion within the limits of reason alone*, trans. and introd. by Theodore M. Greene and Hoyt H. Hudson (New York: Harper and Row, 1934), p. 38. For a more detailed discussion of Hegel's account of the Fall and its philosophical implications see M. J. Inwood, *Hegel*, The Arguments of the Philosophers (London: Routledge and Kegan Paul, 1983), pp. 93–112.

event is, in fact, a necessary event in the life of the Spirit.[11] By dint of an essential rupture, we pass from a merely natural and immediate unity – an abstract identity – to a disunity, and from instinct we pass to reason. Fallen from innocence, we seek knowledge and, as Hegel tells us, 'Philosophy is knowledge'.[12] The philosopher can truly affirm *O felix culpa!* for, in Hegel's view, the Fall not only hastens our ascent to God but does so through the emergence of philosophy. It is on the basis of this view that Hegel confidently claims that 'Philosophy is thus the true theodicy'.[13] For Hegel, the philosopher's task is the dialectical sublation of this first rupture and of all consequent ruptures: with the *Aufhebung's* relentless movement of idealisation, identity and difference are gathered into a higher identity. Passing through language, through 'the *sign* in general', as its natural medium, the Spirit constitutes the sign itself as an identity of an identity and a difference, that is, as an identity of signified and signifier.[14] The sign is therefore a means whereby the Spirit seeks to achieve self-realisation in an ultimate plenitude of presence. And insofar as philosophy is the most concrete manifestation of this self-realisation, the sign is once more conceived, within philosophy, with respect to presence – as a passage leading to presence.

Derrida contests neither the importance nor the historical necessity of seeing philosophy this way. On the contrary, he accords Hegel pre-eminent status as philosopher by virtue of the rigour and passion with which he seeks to suspend difference in identity, the other in the same. It is easy to understand, and to share, this admiration. Unlike all who preceded him, Hegel attempted to overcome difference within both metaphysics and history. Yet Hegel's is not simply a discourse against difference: the dialectic thinks absolute difference, makes it part of its trajectory, and never excludes it. The upshot of the labyrinthine

11 See, for example, *The phenomenology of mind*, trans. and introd. J. B. Baillie (New York: Harper and Row, 1967), pp. 579, 771; *Lectures on the philosophy of religion*, trans. E. B. Speirs and J. Burdon Sanderson (1895; rpt. London: Routledge and Kegan Paul, 1962), Vol. I, p. 276 and Vol. II, p. 203.

12 Hegel, *Logic*, p. 44.

13 Hegel, *Lectures on the history of philosophy*, trans. E. S. Haldane and Frances H. Simson (1892; rpt. London: Routledge and Kegan Paul, 1955), Vol. III, p. 546.

14 Hegel, *Science of logic*, trans. A. V. Miller (London: George Allen and Unwin, 1969), p. 729. Derrida discusses this passage in 'The pit and the pyramid:

arguments of Book 2 of the *Science of logic*, 'The doctrine of essence', is that both identity and difference are mediated, within themselves, by their other, such that each *contains* the other. And if this is so, identity and difference are not finally different. There is a fundamental *identity* of identity and difference, and this supplies the ground of metaphysics, taken as a *telos* or, after the fact, as an *archè*.[15] Difference is not eliminated here, but identity is revealed to be logically prior to it. What is worked out synchronically in the magisterial *Science of logic* is established diachronically in Hegel's various lectures on history and the histories of philosophy, religion and art. There Hegel traces the dialectic's troubled passage from abstract identity, through the emergence of difference (whose equivalent in Christian soteriology is the Fall), to the spirit's gradual ascent to ultimate self-presence and self-mediating identity in God, the *itinerarium mentis in deum*. Philosophy will therefore have the same content as the Christian religion, yet will be cast in a different form. Whereas religious knowledge remains at the level of representation *(Vorstellung)*, expressed in myths and images, philosophy seeks out their cognitive basis, the Notion *(Begriff)*. So although philosophy and religion are acknowledged to differ they ultimately cohere in a deep identity. The dialectic thus proceeds in a double movement: it attempts the classical metaphysical exigency of resolving differences into the *archè* or the *telos*, and seeks to gather all history – the difference between the *archè* and the *telos* – into an ultimate self-present and self-mediating identity.

While Derrida affirms the historical necessity of this idea of philosophy, he also argues that it can never be realised. The fall from full presence, he contends, has always already occurred: the concept of a full presence, of an ideal self-mediating identity which absolutely precedes or succeeds all difference, is a delusion. We have seen that in the *Paradiso* Adam is the sole created being who stands outside language. He does so by determining language, then by escaping its determinations. And we have

introduction to Hegel's semiology' in *Margins of philosophy*, trans. Alan Bass (Chicago: University of Chicago Press, 1982).

15 See *Science of logic*, Book 2, Chap. 2 , Part C (esp. p. 431). Cf. Hegel's earlier formulation that 'the Absolute itself is the identity of identity and non-identity', *The difference between Fichte's and Schelling's system of philosophy*, trans.

also seen a patent instance of what this makes possible: that Adam can elicit a purely ideal meaning from Dante's mind. Whilst this may seem a fanciful example it is not so far removed from Husserl's account of meaning as a purely interior soliloquy, as detailed in the *Logical investigations*.[16] Interestingly enough, the first thing Husserl does is to distinguish between two kinds of sign, the expressive (which carries its own meaning) and the indicative (in which there is a gap between empirical sign and ideal content). And this move is followed by a concerted attempt to deny indicative signs an essential role in constituting meaning. Husserl's account of meaning, in Derrida's view, is a particularly rigorous instance of a far more general philosophical desire to explain meaning wholly by way of simples or moments of undivided presence. So, whether we are talking of Husserl or Dante, philosophical essays or literary texts, all discourse appears to be structured by a distinction between presence and a fall from presence. And one common instance of this distinction is between presence and sign.

This distinction between presence and sign will serve as an example of Derrida's general argument. The argument has both a negative and a positive side: it begins as a critique of the 'metaphysics of presence' and ends by proposing a new way of reading all those discourses which have been dominated by that metaphysics. The negative side has attracted the greater attention, often being taken to be the only thing which concerns Derrida, so I shall take a little more time with it. Derrida wishes to argue two related points: that a discourse is metaphysical to the extent to which it claims that presence absolutely precedes representation, and that this can occur in many ways and be phrased in many different vocabularies. For example, the distinction between the intelligible and the sensible may not always be used to promote metaphysical positions, but it becomes metaphysical when intelligibility is taken to mean 'present to consciousness'. Similarly, it is possible to use the

H. S. Harris and Walter Cerf (Albany: State University of New York Press, 1977), p. 83.
16 Husserl draws the distinction between expression and indication in Chapter 1 §1 of Investigation I. See his *Logical investigations*, trans. J. N. Findlay (London: Routledge and Kegan Paul, 1970). Derrida takes this distinction as his point of entry in *Speech and phenomena*, trans. and introd. David B. Allison with a preface by Newton Garver (Evanston: Northwestern University Press, 1973).

Saussurian vocabulary of signifier and signified without being wholeheartedly committed to metaphysics, yet if one uses 'signified' to mean a concept that is present to consciousness then one is complicit with metaphysics. A discourse is metaphysical, then, if the concept is fashioned as a moment of pure presence, and the sign as representing the concept in its absence. Within these terms, the sign *fails* to represent the concept purely and simply; it introduces the complicating elements of materiality and difference which serve to delay and defer the expected recovery of the concept. This, accordingly, is the basis of the case for valuing the concept over the sign. However, argues Derrida, the sign's failure is structurally determined, and this is the starting-point for his case against the metaphysics of presence.

I begin by making two straightforward points: first, it is a structural characteristic of the sign that it can always be repeated; and second, what we *mean* by 'sign' is that it is what it is in the absence of its animating presence. Now the distinction between 'presence' and 'sign' is a version of the more general distinction between the intelligible and the sensible. Since it always functions in the absence of a presence, the sign has no self-presence by which its intelligible content can withstand the accidents of empirical differences. The sign always works with *two* modes of repetition: its task, as understood metaphysically, is to repeat its originating presence, in order that the intelligible be repeated in the sensible. But the sign, since it is a *sign*, is also open to being repeated itself, so the sensible mark can always be repeated outside its original context. Indeed, the sign cannot be what it is without this possibility of repetition. The first mode of repetition seeks to preserve the sign's intelligible content, while the second mode of repetition puts the identity of that intelligible content in jeopardy. And the problem is that the sign can never put that second mode of repetition out of play: the metaphysical task of the sign is forever stymied by the sign itself.

We need to distinguish between different assumptions here. The first is to do with context: 'no meaning can be determined out of context, but no context permits saturation'.[17] The second concerns repetition: that there is a 'logic which links repetition

---

17 Derrida, 'Living on', in Harold Bloom *et al.*, *Deconstruction and criticism* (London: Routledge and Kegan Paul, 1979), p. 81.

to alterity'.[18] It is important to recognise that the second claim is not that a sign *does* change its meaning if repeated but that a sign's meaning is always *open* to change. The signature on a bank note, for instance, may be repeated endlessly, but its meaning will not change unless it is repeated in a context other than that of a bank note. Yet the signature is certainly open to change; its very structure allows for the possibility of its being repeated outside its original context – by a doodler or a counterfeiter, for example. So, the sign's meaning will in fact change only if it is repeated in a different context. Stated formally, Derrida's argument would run as follows. No context can circumscribe a sign's meaning; the sign's meaning will alter if repeated in a different context; but the sign is structurally open to repetition: therefore, alterity is a structural feature of the sign. The upshot of this argument is that in being subject to the second mode of repetition, the sign must fail to perform its first and primary mode to the extent to which it does not signify the presence purely and simply.

But surely such words as 'primary' and 'fail' are beginning to lose their basis as the consequences of this argument become evident. We have already admitted that, by dint of its structure, the sign can always be repeated outside its original context, and that the sign's intelligible content is therefore always open to modification. However, if this possibility is *always* open, it is an essential possibility and therefore part of the sign's structure. We cannot then speak of the sign's *failure* to repeat a presence, because the possibility of accidents enables the sign's intelligible content to emerge. And if we are to talk of primacy, we are obliged to ascribe it to this condition of possibility rather than to presence of any kind.

The second mode of repetition will always introduce a remainder of signification which does not answer to the sign's animating presence. 'Remainder' can be misleading, however, for this 'improper' signification cannot be kept in isolation from the 'proper' signification. The possibility of the sign being repeated is one of its structural traits: we cannot distinguish between proper and improper significations upon the basis of the sign's identity, since that cannot be realised apart from repetition. Nor can we do so on the basis of an appeal to the

18 Derrida, *Margins of philosophy*, p. 315.

13

sign's animating presence, since that presence cannot restrict the sign's movement of repetition. We therefore have the following situation. The presence in question cannot be signified purely and simply; further, there is no fixed point of any kind which can help us find an angle of deviation between what *is* signified and what *should* be signified. In short, we must conclude that this pure presence has never been given to consciousness: all we can say is that it is a trace of a presence. And if we follow this train of thought to its logical conclusion, we are bound to admit that this trace is of a presence which has never presented itself, so that, strictly speaking, we must talk of a trace of a trace. Although this reasoning leaves us with elements to refine, plainly its conclusion is that there is a mode of repetition which is held to be prior to presence.

From Derrida's perspective, what we have, we might say, is a trespass of the sign – a demonstration that what is taken to mark only the sign is, in fact, a determined modification of the enabling condition of both signs and concepts. So, the mode of priority with which we are concerned is that of the transcendental, the condition of possibility for phenomena. As the phenomenon of repetition is seen, after the fact, to be a modification of a transcendental, Derrida uses the one word – here, 'repetition' – to name *both* the phenomenal *and* the transcendental. The foregoing argument is but one instance of a general strategy. Over the course of his various essays Derrida argues that *différance, supplément, trace*, and so on, are prior to presence; and each time he uses these words in *both* the above senses – a practice which can lead to some confusion, and one I shall later discuss. The general point, though, is clear: the sign trespasses over its assigned limits, thereby blurring any qualitative distinction between the concept and the sign. And this 'trespass of the sign', as I have called it, is one instance of the general mode of critique known today as 'deconstruction'. According to this critique, there is not a fall *from* full presence but, as it were, a fall *within* presence, an inability of 'presence' to fulfil its promise of being able to form a ground. Full presence, for Derrida, is not a prelapsarian ideal or an eschatological hope, but an illusory goal – the illusion being that there is in fact something outside the sign system which can escape its determinations. If one accepts this, it follows that to the precise extent that one identifies God with full presence, as the determinate origin or end of being, one's theology will fall within the scope of Derrida's critique.

Without doubt, this critique of full presence has as its object far more than traditional Christian theology. For even if one rejects the proposition that there is a God, one does not thereby reject all appeals to full presence. Atheists can argue without embarrassment that meaning is delimited by an appeal to full presence, be it a present or presentable object or a consciousness whose states and internal modifications are present to itself; and *mutatis mutandis* the same sort of argument can be furnished with respect to being. We have seen that, for Derrida, the sign does not, and cannot, purely and simply represent the concept. Now we can take 'represent' in a strong sense as 're-presenting' – which is, broadly, the idealist position – or in a weak sense, as 'standing for', which is, equally broadly, the empiricist position. Regardless of the differences in their ontologies, both idealism and empiricism fall within the metaphysics of presence to the extent to which they characterise meaning by way of simples. Given that 'presence' is an epistemological as well as an onto-logical category, Derrida's critique has a very wide scope indeed, taking within its sights both empiricism and rationalism, realism and idealism – in short, as Derrida avers, philosophy and theology in their entirety. Derrida takes theology and philosophy to think 'a *fall* in general', from the primordial to the derivative, from presence to sign, from the proper to the figural, and so on;[19] and it is 'the notion of "fall"' and the entire system of which it is a part which forms the 'constant target' of Derrida's critique.[20]

It is time to pause for a moment and register the variety of topics which Derrida addresses under the general title of 'fall'. It will suffice, I think, to stay with *Of grammatology*, Derrida's most programmatic text, for here one can see a plain emphasis upon a commerce between the Fall and a notion of 'a *fall* in general'. Our discussion took as its starting point Derrida's remark that 'The sign is always a sign of the Fall', and it has led us to a number of metaphysical and epistemological issues. With different ends in view, we could have focussed instead upon the way in which Derrida pictures Saussure as an Adamic figure, as the 'first man'

19 Derrida, *Margins of philosophy*, p. 63. See further *Writing*, p. 27.
20 Derrida, *Positions*, p. 53.

of semiology who experiences a mixture of pleasure and guilt in his later, errant analyses of anagrams in Latin poetry. This sort of relation between interpretation and guilt could easily lead us to the central figure of Derrida's text, Jean-Jacques Rousseau. In his discussion of Rousseau on the origins of society, language and Rousseau's own sexual desires, Derrida foregrounds the notion of the fall. The presumed relation between the awakening of sexual desire and the Fall of Adam and Eve hardly need be stressed. But what makes Derrida's analysis of particular moment is the complicity he discerns between Rousseau's account of the fall from sexual innocence to experience and guilt, man's fall from a state of innocence to a state of corruption in contemporary civilisation, and the fall from speech to writing as detailed in the *Confessions* and the *Essay on the origin of languages*.[21] And finally we could pass, as Derrida does, from Rousseau to Claude Lévi-Strauss, and examine the 'Rousseauism' of *Tristes tropiques*. Here Derrida fastens upon Lévi-Strauss's Adamic description of the Nambikwara Indians and how the anthropologist links writing with their fall from innocence: 'Writing, on this its first appearance in their midst, had allied itself with falsehood'.[22]

We shall explore various facets of 'Adamicism' as this study develops, and we shall examine the force of Derrida's notion of 'complicity' in due course; but now we will return to the metaphysical and methodological issues at hand. I have argued that the notion of 'fall' is for Derrida constitutive of metaphysics and thus passes under his critique. Even when one is not actively *thinking* a fall, to the extent to which one does not put the notion of 'fall' in question, one nonetheless remains within metaphysics.[23] This is an extraordinary claim by any criterion and is all the more so when one realises how boldly Derrida has reduced the *whole* of western thought to metaphysics. Even Martin

21 See Jean-Jacques Rousseau, *Essay on the origin of languages*, in *On the origin of language: Jean-Jacques Rousseau, Essay on the origin of languages, and Johann Gottfried Herder, Essay on the origin of language*, trans. with afterwords, John H. Moran and Alexander Gode (1966; rpt. Chicago: University of Chicago Press, 1986), Ch. 5. In his afterword to the English translation of this essay, John H. Moran remarks of Rousseau's work in general, that 'This etiology of the human condition, a secular version of the Fall, is the dominant theme of his work', p. 75.

22 Quoted by Derrida as the epigraph to *Of grammatology*, II, i, p. 101.

23 Derrida, *Positions*, p. 19.

Heidegger, whose thought is devoted to overcoming meta-physics, and who explicitly distances himself from the theological idea of the Fall, remains caught up in metaphysics in exploring the theme of *Dasein's* fall from primordial to derivative time.[24]

So far we have been assuming that there is a real distinction between philosophy and theology, but if Derrida is right the discourses are fundamentally linked by the way in which they relate to presence and so can be gathered under the general title of metaphysics:

> The difference between signified and signifier belongs in a profound and implicit way to the totality of the great epoch covered by the history of metaphysics, and in a more explicit and more systematically articulated way to the narrower epoch of Christian creationism and infinitism when these appropriate the resources of Greek conceptuality.[25]

The passage from the presence of the signified to its representation in the signifier is, upon Derrida's reading, a 'fall' from the intelligible to the sensible. That is, the story of Adam's Fall is not merely a religious myth; when demythologised, by Hegel or by Derrida, it yields a plain statement of a *philosophical* state of affairs: that the intelligible is valued over the sensible, presence over representation, the simple over the complex, immediacy over mediation, and so forth. In each case, Derrida insists, the latter is implicitly taken as a *fall* from the former.

Like Hegel, Derrida construes philosophy as a demythologising of theology which is orchestrated by theology.[26] For Hegel this is positive: philosophy is the *true* theodicy; for Derrida,

---

24 Thus Heidegger observes that his analysis of fallenness 'has nothing to do with any doctrine of the corruption of human nature or any theory of original sin', *History of the concept of time*, trans. Theodore Kisiel (Bloomington: Indiana University Press, 1985), p. 283. Despite this, Heidegger construes philosophy as a fall from thinking. See Derrida's remarks in *Margins of philosophy*, p. 63.

25 Derrida, *Of grammatology*, p. 13.

26 I follow Copleston in calling Hegel's undertaking a 'demythologising' but it should be stressed that, unlike Bultmann (with whose name the term is now primarily associated), Hegel does not seek to eliminate myth from religious discourse. Rather, Hegel seeks to express the truth of the religious myths in a form adequate to their content which is, in his view, philosophy. For Hegel, philosophy is the *allegory* of theology, a notion to which we shall return in ch. 2. See Hegel's remark on allegory in *Lectures on the philosophy of religion*, ed. Peter C. Hodgson (Berkeley: University of California Press, 1984), p. 399. Also see Copleston's remarks in his 'Hegel and the rationalization of mysticism', in *New studies in Hegel's philosophy*, ed. Warren E. Steinkraus (New York: Holt, Rinehart and Winston, 1971), p. 198 n. 28.

though, it is negative: philosophy merely re-thinks the 'Fall' by way of a 'fall in general'. Or more precisely: where Hegel thinks of the Fall and original sin as the provenance of philosophy, Derrida takes the thought of the fall from the primordial to the derivative to be philosophy's original sin. In fact, upon Derrida's analysis, there is a greater bond between theology and philosophy than Hegel recognised; for both discourses are established as metaphysics by dint of the structure of the sign.[27] Thus we have, on the one hand, the claim that the sign 'by its root and its implications, is in all its aspects metaphysical' and, on the other hand, that 'the intelligible face [the signified] of the sign remains turned toward the word and the face of God'.[28] Indeed, Derrida contends that western philosophy has a particular programme – in short, 'the metaphysics of presence' – and that this programme is of a piece with western theology, even at those times when there appears to be no point of contact between them:

> Even when the thing, the 'referent', is not immediately related to the logos of a creator God where it began by being the spoken/thought sense, the signified has at any rate an immediate relationship with the logos in general (finite or infinite), and a mediated one with the signifier.[29]

For Derrida, then, it is not that the Hegelian demythologising of theology does not go far enough; it goes in precisely the wrong direction, from representation to pure presence, when the root of the problem is 'presence' itself. We must therefore broach the deconstruction of 'presence', and to do that we must focus upon what is both indispensable and threatening to it, the concept 'sign': 'It is thus the idea of the sign that must be deconstructed through a meditation upon writing which would merge, as it must, with the undoing [sollicitation] of onto-theology, faithfully repeating it in its *totality* and *making* it *insecure* in its most assured evidences'.[30] But the sign is always a

---

27 For Hegel the sign is to be considered within psychology not metaphysics or theology. See his *Philosophy of mind* (1845), trans. William Wallace (Oxford: Clarendon Press, 1971), §458 ff. Derrida discusses Hegel's semiology in *Margins of philosophy*, pp. 69–108.

28 The first quotation is taken from *Positions*, p. 17 and the second from *Of grammatology*, p. 13. Derrida also remarks, in the *Positions* passage, that the sign 'is in systematic solidarity with stoic and medieval theology'.

29 Derrida, *Of grammatology*, pp. 14–15. Cf. p. 73.

30 Derrida, *Of grammatology*, p. 73.

sign of the Fall. The story of the Fall shows us man's propensity to undo himself, while deconstruction, a discourse upon a more general notion of fall, shows us the propensity of linguistic constructs to undo themselves.

N.B.

In demonstrating that what seems to be a fall *from* is in fact a fall *within*, Derrida completes the negative labour of deconstruction and turns towards its positive project: to develop a new way of reading texts, one which is utterly faithful to the letter of what is written. The tasks are closely related. Deconstruction involves a re-thinking of the history of western metaphysics; it marks that history by exposing the limits within which it operates, and exceeds it by showing that metaphysics cannot master those limits. These moments of excess are found within the texts of metaphysics, in words we shall analyse later – *supplément*, *parergon*, *pharmakon*, amongst others – and it is precisely in reading these words against the presuppositions of the meta-physical tradition that its limits are made visible. Yet often Derrida does not read a text to put pressure on western meta-physics but rather to affirm those elements forgotten or repressed by previous readings. In other words, he does not stop at showing that a text does overrun its limits, but he explores the streams, the runnels and deltas which that overflow causes, along with the sediment it brings to the surface only to deposit elsewhere. Here he is not so much concerned with the notion of a fall as with what *befalls* a text, the chances and changes it encounters when lifted from its original context or read in other ways.

What is at issue can be seen in a sentence which appears in many of Derrida's texts, '*La signature tombe*'; it means both 'the signature falls' and 'the signature encrypts'. Normally, one thinks of the signature's rightful place as outside a text where it serves to gather the text into a unity, to declare the existence of an authorial consciousness which was the text's source, to affirm the author's legal right over the text – in short to control textual meaning. To sign a text, Derrida argues, is to declare oneself as an absent presence. This does not, however, indicate merely a provisional absence, when one happens to be unable to stand by the text, but a generalised absence, such as after one's death. For it is a structural trait of the sign that it can be repeated outside its original context, at any time and in any place. Or as Derrida boldly puts it: 'the "signature" event carries my death in that event'.[31] The point is that there is no authorial presence outside the text, signified by an appended proper name, which can absolutely control the text's meaning. The signature cannot remain outside the text, a sign of a present consciousness; it 'falls to the tomb', as Derrida says, leaving no firm position outside the text to govern interpretation of the text. An author's text is his or her crypt on which a proper name is emblazoned.

Not only is the signature a name written on a crypt but also it becomes a crypt itself. On the face of it, the signature marks the place where a living author once wrote – it is a tomb; yet also it forms a code, a crypt, within the text. In a number of recent studies Derrida traces a fall from an author's proper name outside the text to a common name within the text. Thus in Derrida's study of the contemporary French writer Francis Ponge, *Signéponge*, we see that certain texts signed 'Francis Ponge' already have traces of that name inscribed within them.[32] There is a disconcerting slippage from nomination to signification such that the things evoked in the text (a sponge, a Turkish towel, pumice stone) reverberate with the poet's proper name (*éponge, serviette-éponge, ponce*). Unable to remain wholly outside the text, the writer's proper name very improperly begins to act like any other signifier, allowing Ponge's texts to be decoded along the lines of homonyms and anagrams of the poet's proper name. (Here Derrida could be seen as standing where Saussure feared to go when he abandoned his work on Latin anagrams.) Derrida has a philosophical thesis to propose, that no uninterrupted boundary can be drawn between reference and meaning, but that point could be made in a few pages. His attention is attracted by the ways in which textual accidents befall proper names, how signification overruns nomination, exceeding it without return. The positive import of Derrida's theory is that nothing can be overlooked when interpreting a text; anything can be detached from its original context, even a proper name, and inscribed within another context where it becomes meaningful. Although the theory of the signature is a discourse on being – the status of the author's presence and absence – it is also a practice of reading.

31 Derrida, *Glas*, trans. John P. Leavey, Jr and Richard Rand (Lincoln: University of Nebraska Press, 1986), 19b.
32 Derrida, *Signéponge/Signsponge*, trans. Richard Rand (New York: Columbia University Press, 1984).

Having explored what is at issue with deconstruction, in both its negative and positive aspects, and one or two of the basic problems it poses for theology, we return to our guiding question – how are metaphysics and theology related? – and pose several smaller questions which I shall try to answer as I continue.

Are *all* theologies complicit with 'metaphysics' in Derrida's sense of the word? Both theology and philosophy are gathered under the one title of 'onto-theology' yet, unlike philosophy, the texts of theology are never thereafter subjected to specific critical inspections. While Derrida freely admits that particular philosophical and literary figures trouble the borders of onto-theology, the thought that the same may hold of theological figures is never explored.

Are there any important differences between the deconstruction of philosophy and the deconstruction of theology? Derrida maintains that philosophy is *always* a discourse on presence, and if that is so it is always open to deconstruction. It may well be that theology has also been, at least in part, a discourse on presence; but there does not seem to be a compelling reason why theology *should* be a discourse on presence. One could argue that the deconstruction of theology would consist in the deconstruction of that which is *metaphysical* in theology, a movement which would lead to the development of a non-metaphysical theology.

Is it possible to read the deconstruction of theology as a *theological* process? If the Fall requires us to adopt a negative theology as a supplement to our positive statements about God, what Derrida defines as the philosophical equivalent of the Fall, the '*fall* in general', requires a negative philosophy, a deconstruction, to wrestle philosophy away from its theological model. In both instances, however, our focus is upon the sign: negative theology and deconstruction both take the sign as the harbinger of metaphysics, and both seek, in their different ways, to put it into question. So there is reason to think that, regardless of how deconstruction confronts theology, a dialogue between deconstruction and negative theology may be possible.

2 Clarifications

For Dante and the long tradition he represents, interpretation is based upon signs which in turn have their ontological basis in God. There is a fall from God's presence to representation, and

21

the aim of interpretation is to recover that original presence. More generally, the whole of history, from creation to apocalypse, can be viewed as a passage from one moment of full presence to another, an epoch of signs and interpretation. At the level of figuration we have an unreflective theology; its cognitive basis supplies a familiar metaphysics of presence – what Derrida insists is '*the only* metaphysics';[33] and it has manifest hermeneutical consequences. With regards to scripture, for example, when the *sensus litteralis* fails to yield a definite meaning in accordance with received doctrine, the fact that the sign's ontological basis is God's presence guarantees that God has underwritten an allegorical meaning, a *sensus spiritualis*. If for Dante we have an ascending series of interpretation, signs and God, for Derrida we have the same series but seen as descending. The deconstruction of the concept 'sign' shows that conceiving the sign as a modification of a full presence (that is, conceiving it metaphysically), is neither inevitable nor rigorous. What Derrida effectively demonstrates is that the metaphysical conception of the sign is not the basis of interpretation but is an interpretation itself: the sign's 'ground' is argued to be interpretation, not God. There are different strands to this conclusion, one regional and one universal. We have the Saussurean point that a sign's expressive power derives from its relations with other signs and is not instituted from outside the system, by nature or God. There is also the Nietzschean line, that everything is always already an interpretation, that there is no unique transcendent point from which one can judge conflicting interpretations – in short, as Nietzsche himself puts it, that God is dead.

The combined force of these arguments is that God no longer has a decisive role with respect to interpretation. And with this we come to the basis of the view, common enough in print but ubiquitous in discussions, that deconstruction has a case to prosecute against religious belief and against Christianity in particular. 'We have no trouble recognizing this [deconstruction] as a swipe at Christianity from *archè* to *telos*', as Schneidau puts it.[34] Derrida's specific remarks on this topic are few and far between; but, it will be remembered, we are not so much con-

33 Derrida, *Of grammatology*, p. 3.
34 Herbert N. Schneidau, 'The word against the word: Derrida on textuality', *Derrida and biblical studies*, ed. Robert Detweiler, *Semeia*, 23 (1982), p. 14.

cerned with Derrida's intentions and individual interests as with the mode of critique he practises and its import for discourse on God. This common view takes two main forms. Eugene Goodheart talks of 'Deconstructive or anti-theological skepticism'; Eric Gould claims that deconstruction is 'counter-theological'; while Mikel Dufrenne settles with 'non-theological'.[35] There is less variety in the second group, for Umberto Eco, Peter Kemp and Mark C. Taylor agree that deconstruction is 'atheistic'.[36] There is a salient difference between these claims (one refers to a discourse on belief and one to belief itself), and I do not think that either is entirely satisfactory: so I shall examine the springs of this common view of deconstruction. And as a good deal of discussion in this area is beleaguered by a confusion of Derrida's already perplexing terms, much of my time will be taken up with clarifying Derrida's vocabulary. Established so far is that no sign-system can be grounded in a moment of presence. We have agreed to take 'presence' as both an ontological and an epistemological category. And to deal directly with matters at hand, we can also agree, for now, to understand by 'ground' any presence which absolutely originates or terminates a sign-system.

At a certain level of generality it is possible to discuss Derrida's case against onto-theology in terms of this vocabulary. However, for reasons I cannot weigh until later, Derrida draws his tools of criticism from the discourse under inspection. Key words – *parergon, hymen, pharmakon* – are not so much *used* for analysis as they are *used up* in the analysis. Thus the vocabulary of one essay differs quite markedly from that of another, not because Derrida is in search of a better vocabulary but because he values immanent critique. When reading the *Critique of judgement*, for example, Derrida organises his analysis around a word used by Kant, *parergon*, which means 'beside the work', 'hors d'oeuvre' or 'supplement' and which Kant uses to discuss frames of paintings, draperies on statues, the colonnades of palaces, and so on. At first sight, the discussion of parerga seems

---

35 Goodheart, *The skeptic disposition in contemporary criticism* (Princeton: Princeton University Press, 1984), p. 13; Gould, 'Deconstruction and its discontents', Denver Quarterly, 15 (1980), p. 101; and Dufrenne, *Le poétique* (Paris: Presses Universitaires de France, 1973), pp. 21ff.
36 Eco, *Semiotics and the philosophy of language* (London: Macmillan Press, 1984), pp. 156, 163. Kemp, 'L'éthique au lendemain des victoires des athéismes', *Revue de théologie et de philosophie*, 111 (1979), *passim*. Taylor, *Erring: a postmodern a/theology* (Chicago: University of Chicago Press, 1984), p. 6.

marginal to the *Critique of judgement*. After all, Kant has far larger concerns at hand: to develop his æsthetic theory, he needs to distinguish keenly between cognitive and æsthetic judgement. In a characteristic move, Derrida uses the terms of Kant's discourse on the frame to analyse how Kant frames the nature of judgement; and it is the lack of fit between the two which provides Derrida with his most illuminating remarks on the text. It is also characteristic that Derrida fastens upon Kant's discussion of borders and frames because the German word *Kant* means 'edge' or 'border': Kant's proper name falls into his text as a common name, one which both organises and disorganises his discussion of art. The point of Derrida's analysis, here as elsewhere, is to show that textual meaning cannot be delimited wholly and homogeneously – that is, cannot be *totalised* – from within or without.

There are particular words, though, which appear throughout Derrida's work, and one of the most common of these is 'text'. Perhaps the most straightforward way of seeing what is at issue here is to consider Derrida's distinction between 'book' and 'text', two words which are usually taken to be synonymous. Derrida focusses upon the literary commonplace that the book is a unified whole – that it is totalised by authorial intention or by the reader's consciousness; then he augments this with appeals to the familiar metaphor that Nature is God's book, ultimately totalised by divine consciousness.[37] The book, in fine, is that writing which is totalised by a consciousness, human or divine. At a certain period of history – roughly co-inciding with modernism – there emerges a new kind of writing in which signs plainly cannot be totalised by concepts. It is signalled by Mallarmé's remark to Degas, 'Ce n'est point avec des idées qu'on fait des sonnets, Degas, c'est avec des mots,' and experienced to its fullest extent in Joyce's *Finnegans Wake*.[38] This new writing, Derrida argues, challenges the metaphysical concept of the book, and in the lexicon of modernism it is called 'the text'.

In considering the deconstruction of 'sign' we saw that Derrida's argument turns upon the disclosure of a relationship between 'repetition' in a phenomenal and in a transcendental

---

37 For Derrida's comments upon 'the Book' see *Writing*, p. 10, and *Dissemination*, trans. and introd. Barbara Johnson (London: Athlone Press, 1981), p. 44.
38 Stéphane Mallarmé, *The poems*, trans. and introd. Keith Bosley (Harmondsworth: Penguin, 1977), p. 19.

sense, and that he insists upon calling both modes 'repetition'. The same manoeuvre can be found elsewhere in Derrida's work with all those categories which he holds to be systematically devalued with respect to an imagined plenitude of presence. Thus with the couples 'speech–writing', 'identity–difference' and 'book–text', it is 'writing', 'difference' and 'text' which are taken both phenomenally and transcendentally. And so, without retracing an argument whose general contours we have already marked, we can say that while Derrida uses the common word 'text' to signify a mode of phenomenal writing, he also uses it to signify the condition of possibility for both 'text' and 'book'. 'Text' therefore has a very considerable range, but its true scope is even larger. This is so for two reasons. First, it is Derrida's contention that as 'metaphysics' names a desire rather than an actual state of affairs, there is in fact no such thing as a book: all writing is textual and, for that reason, resists total-isation. Second, just as, for Derrida, verbal signs do not exhaust the general category of 'sign', so too written texts do not cover the entire category of 'text'. The deconstruction of 'sign' leaves us not with a presence but with the trace of a trace; and, by the same token, the deconstruction of any signifying system – a consciousness, a society, an epoch, or whatever – leaves us with a text, 'a differential network, a fabric of traces referring end-lessly to something other than itself, to other differential traces'.[39]

These different senses of 'text' should be kept in mind when dealing with Derrida's more aphoristic remarks such as *'There is nothing outside of the text'*.[40] Here Derrida is not suggesting, as some literary critics would seem to believe, that it is improper to pass from a phenomenal text to the reader's or writer's life and thus to social and political concerns. Deconstruction is not a formalism. Derrida's point is merely that any knowledge one can

39 'Living on', p. 84. For Derrida's insistence that 'text' is not reducible to 'written text', see further down p. 84 and *Positions*, p. 44. Derrida's broad sense of 'text' is not only a consequence of his broad sense of 'sign', it is also anticipated by Freud's usage. Thus Ricœur's remark upon Freud: 'For him, interpretation is concerned not only with a scripture or writing but with any set of signs that may be taken as a text to decipher, hence a dream or neurotic symptom, as well as a ritual, myth, work of art, or a belief', *Freud and philosophy*, trans. Denis Savage (New Haven: Yale University Press, 1970), p. 26.
40 Derrida, *Of grammatology*, p. 158.

glean of the writer's life and intentions will not provide one with a privileged point of access to the text; it will involve one in yet another network, such as, for example, the writer's various relations with other writers, living and dead, the writer's construction of a text of history, as well as the various texts in which the writer is always already inscribed. The doctrine that there is nothing outside the text is neither esoteric nor difficult: it is merely that there is no knowledge, of which we can speak, which is unmediated. What Derrida adds to this familiar epistemological thesis is the contention that this knowledge is always in a state of being constituted and never arrives at a state of final constitution: there is no immediacy, even in mediation; no self-identity, even in difference. And what distinguishes Derrida from others, such as Maurice Merleau-Ponty, who hold this view, is not so much a matter of position as a matter of thoroughgoing detection. For Derrida locates the desire for immediacy and self-identity even in texts by those writers (Husserl, Heidegger, Lacan, Levinas, and so on) who claim to pass beyond the metaphysics of presence, as well as locating textual strata in the classical texts of metaphysics (by Plato and Hegel) which put their claims into question.

I am now in a position to state what I take to be Derrida's basic contention, and to do so in straightforward terms. It is this: no text can be totalised from within or without, and this is so by dint of the conditions of possibility for textuality. And the question to which we can turn is how it can be argued, on the basis of this contention, that deconstruction is 'non-theological' or 'atheistic'. We can begin by eliminating one common misconception. The deconstruction of a binary couple such as 'presence–absence' does not make any claim as to the validity of the use of that opposition in an empirical or ideal situation. If I wear my grey jacket it is empirically present to me, and if I have it dry-cleaned it is empirically absent from me, as the receipt will signify. At this level, there is no question of whether my jacket is present or absent. Deconstruction comes into play here only when I try to take my sense impressions as moments of simple presence on the basis of which experience as such can be explained. Similarly, deconstruction can make no claim as to the reality or non-reality of God, but it will come into operation if I use 'God' to ground my account of phenomena; and this is so as long as I regard God as the highest being and the ground of being. I shall refine this account by seeing how deconstruction comports with several common views of atheism.

The first account of atheism to heed is also the one which makes the strongest claim. Ernest Nagel formulates it as follows: 'I shall understand by "atheism" a critique and a denial of the major claims of all varieties of theism'.[41] From what we have already encountered, deconstruction plainly offers a critique of one of theism's longstanding claims, that God is the ground of all meaning. More generally, it puts in question a good deal of the vocabulary of presence which theists habitually use to talk of God. Nagel is not entirely clear if a critique of theism should *lead* one to deny it or if the denial is in *addition* to the critique, but either way deconstruction does not fit the picture. Deconstruction offers a critique of theism, to be sure, but it is directed to the 'ism' rather than the 'theos'; that is, it offers a critique of the use to which 'God' is put, but does not make any claim whatsoever about the *reality* of God. In fact, to the extent to which deconstruction is a critique of theism it is also a critique of any discourse which denies there is a God.[42] To press a useful distinction into service: deconstruction is a 'general critique' – it addresses the general conditions of establishing a consistent and complete account – whereas what Nagel has in mind is a 'restricted critique', one which addresses the specificity of a discourse's claims. So if we call a position 'atheistic' by virtue of the fact that it offers a *critique* of theism or because it *denies* that there is a God, we cannot properly attach this label to deconstruction.

But a position can be called atheistic on other grounds, for example if the notion of God is entirely *incompatible* with the views it advances. And this is the case, I take it, with Jean-Paul Sartre who would want to claim that the Christian God is in-

41 Nagel, 'Philosophical concepts of atheism', in *Critiques of God*, ed. Peter Angeles (Buffalo, NY: Prometheus Books, 1976), p. 4.
42 Derrida makes the point that this mode of atheism is itself 'metaphysical' and 'theological' in his sense of the terms. See *Of grammatology*, p. 323 n. 3. We know, too, that while Derrida contends that uncritical valuing of the signified is theistic (*Of grammatology*, p. 13) he also claims that the prizing of the signifier is atheistic (*Dissemination*, p. 54). As Derrida emphasises time and again, deconstruction does not consist in a simple reversal of the signified-signifier hierarchy (which would be necessary to establish deconstruction as atheistic) but it also requires a phase of displacement; and this supports my case that deconstruction is neither theistic nor atheistic in any normal sense of the words. For Derrida's emphasis see, for example, *Dissemination*, p. 6 and *Positions*, pp. 41–42.

compatible with human freedom as he conceives it. From what we know of deconstruction it is plain that it is not atheistic in this sense, for there is no view about being or meaning or morality that it positively asserts. It may be that individual deconstructionists hold views which they do think are incompatible with the idea of God, but they hold these on social, moral or other grounds, and not by dint of a commitment to deconstruction. And *mutatis mutandis*, it may be that individual deconstructionists do believe in God though not, of course, the God who functions as a transcendental signified. It is not inconsistent to argue that *no* theory can be totalised and that *some* views have more coercive power than others. One may think, for example, that there is more to be said for the philosophical view that there are no simples than for the view that there are simples, whilst at the same time holding the metaphilosophical view that neither account is free from problems generated by its own will to totalise and, further, that no such account is corrigible. And this, I contend, is exactly Derrida's view. To relate this to the issue at hand, one may hold that there *is* a God but that there is no *concept* of God to which one can appeal that can ground one's discourse about God or the world.

A third, and equally important, inflection of atheism is found in the work of Emmanuel Levinas. To be an utterly separate being, enclosed within the self and therefore outside the ethical life, is to be an atheist. This is the soul's natural state, its mode of positing itself, which precedes both the affirmation and the denial of the divine.[43] Here atheism is not necessarily to be distinguished from theism, for in Levinas's terms much religious belief is itself prior to the revelation of God. By this Levinas means that many religious people fail to recognise that God reveals Himself only in the other person, as irreducibly Other, and portray Him instead as a being able to be described by philosophical language. While it would be premature to call this a deconstructive way of conceiving atheism – the notion of a soul's 'natural state' would have to come under inspection – it is not incompatible with deconstruction. More immediately useful, however, is Martin Heidegger's view that 'Philosophical research is and remains atheism' by which he means that while

43 Levinas, *Totality and infinity: an essay on exteriority*, trans. Alphonso Lingis (The Hague: Martinus Nijhoff, 1979), p. 58.

philosophy does not deny the reality of God it equally does not presuppose God.[44] One can agree with Heidegger here without committing the philosopher as individual agent to atheism: as Pascal shows, it is possible to believe in God and not explicitly appeal in one's theoretical work to notions such as *causa omnium*, *causa causans*, *causa sui* and so on. In this sense, then, deconstruction can be taken as atheistic.

Let us pursue this matter by returning to Derrida's distinction between 'book' and 'text'. 'Here or there we have discerned writing: a nonsymmetrical division designated on the one hand the closure of the book, and on the other the opening of the text', he begins. 'On the one hand the theological encyclopedia and, modeled upon it, the book of man. On the other a fabric of traces marking the disappearance of an exceeded God or of an erased man'.[45] This brings us to the basis of Derrida's usage of 'God' and 'theology'. We need not endorse Pascal's sharp distinction between the God of the philosophers and the God of Abraham, Isaac and Jacob to recognise that Derrida is more concerned with the former than with the latter. It is not that Derrida addresses himself to a being that is posited rather than to a Father who is trusted, but that he is concerned with how God has been made to *function* in philosophical and theological systems. Before the Age of Reason, God was generally accorded both an ontological and an epistemological function, as the *fons et origo* of all that is and as the guarantor of determinate meaning. Thereafter, God's epistemological function passed to man, initially by means of the Cartesian *cogito* and subsequently by means of the Kantian transcendental subject. If we stress the notion of God's function in human systems, the controversy between theism and humanism can be pictured as 'a controversy between theism and anthropotheism', as Merleau-Ponty nicely puts it.[46] For Derrida as for Merleau-Ponty the issue is not that one must choose between God and man, between theism and atheism, but rather that one must question the assumption that either can ground an adequate account of being in general and of man in particular. Derrida's quarry is the notion of totalisation, and he closes on

44 Heidegger, *History of the concept of time*, p. 80.
45 *Writing*, p. 294. Cf. '[The book] is the encyclopedic protection of theology and of logocentrism against the disruption of writing. . .', *Of grammatology*, p. 18.
46 Maurice Merleau-Ponty, *In praise of philosophy*, trans. John Wild and James M. Edie (Evanston: Northwestern University Press, 1963), p. 43.

God only to the extent that God has been taken to function as a means of totalisation.[47] So if we understand 'theism' to have an unavoidable reference to a determinate centre, and deconstruction to demonstrate that no centre, in any structure, can be determinate, we may say in this sense, and only in this sense, that deconstruction is atheistic. But it needs to be stressed that we are dealing here with a functional usage of 'God' and not with belief in God; and with this we pass to the potentially less misleading designation 'non-theological'.

In Derrida's distinction between 'book' and 'text' it is the book which is viewed as theological and the text which is implicitly seen as non-theological. So as deconstruction insists that there are no books, only texts, it can be called 'non-theological'. But this hardly gets us far: what we need to know is why Derrida associates the book with theology, and how useful this association is. Derrida points us to Curtius who shows with exemplary scholarship how the *topos* of the book is more intimately related to Christianity than to any other movement, religious or otherwise.[48] Before anything else, the notion of the 'book' as a totality derives from early medieval images of the Bible as 'God's book' in which all the mysteries of the universe are written: the Bible is the book of books.[49] The point of this book symbolism is evident in Dante's lines describing the moment when, at last in the Empyrean, he turns to look at God. Within the 'eternal light' he sees 'ingathered, bound by love in one volume, the scattered

---

47 Derrida is clear how 'God' is to be understood in his writings: 'God is the name and the element of that which makes possible an absolutely pure and absolutely self-present self-knowledge', *Of grammatology*, p. 98. Also see, with regards to function, the discussion of Derrida's original presentation of 'Structure, sign and play in the discourse of the human sciences', most notably the following comment on the function of the centre: 'I believe that the center is a function, not a being – a reality, but a function. And this function is absolutely indispensable', in *The structuralist controversy*, eds., Richard Macksey and Eugenio Donato (Baltimore: Johns Hopkins University Press, 1972), p. 271.

48 E. R. Curtius, *European literature and the Latin middle ages*, trans. W. R. Trask (London: Routledge and Kegan Paul, 1953), Ch. 16 'The book as symbol'. Derrida refers us to Curtius in *Of grammatology*, p. 15.

49 See J. Gellrich, *The idea of the book in the middle ages* (Ithaca: Cornell University Press, 1985), Ch. 1. Gellrich lists several biblical figures of God as an Author: 'the biblical tablets are "written with the finger of God" (Exod. 31.18), his "tongue" is a "pen" (Ps. 45.2), and the "heavens" are a "book" (Apoc. 6.14)', pp. 33–34. For further discussion of the relation between 'book' and 'Bible' see Taylor, *Erring*, Ch. 4.

30

leaves of all the universe'.[50] Here the image of the book is used to affirm that all apparent differences are ultimately unified in God: so 'book' is an image of totalisation. Derrida takes the model of the book to be the 'theological encyclopedia', a formulation we can refine by reference to d'Alembert's preliminary discourse on the *Encyclopédie*. 'The general system of the sciences and arts is a labyrinth', d'Alembert remarks, and what he offers the reader is an overview of this labyrinth. The *Encyclopédie* would place 'the philosopher above this vast labyrinth in a very elevated point of perspective which would enable him to view with a single glance his object of speculation and those operations which he can perform on those objects to distinguish the general branches of human knowledge and the points dividing it and uniting it and even to detect at times the secret paths which unite it.'[51] It is well known that the *Encyclopédie* slights Christian doctrine. What is 'theological' about the encyclopedia is its offer of this God's eye view of the labyrinth of human knowledge, its positing of a secure point for totalisation, or, in other words, a transcendental signified. It is this ambition to read the world, from the vantage point of reason, that animated Leibniz's dream of an encyclopedia.[52] And this ambition is raised to its highest pitch when, in his *Encyklopädie*, Hegel tries to grasp this point in the presentation of absolute knowledge.

50 *Paradiso*, Canto XXXIII, lines 85–88. Curtius cites this passage on p. 332. A similar emphasis upon the book as an image of totality may be found in Hugh of St Victor's figure that universal history is a book in three parts (*lex naturalis*, *lex scripta* and *tempus gratiae*). See Gellrich, *The idea of the book*, p. 34.
51 Cited by Umberto Eco in his *Semiotics and the philosophy of language*, p. 83. The totalising aspect of the encyclopedia is suggested by Charles Bonnet: 'I delight in envisaging the innumerable multitude of Worlds as so many books which, when collected together, compose the immense Library of the Universe or the true Universal Encylopædia. I conceive that the marvellous gradation that exists between these different worlds facilitates in superior intelligences, to whom it has been given to traverse or rather to read them, the acquisition of truths of every kind, which it encompasses, and instils in their understanding that order and that concatenation which are its principal beauty. But these celestial Encyclopædists do not all possess the Encyclopædia of the Universe to the same degree; some possess only a few branches of it, others possess a greater number, others grasp even more still; but all have eternity in which to increase and perfect their learning and develop all their faculties'. Quoted by Michel Foucault, *The order of things: an archaeology of the human sciences* (London: Tavistock,1970), pp. 85–86.
52 See Derrida's remarks upon Leibniz and the concept of 'the Book' in *Writing*, p. 10. For Leibniz's comments on 'the Book', see his *Theodicy*, trans. L. M. Huggard (New Haven: Yale University Press, 1952), pp. 371–72.

I can now be quite precise in saying what 'theological' means for Derrida: any claim that a text is or can be totalised is theological. Thus in an interview Derrida talks, as I have when discussing totalisation, of 'the theological presence of a center' and, in another interview, of 'the motif of homogeneity, the theological motif *par excellence*'.[53] The word 'theological' pertains, then, to the use of any vocabulary in which meaning or being is said to be wholly resolved by reference to an origin, end, centre or ground. Once more we turn to Hegel for a clear instance: 'God is the beginning and end of all things', he claims, 'God is the sacred center, which animates and inspires all things'.[54] These particular words are drawn from the vocabulary traditionally associated with the God of the philosophers, but some qualifications are necessary lest we jump to a hasty conclusion in this regard. We do not need 'God' in a discourse for it to be 'theological' in Derrida's sense; all we need is something which *functions* as an agent of totalisation, and that can be 'man', 'Being', 'substance', 'impression', 'Form', 'logical atom', and so forth. If this is so, 'theological' and 'metaphysical' are convertible words in Derrida's lexicon, and it is evident that Derrida's usage of 'theology' is far closer to its original Greek sense, as the study of the being of the ground, than to its other, more common meaning, as the study of man's relationship in faith with God.[55] Also, we should not be too quick to designate the philosophical concept of God as the sole object of Derrida's critique and thereby uncritically align ourselves with Pascal. For this 'vocabulary of presence', as I shall call it, is not wholly distinct from that of Biblical theology. There God is pictured as Creator and Judge, whose self-designation is 'I AM THAT I AM', and it would be difficult to disentangle these notions from those of 'origin', 'end' and 'self-identity'. Even those theologies which seem to be at the furthest possible remove from philosophy are

53 Derrida, *Positions*, p. 14 and p. 64.
54 *Lectures on the philosophy of religion* (ed. P. C. Hodgson), Vol. 1, p. 150.
55 Derrida's use of 'theology' thus follows Heidegger's practice: 'when we speak here of "theological" and "theology" we must remember that the word and concept "theology" did not first grow in the framework and service of an ecclesiastical system of faith, but within philosophy. There is relatively late evidence of the word *theologia* for the first time in Plato: *mythologia*: this word does not occur at all in the New Testament.' Heidegger, *Schelling's treatise on the essence of human freedom*, trans. Joan Stambaugh (Athens, Ohio: Ohio University Press, 1985), p. 50.

nonetheless informed by the vocabulary of presence, as the following indicate: 'bodily incarnation', 'real presence', 'presence of the risen Lord', 'second coming'. So when the first vocabulary is called into question, the second does not entirely escape – a situation which will interest me later.

To return to the final point of clarification. 'Theological', like 'metaphysical' describes a *desire* for totality, and so a discourse may be called 'non-theological' if it seeks to resist totalisation, that is, if it does not attempt to reduce its heterogeneity. But as 'theological' has exactly the same conceptual scope as 'metaphysical' why, one wonders, does Derrida insist upon the word? If the situation were entirely conceptual, a more apt word than either would be 'monological', for Derrida's quarry is totalisation. The terms for the deconstruction of the metaphysics of presence are given to us within history. The phenomenal text, as found in the modernist period, is required before one can pose the problematic arising from the transcendental sense of 'text'; and the same is true of 'writing'. Without the attempt by William Warburton and others to establish the study of writing – grammatology – as a positive science in the eighteenth century, there could be no speculative grammatology today. However, Derrida argues, the emergence of grammatology as a positive science was frustrated by the religious belief that writing was naturally instituted by God: hence a certain antipathy on Derrida's part with respect to theology.[56] There is also reason to acknowledge the fact that theology, once queen of the sciences, has been taken to provide a model – often unconscious – for the newer discourses. Mill's moral sciences are all seen, in Derrida's eyes, to be haunted, in form if not in content, by the ghost of theology. And in this Derrida is close to a common complaint of analytic philosophers: I mean the sort of reservation Russell expresses when led to doubt if the idea of philosophy 'as a study distinct from science and possessed of a method of its own, is anything more than an unfortunate legacy from theology'.[57]

The words 'God' and 'theological' are used by Derrida in a way that is at once more specific and more general than is ordinarily so. There is no particular case proposed against theol-

56 Derrida, *Of grammatology*, pp. 75ff.
57 Bertrand Russell, *Logic and knowledge: essays 1901–1950*, ed. R. C. Marsh (London: George Allen and Unwin, 1956), p. 325.

ogy, but theology is included within a general critique. Any theology that fashions God just from the vocabulary of presence will be shown to founder upon its own foundation; and this leads us to ask if deconstruction attacks theology from any other directions. We have also seen that 'theological' is a synonym for 'metaphysical' in Derrida's lexicon, and this prompts the related question, to be taken up shortly, if it is the case, as Derrida implies, that all theology is 'theological'?

3 Odium theologiæ

Sometimes one can see further by looking to one side rather than straight ahead. So I shall begin by examining not a passage by Derrida but by a writer who, at one period of his career, was heavily influenced by the programme and vocabulary of deconstruction: Roland Barthes. And I wish to probe Barthes partly because we see, in the following passage, a particularly clear instance of one interpretation of the force of deconstruction, and partly because passages such as this are often invoked as indicating the inevitable theological implications of deconstruction. 'We know now', Barthes writes, 'that a text is not a line of words releasing a single "theological" meaning (the "message" of the Author-God) but a multi-dimensional space in which a variety of writings, none of them original, blend and clash'.[58] So far deconstruction has been presented as a practice of reading, but the deeper implications of this practice are soon drawn out:

> In the multiplicity of writing, everything is to be *disentangled*, nothing *deciphered*; the structure can be followed, 'run' (like the thread of a stocking) at every point and at every level, but there is nothing beneath: the space of writing is to be ranged over, not pierced; writing ceaselessly posits meaning ceaselessly to evaporate it, carrying out a systematic exemption of meaning. In precisely this way literature (it would be better from now on to say *writing*), by refusing to assign a 'secret', an ultimate meaning, to the text (and to the world as text), liberates what may be called an anti-theological activity, an activity that is truly revolutionary since to refuse to fix meaning is, in the end, to refuse God and his hypostases – reason, science, law.[59]

58 Barthes, 'The death of the author', in *Image, music, text*, trans. Stephen Heath (New York: Hill and Wang, 1977), p. 146.
59 Barthes, 'The death of the author', p. 147.

Barthes's case is based upon the familiar conceptual model of interpretation, signs and God. All attempts to arrive at a determinate meaning – that is, all attempts to totalise a text – are held to be theological insofar as they assume, at one level or another, that the sign is ultimately grounded in a pure self-presence. And so the demonstration that in any given text there is a remainder of signification which escapes any conjectured circumscription, is taken to be an anti-theological activity. It is unclear, however, exactly what force is to be attributed to the notion of *refusing* 'God and his hypostases'. Barthes's argument can be formalised along the following lines. The theist's position is presented as 'If there is a God, then a determinate meaning can be found for any given text' to which Barthes replies, 'If I can show you that, in any given text, meaning is structurally indeterminate, then this is in effect a denial of God'. Barthes's reply need not worry the theist since, even if we accept his premise, the conditional 'If – q then – p' may be deduced from 'If p then q'. So Barthes's case goes no way toward establishing an argument against the theist. However, perhaps the force of 'refuse' is not to be taken quite so strictly; perhaps Barthes's aim lies not so much in making out a case against theism but in developing another vocabulary for interpretation, one in which 'God' plays no important role.

This view finds some support in Barthes's comments on western and eastern attitudes toward the sign, offered during an interview with *L'Express*. After explaining the characteristically Derridean point that in a dictionary any signified is also in the position of a signifier, Barthes remarks that 'in the West there comes a point when the dictionary, or, if you prefer, the inventory of everything in the world, comes to a halt with God, who is the keystone in the arch, since God can only be a signified, never a signifier: how could God ever mean anything beside himself?'[60] We pick up his thread with the following remarks: 'All civilizations in which monotheism plays a role are necessarily under the constraint of monism; they stop the play of signs at some definite point. And that is the structural constraint of our

60 '*L'Express* talks with Roland Barthes' (*L'Express*, May 31, 1970) in R. Barthes, *The grain of the voice*, trans. Linda Coverdale (New York: Hill and Wang, 1985), p. 99. Barthes maintains that 'the metaphysical or semantic definition of theology is to postulate the ultimate Signified' in 'L'analyse structural du récit: à propos d'Actes X-XI', in *Exégèse et herméneutique*, ed. Xavier Léon-

civilization'.[61] 'Monism' is used strangely here. What about Catholics, such as Descartes, who were firm dualists? Or, again, what about Plotinus – whose influence on Christian theology surely needs no testimony – who held the doctrine of the Indeterminate Dyad? The situation Barthes describes here is not monism at all but monogenesis.

Christian theology, with its doctrinal emphasis upon purity of origins – *creatio ex nihilo*, Mary's immaculate conception and Jesus's virginal conception – stands as a paradigm of the metaphysics of presence, so much so that Derrida can talk, in the one breath, of 'the philosophical or Christian idea of pure origin'.[62] Now as we know, Derrida argues that the weak link in the conceptual chain 'interpretation– sign–God' is the middle term, the upshot being that we must take interpretation, not God, as the originary term, with all the linguistic and conceptual paradoxes that this involves. Quite plainly, 'interpretation' will differ in meaning depending upon whether the chain is read as ascending or descending. If God is taken as *fons et origo*, interpretation is to be conceived along the lines of recovery and fall. But if 'interpretation' is taken to precede 'sign', it is to be regarded – so Derrida and Barthes contend – as groundless play and affirmation. Meaning, Derrida tells us, 'is a *function* of play, is inscribed in a certain place in the configuration of a meaningless play'.[63] We can postpone a discussion of play to later in this study; but we need now to clarify the status of 'God' in the new model of interpretation.

The new model of interpretation draws its vocabulary from the old model, but the import of the immanent critique which leads Derrida to establish the new model is that the concepts of the new model are prior to those of the old model. The difficulty, however, is that the new model puts into question precisely those words such as 'origin' and 'priority' which it needs to claim for its own. Derrida is therefore forced to adopt paradoxical formulations such as 'non-originary origin', that is, to use the discourse of phenomenality to talk about the condition of possibility of phenomena. This is so with all Derrida's hinge words: *écriture, différance, trace, répétition, jeu, supplément*, and so

Dufour (Paris: Seuil, 1971), p. 201. For Derrida's similar comments see, for example, *Positions*, p. 20.

61 '*L'Express* talks with Roland Barthes', p. 99.   62 Derrida, *Writing*, p. 248.
63 Derrida, *Writing*, p. 260.

forth.[64] Now at the level of the transcendental we have a mode of difference which precedes the notion of identity; it cannot be recuperated by identity, as in Hegel's formulation; it is difference as such or, in Derrida's radical refinement, *différance*. Since it precedes all relation to presence or identity, *différance* can be neither self-present nor self-identical; it is never constituted, only ever constituting: thus Derrida's talk of the play of *différance*. Although we write the word *'différance'* and use it as a concept, as I am doing here and now, what the word signifies in fact is the enabling condition of conceptuality. All concepts, and hence all meaning, are a function of *différance*; and this obviously holds true for the concept of God.

It is from this point that the deconstructive challenge to theology is made. Its main line of attack is the critique of functional transcendence; but Derrida's general critique ramifies into various arguments, which I shall sketch now and examine later. To begin with, we have the basis of a genetic critique of theism; and this, I take it, is the import of Derrida's somewhat opaque question to Emmanuel Levinas: 'and if God was an *effect of the trace?'*[65] It is perfectly plain, however, that God cannot be an effect of *différance*: although it sounds far less dramatic, what Derrida can only mean is that the *concept* of God is an effect of the trace. The deconstruction of theism will show, consequently, that 'God', as used at any point and time of history, is a construction. This may count against *arguments* for God's existence, such as Descartes's, which depend upon the idea of God being implanted in the mind, but it hardly counts against *belief* in God. After all, how we get the idea of something and if that idea is true are entirely different matters, as are arguments *that* God exists and confessions of belief *in* God.

This final distinction may lead one to object that Derrida assumes that God *is* a being or *is* Being itself, whereas God is wholly other than both beings and Being, and so Derrida misses the entire animus of theism, God's infinite otherness. In point of

64 Consider the following: 'The (pure) trace is differance' (*Of grammatology*, p. 62); 'The *pharmakon* is that dangerous supplement' (*Dissemination*, p. 110); 'this movement of play . . .is the movement of *supplementarity*' (*Writing*, p. 289); 'The same is here called supplement, another name for differance' (*Of grammatology*, p. 150); 'It is a question, rather, of producing a new concept of writing. This concept can be called *gram* or *différance*' (*Positions*, p. 26).
65 Derrida, *Writing*, p. 108.

fact, however, Derrida's critique of theism is based precisely upon these views, as expressed by Levinas in *Totality and infinity*. Levinas sets the infinite value of the Other against the totality of the Hegelian Same; but, as Derrida argues, to do this is precisely to play into Hegel's hands. There is no basis for Levinas's assumption that totality is finite and unsurpassable; the point of the *Aufhebung* is that it does not destroy but conserves otherness in the dialectical sublation of the Same and the Other.[66]

In addition, the deconstructive case is conducted with respect to content and form. The main thrust of Derrida's attack is levelled at the reference to a determinate centre in theism. That is, theism is understood as belief in a centre, and theology is consequently seen as a thetic discourse. But as both Barthes and Derrida make plain, they refuse to fix textual meaning in specific theses; and the playfulness of their discourses is intended as an anti-theological gesture. We can postpone the difficulties with this particular case until we have investigated the force of 'play', and return instead to the more general argument of which it is a part. I mean, of course, the view to which our discussion of Barthes has led us: that deconstruction at once discredits an old vocabulary, ineluctably linked with theology, and urges us to accept a new vocabulary which does not do without the old but situates it with respect to the new. Thus the concepts upon which classical discourse on God has been founded – 'origin', 'end', 'self-identity', and so forth – are shown, not speculatively but as the result of specific readings, to be incapable of providing such a foundation. In this sense, theology is shown to founder upon its own foundation, though whether this is theology's *only* foundation and whether theology needs such a foundation are questions to place on notice.

Still, before I pass to other topics it would be useful to register the differences between the two general models that have regulated my discussion throughout this chapter. By dint of an immanent critique we pass from a model in which signification depends upon the positing of a transcendental ground, and in which interpretation can be construed only by way of a fall, to a model in which chance, what befalls a sign, is a condition of possibility for signification in general. We pass from a model in

66 Derrida, *Writing*, p. 120.

which there is a fundamental difference between a sign and the sign of a sign to one in which there is no basis for a qualitative distinction between 'original' and 'counterfeit'. More generally, we pass from a discourse upon the 'ground' to one upon the 'groundless'. We do not have, in any significant sense, a case for atheism; but if we accept Derrida's analysis of the relation between presence and sign, as I think we must, we do have to recognise that a good deal of the traditional doctrinal content attached to 'God' is put under critical pressure.

There are different ways of responding to this recognition. So far I have been guided by the commonly accepted view that deconstruction exhibits an *odium theologiæ*, that it furnishes a powerful critique of the possibility of theology. Those who propound this view generally take deconstruction as the latest and most refined instance of Nietzsche's attack against western morality, philosophy and religion. Deconstruction has therefore become aligned with the slogan 'God is dead', and while there is some reason for this association it is also, in many ways, a misalliance. For as this discussion has shown, deconstruction provides a critique not of theology as such but of the metaphysical element within theology and, for that matter, within any discourse. If we take 'God is dead' to be a statement about the impossibility of locating a transcendent point which can serve as a ground for discourse, then deconstruction is indeed a discourse on God's death. But if we take 'God is dead' to be a formula for unbelief or disbelief, then there is no reason at all to link it with deconstruction. With this distinction in mind, I turn to a completely different reading of deconstruction, one in which the links between deconstruction and theology are positive rather than negative.

2 | Deconstruction otherwise

Introduction

The first chapter described what the relationship between deconstruction and theology is commonly taken to be and what reasons there are for holding this view. However, in trying to be precise about the matter at hand I had to raise but leave unexamined a number of issues which now demand clarification. I have had recourse, for example, to Pascal's distinction between the God of the philosophers and the God of Abraham, Isaac and Jacob; and I have made use of Nietzsche's statement 'God is dead'. The conjunction of Pascal's distinction and Nietzsche's statement inevitably leads one to ask, 'But *which* God is dead?' While no one doubts what Pascal's answer would be, there is a general lack of agreement as to how Nietzsche would reply. There are those, for instance, who regard Nietzsche as diagnosing a malaise in Christendom: real belief in the God of Christianity is dead, and so the Christian God has lost all power over the determination of man.[1] Others understand Nietzsche to affirm that Christian morality has been so discredited, both from within and without, that it can no longer be endorsed by a serious moral agent.[2] Still others approach the text from Nietzsche's epistemology, seeing it as a terse denial that there can be any firm ground for our knowledge of ourselves and our

---

1 See, for example, Martin Heidegger, *Nietzsche*, Vol. IV, trans. Frank A. Capuzzi, ed. D. F. Krell (San Francisco: Harper and Row, 1982), p. 4. Heidegger distinguishes between Christendom – a cultural and intellectual movement – and Christianity, a relationship in faith with God.
2 '"God is dead"... Nietzsche's heart was not in contesting the existence of God, or in the other arguments to which we have referred. His central attack, into which he flung himself with all his force, was upon what he called Christian morality.' Karl Barth, *Church dogmatics*, Vol. 3 'The doctrine of creation', Part 2, p. 238.

world.[3] Finally, there is a small number of critics who see in Nietzsche's aphorism an attempt to jolt us out of received conceptions of God so that we may begin our quest for the God who is beyond all human categories of good and evil, beyond all human notions of being and non-being.

There would be little point in trying to forge a positive link between Pascal and Nietzsche. The most that can usefully be said is that each rejects the God of the philosophers, though for quite different reasons and for very different ends. Still, the various senses in which the word 'God' is used by Pascal, Nietzsche and their commentators reminds us that few words are more overdetermined than this one. It is not just that 'God' tends to play different roles in philosophy and theology but that the traditions have been so tightly interlaced for so long that it is well nigh impossible to distinguish between these roles. In many cases, of course, a sharp distinction is not called for, yet there are times enough when an entire work or an approach demands that a distinction be made. Pascal's *Pensées* is one such work, and along with a host of texts written at various times and in various contexts, it forms part of a tradition commonly known as 'non-metaphysical theology'. ←

Derrida's project involves a thinking back through the history of western thought to find those moments when metaphysics is marked and exceeded by something it cannot fully control. And in this project a special place has been reserved for literary texts: Artaud, Bataille, Blanchot, Celan, Genet, Jabès, Mallarmé and Ponge. What attracts Derrida to literary language is not so much its semantic richness as its rapport with the limits of thought. Literature, for Derrida, is a matter of 'certain movements which have worked around the limits of our logical concepts, certain texts which make the limits of our language tremble, exposing them as divisible and questionable'.[4] It is here, apparently outside philosophy, that one can gain a purchase upon philosophy. 'In literature, for example, philosophical language is

---

3 See, for example, Tracy B. Strong, *Friedrich Nietzsche and the politics of transfiguration* (Berkeley: University of California Press, 1975), p. 205. It should be emphasised, however, that these three positions are sometimes held by the one thinker, as is the case, for example, with Heidegger.

4 Derrida, 'Deconstruction and the other', in *Dialogues with contemporary continental thinkers*, ed. Richard Kearney (Manchester: Manchester University Press, 1984), p. 112.

still present in some sense; but it produces and presents itself as alienated from itself, at a remove, at a distance. This distance provides the necessary free space from which to interrogate philosophy anew'.[5] What Derrida finds in some literary texts is also at work in religious texts; above all, it is in the writings of the mystics and mystical theologians that the vocabulary and concepts of philosophy present themselves as limited and askew, at variance with themselves. Deconstruction is an attempt to find a place from which to question metaphysics, a place that is itself not simply within metaphysics. Such an attempt can be launched from within discourse on God, in those writings which put metaphysics in question in order to speak of God.

If there is a way of bringing theology and deconstruction into conversation, then, it will be by way of non-metaphysical theology, and the dialogue will involve mystics as well as theologians. Yet there are various objections to this conversation taking place, and these must be examined before we can proceed. We have seen that, for Derrida, all theology is *ipso facto* metaphysical, and I have indicated several points of weakness in this claim. Pressing one of these, I have distinguished between the *text* of theology and the 'theological' *function* of context. With this in mind, I pose the following questions. In what ways has deconstruction been framed so that it appears to have an inbuilt resistance to religious questions? What is the deconstructive power of the text of theology?

1 Immanent critique

At the risk of labouring the point, I begin by reiterating the three fundamental tenets of Derrida's case: *all* texts resist totalisation; *no* text is absolutely free from a context or a centre; and *some* texts seem to totalise other texts. If we apply these tenets to the text of deconstruction itself we can easily identify a number of positions which, in attempting to put deconstruction to work, inevitably, and often unwittingly, set a process of totalisation in motion. Most common, perhaps, is the view that deconstruction is concerned only with literary texts, that it is a barely disguised formalism. True, Derrida often begins and ends with the 'words on the page', but his object is to see how that text invites being

5 Derrida, 'Deconstruction and the other', p. 109.

framed by a context it cannot fully master. So there is an inter-
play between the phenomenal and the transcendental senses of
'text' which precludes any simple formalism. Almost as common
is the tempting ploy, often used by Marxists and feminists, to
take 'difference' and 'undecidability' as distinct values in themselves when their critical force lies precisely in their power to
question the ground of values. I wish to stress, however, that
consciously or unconsciously deconstruction has been promoted
by its adherents (especially in the English-speaking world)
within the general context of 'atheism'. The viability of atheism
as a context for deconstruction is not in question here; but what
is in question is the often unspoken assumption that there is a   NB
natural or inevitable link between deconstruction and atheism:
for that is exactly what transmutes a matter of context into a
matter of totalisation.

I shall focus on what is arguably the most influential text on
deconstruction in the English-speaking world: Gayatri Spivak's
'Translator's preface' to *Of grammatology*. We see here a common
framing of Derrida and déconstruction, namely their inclusion
within a 'counter tradition' at work in western thought.[6] Spivak
spends most of her time discussing 'three magistral [*sic*] gram-
matologues: Friedrich Nietzsche, Sigmund Freud, Martin Heidegger' and thereby reads Derrida as the most recent member of
a tradition and, indeed, as the after-the-fact origin of the tradition. And the authority for this tradition turns out to be none
other than Derrida's own citation of these names. Speaking of
the emergence of his own problematic, Derrida asks,

> Where and how does this decentering, this thinking the struc-
> turality of structure, occur? It would be somewhat naïve to
> refer to an event, a doctrine, or an author in order to designate
> this occurrence. It is no doubt part of the totality of an era, our
> own, but still it has always already begun to proclaim itself and
> begun to *work*. Nevertheless, if we wished to choose several
> 'names', as indications only, and to recall those authors in
> whose discourse this occurrence has kept most closely to its
> radical formulation, we doubtless would have to cite the
> Nietzschean critique of metaphysics, the critique of the con-
> cepts of Being and truth, for which were substituted the con-

---

6 The same view is in evidence in Christopher Norris's *Deconstruction* (London:
Methuen, 1982), especially chapter 4. For Norris's decidedly negative view as
to possible relations between deconstruction and theology see his 'Transcendental vanities', *Times Literary Supplement*, 27 April 1984, p. 470.

cepts of play, interpretation, and sign (sign without present truth); the Freudian critique of self-presence, that is, the critique of consciousness, of the subject, of self-identity and of self-proximity or self-possession; and, more radically, the Heideggerian destruction of metaphysics, of onto-theology, of the determination of Being as presence.[7]

Derrida's point is simply that Nietzsche, Freud and Heidegger provide the phenomenal points of departure for his project. In general terms, Derrida questions the relation between the phenomenal and the transcendental: the *themes* of these three thinkers are shown to be in fact part of the *structure* of all discourse. One consequence of this, as Derrida explains, is that no text can fully account for itself. Now there is a slide from the foregoing passage in Derrida's essay to its quotation in Spivak's introduction. From an argument that no text can supply its own context (which mentions Nietzsche, Freud and Heidegger as starting-points), we pass to the implicit view that these thinkers form the natural and inevitable context for reading Derrida's text. It goes without saying, I imagine, that Derrida could plausibly have invoked other names – Georges Bataille, Maurice Blanchot and Ferdinand de Saussure, for example – and this counts against Spivak's attaching any unique significance to those he does name. Clearly, we see here the unwitting beginning of the critical reception of deconstruction: a process of totalising Derrida's text with reference to Nietzsche, Freud and Heidegger.

It is of course possible to find other contexts for reading Derrida. Out of the many, I choose just one: Isaac Luria, Emmanuel Levinas and Edmund Jabès. From the first we see the Kabbalistic emphasis upon the endless interpretability of a text; from the second, the problematic of the trace and the critique of totality; and from the third, the passage from 'book' to 'text'. All three are Jewish, all three address religious questions, and all three are absent from Spivak's text. I do not claim that these names provide a better, more direct point of entry into deconstruction, only that they reveal one of Spivak's gaps in discussing Nietzsche, Freud and Heidegger, namely an avoid-

7 Derrida, *Writing*, p. 280. Quoted by Spivak, 'Translator's preface', *Of grammatology*, p. lxvii.

Spivak limits...

ance of any links between deconstruction and religion. Speaking of the process of deconstruction, Spivak issues a stern warning to the reader: 'Let me add yet once again that this terrifying and exhilarating vertigo is not "mystical" or "theological"'.[8] This is a curious moment in a text which has talked so animatedly about the danger of adding supplements. Spivak has told us repeatedly how the disseminative drift of texts subverts attempts to control textual meaning, but now, it seems, a firm limit is to be placed upon our reading: we are *not* to think of linking deconstruction to theology or mysticism. There is one sense in which Spivak is perfectly correct. Although Derrida often uses the syntax characteristic of negative theology – 'neither this nor that' – he is most certainly not a theologian or a mystic. However, Spivak is not talking here of the *use* to which Derrida puts deconstruction but rather of the *process* of deconstruction itself; and to exclude theology from deconstruction in this way is simply pre-emptive. For if deconstruction puts into question all systematic knowledge of the highest being and affirms the play of the groundless in the positing of any ground, then it is in point of fact close to the reflections of many mystical theologians. There may be no thematic link between deconstruction and mystical theology, but there may well be a structural link, in that mystical theology might be a mode of deconstruction: and such is the general argument of this study.

Keeping Spivak's interdiction in mind, we can take a closer look at how these three thinkers are presented to us. We come to the quotation of Derrida's citation of Nietzsche, Freud and Heidegger only after having digested Spivak's readings of these three; yet while there is much that is interesting and informative here, her readings plainly emphasise a certain aspect of each writer's work. These figures are introduced to us as three merciless demystifiers, three master hermeneuts of suspicion, as indeed they are. But if we are attentive to Derrida's own practice we should be aware that what Spivak foregrounds is linked to what she pushes to the background; and it is evident that one of the elements which Spivak renders marginal is the category of the religious. We see the Nietzsche whose madman announces 'God is dead' but not the Nietzsche whose madman cries 'I seek

8 Spivak, 'Translator's preface', *Of grammatology*, p. lxxviii.

NB

God! I seek God!'[9] We see Freud's attack on the notion of a unified self-consciousness, but not the Freud who deployed Kabbalistic modes of interpretation.[10] And most revealing of all, we see the 'god-less' Heidegger who attempted the *Destruktion* of onto-theology though never the Heidegger who did so because the God of onto-theology was not sufficiently divine.[11]

We can agree, on the whole, that the triptych Nietzsche, Freud and Heidegger does not form a natural or inevitable context from within which to study deconstruction. And we can also agree that even if this context is adopted one is not thereby committed to Spivak's particular readings of Nietzsche, Freud and Heidegger. For it is surely apparent that Spivak frames deconstruction, from the beginning of its career in the English-speaking world, in ways that marginalise any possible positive relationship between it and theology. Moreover, it is clear that Spivak's framing of deconstruction is itself open to a further deconstruction. But we can go still further: even if one assumed that deconstruction was originally intended to have only a nega-tive relation with theology, one could not argue, on Derrida's assumptions, that deconstruction would always be construed along those lines. If Derrida is right to argue, *contra* Lacan, that a letter does not always arrive at its destination, that it can always be deflected in an unforeseen manner, then one must concede the possibility that the letter of deconstruction may arrive else-where, at an altogether unforeseen address, at the Chicago School of Divinity, say, rather than at the head office of the Rationalist Society. All in all, my reading of Spivak's 'Trans-lator's preface' inclines me to agree with Mark C. Taylor when he complains that 'Followers of Derrida have preferred to overlook the theological and religious aspects of his thought, no doubt suspecting that they represent a vestige of the nostalgia which he criticizes so relentlessly'.[12]

But what are the 'theological and religious aspects' of Derrida's thought? A number of theologians, including Taylor,

9 Nietzsche, *The gay science*, trans. Walter Kaufmann (New York: Vintage Books, 1974), §125 (p. 181).
10 See David Bakan, *Sigmund Freud and the Jewish mystical tradition* (1958; rpt. Boston: Beacon Press, 1975).
11 See Heidegger, *Identity and difference*, trans. Joan Stambaugh (New York: Harper and Row, 1969), p. 72.
12 Taylor, *Deconstructing theology* (New York: Crossroad Publishing Company, 1982), p. xx.

46

have been quick to link deconstruction to the 'God is dead' theology of Altizer and Hamilton; but this is foreign to Derrida's thought. 'It would not mean a single step outside of metaphysics if nothing more than a new motif of "return to finitude", of "God's death", etc., were the result of this move', he remarks. And lest there remain any room for doubt he adds, 'It is that conceptuality and that problematics that must be deconstructed. They belong to the onto-theology they fight against'.[13] The dialectical sublation of classical theism and classical atheism, as found in Altizer's doctrine of 'Christian atheism', is just one more instance of the Hegelianism which Derrida weighs and finds wanting. Yet if Derrida does not endorse the theology of the 'God is dead' movement, he does use the phrase 'God is dead' in his own way, to mean that 'God' cannot function as an agent of totalisation. In this sense Derrida can say without contradiction that 'The death of God will ensure our salvation because the death of God alone can reawaken the divine' and, with equal force, that 'The divine has been ruined by God'.[14] Such remarks suggest the possibility of re-thinking the divine in a discourse which, while it cannot abolish metaphysics, is no longer *governed* by metaphysics. But we need not dwell on Derrida's personal views. There is no reason why there should not be a structural relation between deconstruction and mystical theology and some *prima facie* evidence that there is.

2   *Liberator theologiæ?*

The critical object of deconstruction is totalisation. In the account of deconstruction with which we have so far been concerned, totalisation has been understood exclusively with reference to a 'transcendental signified', a purported Archimedian point outside all textual determinations. We have seen how it is possible to understand God as a paradigmatic instance of such a point, and that the view of deconstruction as 'atheistic' may be traced directly to this supposition. This view could be contested by means of an immanent critique, in which it is argued that the 'atheistic' reading of deconstruction is itself open to deconstruction; and I have already broached such a critique. The atheist

13 Derrida, *Of grammatology*, p. 68. Cf. *Positions*, p. 6.
14 Derrida, *Writing*, p. 184 and p. 243.

reading of deconstruction assumes that totalisation occurs only by means of a reference to an exterior *point*; but totalisation can also occur by reference to a *method*. Thus understood, the critical object of deconstruction is not 'God' but 'hermeneutics'. And if this is the case one can develop a reading of deconstruction that is more positive in its relation to theology than has yet been suggested.

I must begin by pointing out a possible source of confusion. The word 'hermeneutics' is sometimes used, very generally, to signify all discourses that reflect upon problems of interpretation. In this sense Richard Palmer can talk of Gadamer, Ricœur and Derrida as practitioners of 'philosophical hermeneutics'.[15] Paul Ricœur, however, talks of two quite different sorts of hermeneutics: the hermeneutics of faith, on the one hand, is characterised by an attempt to recover intended or even unintended authorial meaning; and in this group we may place Schleiermacher, Dilthey and Hirsch. On the other hand we have the hermeneutics of suspicion, as characterised by the work of Marx, Nietzsche and Freud. Here the emphasis is upon the essential incompleteness of the interpretive act, the thought that behind every mask there is another mask.[16] This is a useful distinction, and if we were to adopt it Derrida would be placed amongst the hermeneuts of suspicion. Now while Derrida would acknowledge a hermeneutic element at work in the texts of Marx, Nietzsche and Freud, he himself uses the word 'hermeneutics' to signify any theory of interpretation which is governed, implicitly or explicitly, by an appeal to presence, be it authorial intention or the reader's consciousness. And as these thinkers feature amongst those who put the notion of presence into question, they are not to be gathered purely and simply under the general title of 'hermeneutics'. So in Derrida's sense of the word, while 'hermeneutics' includes the hermeneutics of faith it also takes within its bounds Gadamer's 'philosophical hermeneutics', Ricœur's own hermeneutic project, and all *Rezeptionästhetik*, not to mention the whole of allegorical and philological hermeneutics.

In Derrida's lexicon, then, 'hermeneutics' signifies a method

15 Palmer, 'Allegorical, philological and philosophical hermeneutics: three modes in a complex heritage', *University of Ottawa Quarterly*, 50 (1980), p. 340.
16 See Ricœur, *Freud and philosophy*, pp. 32–36.

of totalisation, as is emphasised when Derrida talks, for example, of 'an *assured* horizon of a hermeneutic question' and of 'a hermeneutic *mastery*'.[17] I have already distinguished between the text of theology and the 'theological' function of context, and I need to extend this distinction into the realm of hermeneutics. The word 'hermeneutics' first appears in post-Reformation theology, specifically in discussions of scriptural exegesis. In the wake of Bultmann's work, though, hermeneutics has moved from a marginal area of theology concerned only with philology and principles of exegesis to assume the centre stage of theological discussion such that, in the early 1960s, Heinrich Ott could claim that 'theology as a whole is hermeneutical'.[18] Whether Derrida would agree or disagree with Ott is largely beside the point, but he would most definitely claim that hermeneutics is essentially theological. And he would not mean thereby that hermeneutics from Schleiermacher to Ricœur is necessarily concerned with the Bible, only that the hermeneutical attempt to account for all textual meaning in the one reading is 'theological'.

The link between hermeneutics and philosophy, in Derrida's senses of these words, is easily established, both conceptually and historically. Overall, Derrida construes philosophy as that discourse which seeks to resolve textual differences in conceptual unities. Philosophy is therefore always an attempt to totalise the text or, more precisely, *écriture*. I invoke Derrida's French here for a specific reason which one or two examples should explain. The basis of Derrida's mode of analysis is a rigorous attention to the way in which particular words and phrases seem to differ from themselves in certain texts. Thus we see how, in reading Rousseau, Derrida fastens upon the word '*le supplément*' which can mean both 'an addition' and 'a substitute'.[19] Rousseau is well aware of the ambiguity of this word but, as Derrida patiently shows, he cannot fully control the way in which the word works in the text he writes. Rousseau's *Confessions* follows a kind of 'kettle logic', in which the narrator maintains I added writing as an unnecessary extra to speech; I replaced speech

---

17 Derrida, *Spurs*, pp. 127, 131. My emphasis.
18 Ott, 'What is systematic theology?' in James M. Robinson and John B. Cobb Jr, eds., *The later Heidegger and theology*. New Frontiers in Theology, I. (New York: Harper and Row, 1963), p. 78.
19 See Derrida, *Of grammatology*, II, 2, esp. pp. 144–45.

with writing; and there never was a fullness of speech in the first place.[20] The three views cannot be gathered together into a coherent whole, not even under the rubrics of 'ambiguity' or 'polysemy', yet each is fully answerable to the text and so the text exceeds any attempt to totalise it. Similarly, in reading Plato's *Phaedrus* Derrida focuses upon the description of writing as a *pharmakon*. The word *'pharmakon'* can mean both 'remedy' and 'poison'. Derrida argues that no attempt to gloss writing exclusively as a poison, as happens in the tradition of Plato translation, can fully explain the text: it will always be possible to develop a reading which takes writing to be a remedy. Scrupulous attention to the ambivalence of one word can recall a certain tradition of reading Rousseau or Plato to its proper limits.

With this in mind, I return to Derrida's own word, *écriture*. The tradition of Derrida interpretation, which includes the tradition of Derrida translation, has almost exclusively taken *'écriture'* to mean simply 'writing'; its other meaning, 'scripture', has been ignored.[21] To point out this difference within *'écriture'* is not to protest that Derrida has been ill-served by his interpreters and translators; it is to observe that the conception of *écriture* as 'writing', pure and simple, has been used to bring Derrida's text (and, implicitly, the text of deconstruction) completely in line with secularism. If we conceive *écriture* as 'scripture' a number of Derrida's remarks readily assume a different expression. We note, for instance, how Derrida defines Judaism as 'the birth and passion of *écriture'* and that it is 'The Jew who elects *écriture* which elects the Jew'.[22] From this second interpretation of *écriture*, it is possible to explain remarks that can only seem puzzling within the orbit of the word's first interpretation. The following should make the point: 'the Jew is but the suffering allegory' and 'The Jew is split, and split first of all between the

20 The term 'kettle logic' is drawn from Freud's *Jokes and their relation to the unconscious*, trans. James Strachey. Pelican Freud Library, Vol. 6 (Harmondsworth: Penguin, 1976), p. 100.
21 There are two exceptions. Susan Handelman notes in passing that *'écriture'* can mean 'scripture', though her concern is to present deconstruction as a 'new religion of *Writing'*, *The slayers of Moses: the emergence of rabbinic interpretation in modern literary theory* (Albany: SUNY, 1982), p. 164. Similarly, Andrew J. McKenna observes, with regard to Barthes, that 'the French word for writing is the same which designates Scripture', 'Biblioclasm: joycing Jesus and Borges', *Diacritics*, 8 (1978), p. 16.
22 Derrida, *Writing*, p. 64 and p. 65. Translation modified.

two dimensions of the letter: allegory and literality'.[23] It is possible to read these remarks as making a claim about the relation between philosophy and literature (that philosophy is always already the allegory of a literary text) but while this reading has some force it is neither the only nor the best available. The point of 'allegory' is most keenly registered here if one recognises that the means whereby Jewish scripture was linked with its 'other' – Greek metaphysics – was through the operations of the allegorical hermeneutic.

We must be careful not to go too quickly here. It could be argued that the allegorical hermeneutic was used precisely by the early Church Fathers – especially Origen and the Cappadocians – to elevate Christian over Jewish doctrine. So, in attacking hermeneutics, Derrida is once more attacking Christianity. This argument has some force; its premises are correct, and Derrida's critique of hermeneutics does have consequences for what is 'theological' in Christian theology; but its force is reduced by the possibility of drawing another conclusion. The allegorical hermeneutic was devised *within* the Jewish faith with the specific aim of preserving that faith in the face of philosophical critique. If one allows this final point it can be argued that the deconstruction of hermeneutics does not call religious faith as such into question but offers a critique of the relation between faith and metaphysics as determined by hermeneutics. I wish to give more substance to this view, and thus to the reading of deconstruction based upon *écriture* as 'scripture'. And as it turns out, Derrida supplies us with an historical point of departure in his phrase 'Alexandrian promiscuity' which, in the context of an essay on Judaism and philosophy, can only be an elliptic reference to Philo.[24]

Philo effects the transformation of an old crossroads, the confluence of Judaism and Hellenism, into a new point of departure, the interpretation of scripture by way of Greek philosophy. Equally at home in the two traditions, both culturally and intellectually, Philo Judæus cannot be separated from Philo Alexandrinus; it is impossible to distinguish Philo's faith as a Jew from his interpretation of that faith as an Alexandrian. Certainly he was not the first to attempt a synthesis of the traditions; he ends a long period, stretching back two centuries or more, of

23 Derrida, *Writing*, p. 75.   24 Derrida, *Writing*, p. 84.

unsatisfactory fusions which, after him, can be seen only as confusions. By and large these sought to overcome ideological conflicts by forcing an identification of Judaism and Hellenism at the level of religious history, by claiming, for example, that Moses was in fact Osiris or Hermes-Tat. Philo, however, is the first to attempt a quite different kind of synthesis, the relating of Jewish faith and Greek philosophy; his programme does not involve the elimination of religious differences as they had unfolded in history but, rather, seeks to draw together Jewish faith and the most persuasive elements of Greek philosophy. Philo's entire enterprise is aptly captured by the word 'interpretation', not only because of the lead role his allegorical method plays in his writings, but also, and more generally, because Philo is an interpreter in the etymological sense of the word, a negotiator of *pretium* or value: he negotiates between what is, for him, of supreme value in both traditions. Such a task was undoubtedly necessary in first century Alexandria: the Jewish Law was quickly becoming unintelligible to the Jews of the Diaspora precisely because the concepts of Greek philosophy were taken, by both Greeks and Jews, as the basis of intelligibility. Individual Jews were beginning to see the Law as thoroughly anachronistic; certain semi-popular fusions of Judaism and Hellenism rendered legal observations pointless.[25] Philo's task was to render as intelligible and familiar what was beginning to appear unintelligible and unfamiliar, that is, to interpret the Torah in accordance with the conclusions of Greek philosophy, and to do so without abandoning the positivity of the Law.

A devout Jew of the Diaspora, Philo was committed to two basic propositions: that the text of the Jewish Bible – in both Hebrew and Greek – is divinely inspired and therefore incapable of error, and that God is absolutely transcendent. Each of these propositions is underpinned by a matrix of theological assumptions, but whereas the second can be harmonised with certain scriptural pronouncements and particular conclusions of Greek metaphysics, the first is exclusively confessional. Philo's difficulty is that these propositions are in conflict: whilst all scrip-

25 See Philo, *On the migration of Abraham*, 91–93, in *Philo* (10 Vols.) ed. F. H. Colson and G. H. Whitaker. Loeb Classical Library (London: Heinemann, 1929–71), Vol. 4. Goodenough remarks that 'Philo was a fastidious observer of the Law', *By light, light* (1935; rpt. Amsterdam: Philo Press, 1969), p. 84.

ture, and especially the Pentateuch, is to be considered inerrant, not all scripture – not even all that is traditionally credited to Moses – appears to square with the doctrine of God's transcendence. Philo's exemplary solution of this problem involves a distinction between the literal or obvious meaning of scripture and its underlying or allegorical meaning. By this means he is able to hold both propositions in tandem; indeed, according to this view, scripture is held to be more subtle, more deeply inspired, than appearances would otherwise suggest.

It is time to take a look at how the allegorical hermeneutic works. God's transcendence is, for Philo, a literal truth; so when he encounters a text such as Numbers 23:19, 'God is not a man', he takes it as a literal expression of the truth; but when faced with Deuteronomy 1:31, in which God is plainly compared with a man ('thou hast seen how that the Lord thy God bare thee, as a man doth bear his son'), the text is to be interpreted allegorically.[26] The doctrine of God's transcendence is, accordingly, the firm criterion for all interpretation of scripture. Yet this doctrine does not provide the stable point of reference for faith it seems to offer. After all, the transcendence of the deity is a conclusion of Greek philosophy as well as the starting-point of Jewish faith, and if Philo were to maintain this doctrinal hierarchy he would thereby allow the scriptures to be interpreted by those who do not accept the Jewish faith. There could be no check, other than that of God's transcendence, on the conclusions of the allegorical hermeneutic: the Law would be in constant danger of being allegorised out of history, and it is the positivity of the Law that Philo is committed to preserve. In order to forestall this possibility Philo returns to the doctrine of the inspired, inerrant text. Quite plainly he cannot prize this doctrine above the doctrine of God's transcendence, but he can consistently maintain that the allegorical hermeneutic can only be deployed by someone who is inspired, and this is exactly what he does. Sowers notes that for Philo 'the inspiration of the Biblical writer and the allegorical interpreter are of the same prophetic type', and there is definite evidence in Philo's texts to support this view.[27]

26 Philo, *On the unchangeableness of God*, xi. 52–53 and xiv. 69. (*Philo*, Vol. 3.) Also see *On the birth of Abel and the sacrifices offered by him and by his brother Cain*, xxx. 101 (*Philo*, Vol. 2).
27 S. G. Sowers, *The hermeneutics of Philo and Hebrews*. Basel Studies of Theology, No. 1. (Richmond, VA: John Knox Press, 1965), p. 41. Goodenough also

This doctrine of inspired interpretation does not necessarily conflict with the view, which Philo also holds, that interpretation has rules which must be followed.[28] Anyone can follow the rules, but the rules need to be followed by the right person, in much the same way as anyone can learn to write iambic pentameters though only poets can write poems. There are various objections that one could raise against this view of inspiration, but they need not detain us here. Of importance for us is that by according neither the doctrine of God's transcendence nor the doctrine of inerrant scripture an uncritical privilege, Philo is constrained to set the allegorical hermeneutic above all possible rivals, from within the Jewish faith and Greek philosophy. The allegorical hermeneutic is to be used because it leads to the truth, and because it leads to the truth it has the status of a true method. Doctrine and hermeneutic are therefore tightly interwoven, and while this gives substantial security to Philo as hermeneut it also means that any attack upon the allegorical hermeneutic will also be, at least in part, an attack against the content of the doctrines it shapes and supports; and this is exactly what happens when Derrida brings hermeneutics into question.

The truth of allegorising is constituted by its disclosure of a true difference, that God is unlike man, and God's difference from man guarantees that any text which represents Him as like man must necessarily differ from itself: it must not mean what it seems to mean. In what way, though, does God differ from man? Is it even possible for us to know? For if we can have

remarks that 'Philo felt himself inspired at times', *By light, light*, p. 76. For Philo's remarks about inspiration and interpretation see *On the change of names*, 139 (Philo, Vol. 5), *On the cherubim, and the flaming sword, and Cain and the first man created out of man*, 27 (*Philo*, Vol. 2); *On the birth of Abel*, 78 (*Philo*, Vol. 2); *On the special laws*, III. 1 (*Philo*, Vol. 5). These remarks upon inspiration and interpretation are often made in tandem with remarks upon the privilege of those initiated into sacred mysteries. In this regard see especially *On the cherubim*, 42 and 48 and *On the birth of Abel*, 60 and 62.

28 Thus Philo writes of interpreting 'in accordance with the rules of allegory', *On dreams*, I. xiii. 73 and again at I. xvii. 102 (*Philo*, Vol. 5). In the second section of this same treatise Philo writes of 'the directions of Allegory' (II. ii. 8); and in another text Philo makes the following remark: 'But we shall take the line of allegorical interpretation not in any contentious spirit, nor seeking some means of meeting sophistry with sophistry. Rather we shall follow the chain of logical sequence, which does not admit of stumbling but easily removes any obstructions and thus allows the argument to march to its conclusion with unfaltering steps', *On the confusion of tongues*, v. 14 (*Philo*, Vol. 4).

positive knowledge of how God differs from us, we can surely know something of God. Now Philo is committed to the view that no positive assertion can be made concerning God, yet this view is nowhere advanced in scripture.[29] The fact that God's transcendence of the world is a conclusion of Greek metaphysics – specifically, for Philo, in Plato's *Timaeus* – as well as a starting-point of Jewish faith, prepares the ground for a translation of a scriptural notion into philosophical concepts. Yet the Jewish starting-point and the Greek conclusion are by no means identical, and Philo modifies both the Aristotelian and the Stoic versions of the cosmological argument before making any translation of scripture into philosophy. After this, however, Philo passes from God's 'unlikeness' to his 'incorporeality' and 'simplicity', and from God's 'unity' to His 'simplicity'. In each case a scriptural notion is translated into an Aristotelian concept. What is new in Philo, at least according to Harry Wolfson, is that Philo argues for God's incomprehensibility on the sole basis of His incorporeality, and from here to the conclusion that God is unnameable and ineffable.[30]

We must be careful to distinguish between the warp and the woof of Philo's argument. It is plain that Philo's allegorical hermeneutic seeks to totalise Jewish scripture, and that the agent of totalisation is not Greek metaphysics, as is usually thought, but the allegorical hermeneutic itself. And I have already adduced reasons why Derrida would strongly object to this view of interpretation and, for that matter, to this view of translation. But it is also plain, I think, that Philonic hermeneutics does a good deal more than establish a positive relationship between scripture and metaphysics; it also goes some way towards developing an account of how one can talk about this transcendent God: that is, it gives rise to a negative theology. Andrew Louth is right, then, to suggest that 'Philo certainly has some claim to be called the Father of negative theology',[31] but

29 Philo, *Allegorical interpretation*, III. lxxiii. 206 (*Philo*, Vol. 1).
30 Wolfson, *Philo* (Cambridge, MA: Harvard University Press, 1948) Vol. 2, p. 111 and p. 154.
31 Louth, *The origins of the Christian mystical tradition* (Oxford: Clarendon Press, 1981), p. 19. Also in agreement is Julius Guttmann who remarks that 'Philo went far beyond Plato, and for the first time gave to the notion of divine transcendence the radical twist of later negative theology', *Philosophies of Judaism*, trans. Silverman (New York: Holt, Rinehart and Winston, 1964), p. 25.

what escapes Louth's attention, and the sustained attention of scholars generally, is that there is a relation between the allegorical hermeneutic and negative theology. And it is this relation which distinguishes Philo from other contenders for the title 'Father of negative theology', especially Parmenides. I wish to reserve discussion of this relation until I discuss the different kinds of negative theology. I reserve, too, the question of the relation between the deconstruction of hermeneutics and negative theology. All this will concern us in part III, while now we examine the relation between scripture and metaphysics in closer detail.

It may seem odd to argue, as I am doing here, that deconstruction can be read as directed against Philonic hermeneutics. After all, Derrida makes only one allusion to Philo, and even there he does not mention him by name. Yet in talking of Philo we are not so much dealing with the individual *author* of a particular set of texts as with a *tradition* of hermeneutics whose historical provenance we take to be those texts. Aristobulus or Pseudo-Aristeas could be cited as originating the allegorical hermeneutic, and one could look elsewhere, for example to Rabbinic allegory, to find another point of origin; but I choose Philo partly because of the acuteness of his formulations, partly because of the richness of his exegesis and partly because of his influence throughout the Patristic era. So I am not committed to the monogenesis of 'hermeneutics'; nor do I make assumptions about Derrida's reading. Also, while I cannot help but base my case on those texts signed 'Jacques Derrida' our chief interest is in the general strategy of deconstruction, and my claim is that deconstruction, being what it is, must take the allegorical hermeneutic as one of its critical objects.

I have spoken of a tradition which answers to Philo, and I need to give some substance to this claim. Philo's allegorical hermeneutic opened a path that the Alexandrian catechists Clement and Origen were to follow and extend in accordance with their theological directives, and which was to be pursued by later Fathers, such as St Gregory Nyssa, whose authority as representatives of Nicene orthodoxy was to extend, in part, to the hermeneutic itself. In the homilies of St Ambrose, preached in the late fourth century, Philo's hermeneutic is still dominant, and its significance for later theology is underlined by St Augustine's testimony in the *Confessions* that it was instrumental in his

56

conversion to Christianity. Not surprisingly, it is Augustine who later defends allegorising against Faustus the Manichee and who, in *On Christian doctrine*, preserves important features of the method for its further dissemination in the Middle Ages and beyond. Philo's significance is not, however, wholly contained within the history of theology as such. Wolfson contends that Philo inaugurates the philosophy that was to dominate the entire period that closes with Spinoza's *Tractatus theologico-politicus*, an era of what we might call *Philo*-sophy.[32] Somewhat more cautiously, Hegel makes 'cursory mention' of Philo's role in the Spirit's quest for absolute self-realisation but emphasises that 'In him we for the first time see the application of the universal consciousness as philosophical consciousness'.[33]

The selection of Hegel out of a vast range of historians of philosophy is not arbitrary but crucial in this context. For only by a discussion of Hegel can we see what is at stake in the relation between Philo and Derrida. Philo's hermeneutic has been claimed to generate the very idea of philosophy that governed thought from the first century to the seventeenth; Hegel's dialectic is the means by which he orchestrated the history of philosophy into what, for him, constituted philosophy as such; and Derridean deconstruction is held to call into question the status and heritage of this conception of philosophy. Towards the end of the essay in which Derrida alludes to Philo, an essay addressing problems in the philosophy of Emmanuel Levinas (including the problem of whether there is, in fact, a Jewish philosophy), Derrida notes that 'the strange dialogue between the Jew and the Greek [has] the form of the absolute, speculative logic of Hegel'.[34] The significance of this remark is evident when one recalls that Derrida uses 'Hegel' as a synecdoche for western philosophy as such. It was of course Heidegger who instituted the familiar image of Hegel as 'the last Greek', the point being

32 'The historical significance of Philo is that his revision became the foundation of the common philosophy of the three religions with cognate Scriptures – Judaism, Christianity, and Islam. This triple religious philosophy, which originated with Philo, reigned supreme as a homogeneous, if not a completely unified, system of thought until the seventeenth century, when it was overthrown by Spinoza, for the philosophy of Spinoza, properly understood, is primarily a criticism of the common elements in this triple religious philosophy.' Wolfson, 'Philo Judæus', *The encyclopedia of philosophy*, 1967 edition.
33 Hegel, *Lectures on the history of philosophy*, Vol. II, p. 387.
34 Derrida, *Writing*, p. 153.

that Hegel's project works with, translates and extends the founding concepts of philosophy: *logos, morphe, ousia, telos* and the rest. In Derrida's lexicon 'Athens' and 'Hegel' stand for serious philosophy: any philosopher, to the precise extent to which he or she *is* a philosopher, is both Greek and Hegelian.

But why is Philo of importance to Hegel? And why is the allegorical hermeneutic of consequence to philosophy? For Hegel, history is always the history of the spirit, and Philo is gathered into the history of philosophy because he overcomes the difference between Greek philosophy and the Jewish Law: Philo releases the spirit from the letter by revealing 'Plato present in Moses'.[35] Hegel approves of Philo because Philo shows the spirit of philosophy to be within its opposite, the Jewish Law, and thereby makes for the sublation of Judaism and Greek philosophy. So, the allegorical hermeneutic is the *vehicle* of the Hegelian dialectic within history. But it is more than this: in its overcoming of specific oppositions in a synthesis which at once maintains and surpasses both the Greek concept and Jewish faith, the allegorical hermeneutic *prefigures* the Hegelian dialectic itself. We have already noted Hegel's high estimation of the Greeks, and of Greek philosophy, but we must also stress Hegel's view of the relation between the Greeks and the Jews.

Hegel's view of Judaism is a good deal more complicated than has sometimes been suggested, but insofar as Hegel maintains a consistent thread in his criticisms, his objections gather around the Jewish observance of the letter of the Law. In his *Lectures on the philosophy of religion* Hegel talks of 'the most trifling regulations' to be found in the Torah, of 'an abstract obedience which does not require any inwardness' and remarks that 'The laws, the commands, are to be followed and observed merely as if by slaves or servants'.[36] Similarly, in the *Phenomenology of mind* Hegel complains that the Jewish consciousness fails to mediate and reflect itself and has been turned into 'a rigidly fixed extreme' which necessitates a 'complete reversal'.[37] From the perspective of the dialectic, the Jews represent the unhappy consciousness brought about by their condition of absolute bondage to the Lord God. The Spirit strives to attain self-

35 Hegel, *Lectures on the history of philosophy*, Vol. II, p. 388.
36 Hegel, *Lectures on the philosophy of religion*, (Speirs edition), Vol. II, pp. 211, 215–16.
37 Hegel, *Phenomenology of mind*, pp. 366, 367.

sublate: opposite y posit -
to negate or deny -.
to reduce to subordinate. position by adding
what it needs, to be intelligible.

consciousness in Judaism but is frustrated by the rigidity of the Jewish Law: its absolute devotion to the letter, its conception of God as totally other than man.

Although the Jewish consciousness, through its strict adherence to the letter of the Law, stands convicted by Hegel as 'a rigidly fixed extreme', it nonetheless contains an aspect of the truth. The Hegelian dialectic develops by way of contrasting facets of the truth and not by simple oppositions of truth and falsity. Emile Fackenheim is therefore right to insist that Hegel's philosophy does not 'simply side either with Athens or Jerusalem' and that 'the truth in each reveals a falsehood in the other'.[38] Jewish literality is revealed as overly particularised but, unlike Neoplatonism, it does not deny the Spirit's historical form, a danger Hegel associates with Gnostic interpretations of scripture and also, though perhaps less justly, with Philo's allegorising of the Torah. The dialectic preserves the Jewish insistence upon the letter, and indeed preserves the *otherness* of the letter, but there can be no denying the fact that the dialectic values the spirit over the letter and, to that extent, Athens over Jerusalem. Hegel quotes the Pauline pericope 'The letter killeth but the spirit gives life' with express approval in those instances, such as the writings of the orthodox Fathers, where the truth of the Spirit is known in a concrete rather than an abstract spirit.[39] Philosophy, the 'witness of the Spirit in its highest form',[40] develops in history, to be sure, but the index of its development is the superior status granted by Hegel to the signified over the signifier. The dialectic develops out of, and abides within, the Greek *logos* which, in separating being from language, promises the possibility of an absolute knowledge of the Spirit in and for itself. What is passed over by the dialectic is the Hebrew *davhar* which, as both word and act, constitutes discourse as act and values scripture over nature. If the dialectic uses the letter to give rise to the spirit, and if the Spirit is the *meaning* of history, as Hegel holds, then the Hegelian philosophy is an *allegory* of history.

It is worth taking a moment to draw out the import of this final

38 Fackenheim, *The religious dimension in Hegel's thought* (Bloomington: Indiana University Press, 1967), p. 174.
39 Hegel, *Lectures on the history of philosophy*, Vol. III, pp. 12–13, p. 15. Also see his *Lectures on the philosophy of religion* (Speirs edition), Vol. II, pp. 343–46.
40 Hegel, *Lectures on the philosophy of religion* (Speirs edition), Vol. II, p. 340.

point. I have argued that, for Derrida, 'hermeneutics' in general is to be understood as an attempt to totalise *écriture*. In the more specific vocabulary in which our discussion has been conducted, hermeneutics is the reading of scripture in terms of philosophy, and Philonic allegory is the *locus classicus* of this hermeneutic mode. I have also argued that for Derrida 'hermeneutics' is a far more widespread tradition than is usually allowed to be the case, and I have taken Philo and Hegel as apparently different indices of this general tradition. We have also seen in the first chapter that Hegel's philosophical project is a demythologising of religious cognition. For Hegel, religion has access to the true content of cognition, but its form remains in the realm of representation (*Vorstellung*); it is the task of philosophy to provide the form adequate to this true content, and that form is the Concept (*Begriff*). In short, the Hegelian dialectic, at least in its highest reaches, is the translation of religion into philosophy, which is to say that it is, in Derrida's sense of the word, a hermeneutic. Both Philo and Hegel accord a privilege to the spirit over the letter, and both see the distinction between the spirit and the letter as tending to converge with the distinction between the intelligible and the sensible. So, once more in Derrida's sense of the word, both Philonic allegory and the Hegelian dialectic are examples of 'metaphysics'.

This discussion has led to the following conclusions. In general terms the tradition of onto-theology is supported by a particular mode of interpretation, which we have called 'hermeneutics', and its fundamental assumption is the identification of the 'spirit' with the 'intelligible'. The deconstruction of onto-theology therefore consists in the deconstruction of this tradition of hermeneutics, which is achieved by showing that it is impossible to totalise *écriture*. If we take *écriture* to signify 'scripture' what we have, in sum, is the view that scripture performs the deconstruction of the metaphysical element within theology. With this in mind, we listen to Derrida: 'The difference between signified and signifier belongs in a profound and implicit way to the great epoch covered by the history of metaphysics, and in a more explicit and more systematically articulated way to the narrower epoch of Christian creationism and infinitism *when these appropriate the resources of Greek conceptuality*'.[41] What is

41 Derrida, *Of grammatology*, p. 13. My emphasis.

submitted to critique, consequently, is not Christianity but hermeneutics. The *text* of theology is not called into question as such; if anything, it seems that deconstruction provides us with the basis for a non-metaphysical theology.

What I have done so far in this chapter is apply Derrida's mode of critique, not so much to his own text but to the critical reception of that text. In so doing I have remained within the field of immanent critique, following Derrida's remarks concerning the 'question of method' with regards to reading Rousseau:

> This question is therefore not only of Rousseau's writing but also of our reading. We should begin by taking rigorous account of this *being held within* [*prise*] or this *surprise*: the writer writes *in* a language and *in* a logic whose proper system, laws, and life his discourse by definition cannot dominate absolutely. He uses them only by letting himself, after a fashion and up to a point, be governed by the system. And the reading must always aim at a certain relationship, unperceived by the writer, between what he commands and what he does not command of the patterns of the language that he uses. This relationship is not a certain quantitative distribution of shadow and light, of weakness or of force, but a signifying structure that critical reading should *produce*.[42]

If we apply this methodology to Derrida's own text, the question of Derrida's intention with respect to 'deconstruction' can be only one factor amongst others. For all we know, it may well be that Derrida intends *écriture* to signify 'writing' and that he has no complaint to make with the way in which deconstruction has been received. But the point is that Derrida's text cannot help but signify both 'writing' and 'scripture'. *Ecriture*, I have argued, is a structurally undecidable word in Derrida's text in precisely the same way as *pharmakon* and *supplément* are in Plato and Rousseau. It is one of Derrida's central tenets that no reading can totalise a text, and if this is the case, it must also be so with respect to Derrida's writing. This text has been read as though a certain link with atheism formed a natural and inevitable context, but by Derrida's own principles this cannot be the case. Established thus far is that deconstruction, as a general mode of enquiry, has positive links with theology. But it is also possible

42 Derrida, *Of grammatology*, p. 158.

to lend some support to a reading which contests the framing of Derrida's enquiries in completely secular terms, and it is to this that we turn our attention.

We have seen that the 'atheist' account of Derrida's text relies upon the argument that God is pure presence and that Derrida's critique of the sign entails that it is impossible for a presence ever to present itself. We need not discuss the strength of this argument, for it fails on purely immanent grounds. If one accepts Derrida's critique of the sign, one must also accept that no context can totalise a text, including Derrida's own text. It is always possible to show how the text can be contextualised in a different manner, and in this instance all one has to do is to attend to Derrida's regard for the text of Jewish theology. Thus rather than take the argument that there is a fall in presence to count directly against the possibility of belief in God as full presence, one can consider it in the context of the Lurianic doctrine of God's *zimzum*, His withdrawal into Himself to provide a space and an occasion for creation.[43] Derrida's constant target is the notion of a full presence, and this target includes God only in those instances where God is conceived as full presence. And Derrida agrees with Moses Mendelsohn that the God of Judaism 'does not manifest himself, he is not truth for the Jews, total presence or parousia'.[44] The concepts of 'truth', 'total presence' and 'parousia' are called into question, not the concept of 'God' as such.

To take several further examples. It is doubtless the case that Derrida takes the elevation of speech over writing to be of a piece with the Christian doctrine of Christ as the divine *Logos*; but the deconstruction of the speech/writing hierarchy does not necessarily count against religious commitment. The views that writing evolves simultaneously with or prior to speech are not uncommon in eighteenth-century thought. David Hartley was compelled by his associationism to hold that speech and writing evolved *pari passu*, and this conflicted with neither his faith nor his theology.[45] Similarly, Johann Herder, a distinguished theo-

---

43 See Derrida, *Dissemination*, p. 344. Also see Thomas J. J. Altizer's comments on Derrida and God's *zimzum* in 'History as apocalypse', *Deconstruction and theology*, pp. 148–49.
44 Derrida, *Glas*, p. 51a.
45 See Hartley, *Observations on man, his frame, his duty, and his expectations* (1749; rpt. Gainsville, FL.: Scholars' Facsimiles and Reprints, 1966), Part I Ch. 3 Sec. 1 (p. 299).

logian, once maintained that writing precedes speech.[46] And finally, the view that writing precedes speech was common amongst the eighteenth-century *illuminati*, for whom it had a positive religious significance.[47] One could go still further and detail how the notion of textual dissemination is largely anticipated by the Kabbalah,[48] and how Derrida's statement 'There is nothing outside of the text' recalls the Jewish legend that Yahweh looked into the Torah and then created the heavens and the earth.[49] And one could point to the fact that Derrida signs his essays on Jabès pseudonymously as 'Reb Rida' and 'Reb Derissa', thus playfully casting himself in the role of rabbi (Reb Derrida). The point is clear: there is a body of textual evidence to frustrate any attempt simply to align Derrida's text with secularism. If Hegel is pleased to find Plato present in Moses, it is Derrida's delight to find Moses present in Plato.

It could be objected here that Derrida is being ironic in setting Jerusalem against Athens, that he is merely using Jewish mystical motifs without any commitment to them. This objection has some force, and I shall attend to the role of irony in Derrida's texts in chapter 5. I do not think, however, that this objection meets my main point. For I am not arguing that Derrida's text has an apologetic intention, only that if one accepts Derrida's general argument then one cannot regard *écriture* as 'writing' to the complete exclusion of 'scripture'. And what is said with respect to Derrida's text is *a fortiori* the case with what I have called the text of deconstruction. Even if one were to admit that Derrida is being ironic in setting Jew against Greek, it would not count against my general conclusion that the deconstruction of

---

46 See J. H. Stam, *Inquiries into the origin of language: the fate of a question* (New York: Harper and Row, 1976), p. 170.

47 Stam, *Inquiries*, p. 206.

48 'More audaciously than any developments in recent French criticism, Kabbalah is a theory of *writing*, but this is a theory that denies the absolute distinction between writing and inspired speech, even as it denies human distinctions between presence and absence. Kabbalah speaks of a writing before writing (Derrida's "trace"), but also of a speech before speech.' Bloom, *Kabbalah and criticism* (New York: Seabury Press, 1975), p. 52. Also see p. 80.

49 'Jewish folklore is replete with parables that ascribe such precedence to Torah', remarks Shira Wolosky in 'Derrida, Jabès, Levinas: sign-theory as ethical discourse', *Prooftexts*, 2 (1982), p. 291. Also see *Of grammatology*, p. 16 and especially *Writing*, pp. 74–76 in which the religious echoes attending *écriture* and *texte* can be plainly heard.

hermeneutics is performed by scripture. (And there is good reason not to accept this antecedent in all cases; it may be the case that Derrida uses the Jewish motifs in an ironic manner in his essays on Jabès, but there is no conscious irony in his essay on Levinas.)

3 The context of discussion

Throughout this chapter we have been engaged in immanent critique. I have argued that it is impossible for an atheist reading to totalise the text of deconstruction, and I have shown how such attempts are blind to a theistic reading of deconstruction. Now in developing this theistic reading I am not arguing that it is the one true reading of Derrida's text or what I have been calling the text of deconstruction: such a claim would immediately fall victim to the critique I have elaborated. I wish to uncover a relationship between deconstruction and theology, but my contention is that this relationship is structural, not thematic. My interpretation of deconstruction is therefore at odds with both the atheist and theological appropriations of deconstruction, for both of these confuse, in different ways, the *process* of deconstruction with certain of its Derridean *themes*. In this section I wish to place the discussion of theology and deconstruction in a slightly broader context and also isolate a number of common errors in theological appropriations of deconstruction.

I begin with a brief taxonomy of the debate between theology and deconstruction. This debate may be resolved into five distinguishable, though not wholly distinct, areas. (1) The first and perhaps most common view is that deconstruction is directed against theology as such, a position endorsed with equal vigour by atheists and theists of various persuasions, and one I have already taken stock of in the first chapter. (2) There is a fine, though fluid, line separating this first group from the views of the 'death of God' theologians who are perhaps the most keen of all the specific groups to claim a common lineage with Derrida. Carl Raschke attempts to sum up this group's position in the formula that deconstruction is 'in the final analysis *the death of God put into writing*' and Mark C. Taylor, a little more lucidly, claims that 'Deconstruction is the hermeneutic of the death of God and the death of God is the (a)theology of Deconstruction'.[50] This sounds impressive, but the very phrase 'death of God' is itself far from clear, and is rejected by Derrida himself. Thomas Altizer, the *sovereign* suzerain of this group, goes as far as to suggest that Derrida may 'bring the whole tradition of modern Christianity to an end, and thereby make possible a new Christian beginning',[51] a curious view given that Derrida calls both 'end' and 'beginning' into question. (3) Taking a different tack from both these groups are those who wish to link deconstruction to a more orthodox theological position.[52] Judson Boyce Allen, for one, talks of 'a human soul deconstructed by sin'; and Robert Magliola, for another, goes so far as to claim that 'the mystery of the triune God can be *apprehended anew* in terms of "deconstruction"' and observes that the declarations of the Council of Nicea 'effectively deconstruct the subordinationist model'.[53]

Magliola also belongs to a fourth group which directs attention to parallels between deconstruction and the practices or the theologies of non-Christian religions. We may divide this group into the following sub-groups: (4a) those who emphasise connections between deconstruction and Buddhism or Taoism; and (4b) those who finds points of intersection between deconstruction and Judaism. Magliola finds deconstruction anticipated in the Buddhism of Nagarjuna; Michelle Yeh compares Derrida's thought with the Taoism of Chuang Tzu, while Nathan Katz finds links between deconstruction and certain Buddhist prac-

---

50 Raschke, 'The deconstruction of God', in Altizer *et al.*, *Deconstruction and theology*, p. 3. Taylor, *Deconstructing theology*, p. xix.
51 Altizer, 'History as apocalypse', in Altizer *et al.*, *Deconstruction and theology*, p. 151.
52 The literature of this particular area is quite considerable. The following references indicate the variety of 'mainstream' theological responses to deconstruction. Louis Mackey attempts to counter the popular view that deconstruction is nihilistic and atheistic in 'Slouching towards Bethlehem: deconstructive strategies in theology', *Anglican Theological Review*, 65 (1983), pp. 255–72. H. Meschonnic offers a wide-ranging discussion of Derrida and the sacred in 'L'écriture de Derrida' in *Le signe et le poème* (Paris: Gallimard, 1975), pp. 401–92. William Dean attempts to link deconstruction and process theology in 'Deconstruction and process theology', *The Journal of Religion*, 64 (1984), pp. 1–19. And finally, a cross-section of recent thought in this area is to be found in *Derrida and biblical studies*, ed. Robert Detweiler, *Semeia*, 23 (Chico, CA: Scholars Press, 1982).
53 Allen, *The ethical poetic of the later middle ages* (Toronto: University of Toronto Press, 1982), p. 250. Robert Magliola, *Derrida on the mend* (West Lafayette, Ind.: Purdue University Press, 1984), p. 134 and p. 137.

tices, especially Tibetan hermeneutics.[54] More sustained attention, however, has been focussed upon Derrida's sources in Rabbinic and Kabbalistic writings and upon evident parallels between Derrida's interpretive practice and Jewish hermeneutics. Thus Susan Handelman sees deconstruction as part of a far more sweeping movement – including Freud, Lacan and Bloom – whose members consciously or unconsciously are reviving elements of rabbinic hermeneutics; while Harold Bloom himself argues persuasively that Derrida's theory of *écriture* and *archi-écriture* is a belated rival of the Jewish mystical-hermeneutical writings in the Kabbalah.[55] Altizer also emphasises that Derridean deconstruction is underwritten by Lurianic Kabbalism and points to the importance of specific Lurianic doctrines in Derrida's thought.[56] (5) The final area of argument concerns possible relations between mysticism and deconstruction, and this is of particular relevance to this study. Gayatri Spivak, introducing *Of grammatology* to English-speaking readers, insists, as we saw, that deconstruction 'is not "mystical" or "theological"'.[57] Yet John Caputo talks of deconstructing 'Thomistic metaphysics, to break open its metaphysical encasement and to expose the contents of its essentially mystical significance'; and John Dominic Crossan suggests that 'what Derrida is saying leads straight into a contemporary revival of negative theology'.[58] Hailed both as a support for atheism and as

54 See respectively: Magliola, *Derrida on the mend*, pp. 87–129; Michelle Yeh, 'The deconstructive way: a comparative study of Derrida and Chuang Tzu', *Journal of Chinese Philosophy*, 10 (1983), pp. 95–126; and Nathan Katz, '*Prasanga* and deconstruction: Tibetan hermeneutics and the yana controversy', *Philosophy East and West: A Quarterly of Asian and Comparative Thought*, 34 (1984), pp. 185–204. Also see Zhang Longxi, 'The *Tao* and the *Logos*: notes on Derrida's critique of logocentrism', *Critical Inquiry*, 11 (1985), pp. 385–98.
55 See Susan A. Handelman, *The slayers of Moses*, Ch. 7. An interesting precursor of this mode of analysis is David Bakan's *Sigmund Freud*. Also see Harold Bloom, *Kabbalah and criticism*, esp. pp. 52–53, 80.
56 'Two Lurianic doctrines in particular are related to Derrida's thinking: (1) on *zimzum* (God's retraction or withdrawal into himself in order to make possible the creation); and (2) on *shevirat ha-kelim* (the "breaking of the vessels").' Altizer, 'History as apocalypse', pp. 148–49. The most thorough account of the relations between deconstruction and the various currents of Judaism is to be found in Shira Wolosky's 'Derrida, Jabès, Levinas', pp. 283–302.
57 Spivak, 'Translator's preface', *Of grammatology*, p. lxxviii.
58 Caputo, *Heidegger and Aquinas* (New York: Fordham University Press, 1982), p. 247; and Crossan, *Cliffs of fall: paradox and polyvalence in the parables of Jesus* (New York: Seabury Press, 1980), p. 11. Two further books which take up a Heideggerian line, not dissimilar from Caputo's, are Joseph S. O'Leary

an aid to Trinitarian theology, deconstruction has been rapidly and often uncritically adopted by positions ranging across the entire theological spectrum.

Are we to conclude from these contrasting and contrary sets of quotations that deconstruction can be pressed into the service of any position? I do not think so. It can of course be argued that the *concept* 'deconstruction' is anterior to the *word* 'deconstruction', and the argument has some force; but it does not go far toward justifying all or even many of the above claims, for very few of them rest upon the concept 'deconstruction'. Paul de Man ruefully observes how deconstruction 'has been much misrepresented' but that he has 'the fewer illusions about the possibility of countering these aberrations since such an expectation would go against the drift of my own readings'.[59] There is a difference between holding the view, as de Man does, that the identity of a discourse, such as deconstruction, is constituted after the fact by differing interpretations of that discourse – including parodies, strong and weak misreadings, and so on – and the view that all interpretations are equally valid. There are good arguments one can bring in support of the first view but none in favour of the second; though here de Man's *laissez faire* policy allows the views to be conflated. De Man may not think he can practically counter these aberrations, but in calling them 'aberrations' he implies that he has some notion, albeit negative, of what deconstruction truly is or should be. It is important to use both the word 'deconstruction' and the concept 'deconstruction' as rigorously as possible, and as this is not done in the majority of cases in (1)–(5) it is worthwhile to point out what is aberrant in them, and in this way distinguish our position from those adumbrated above.

First of all we recall the definition of 'deconstruction' with which we have been working. To deconstruct a discourse is to show, by reference to its own assumptions, that it depends upon prior differences which prevent that discourse from being totalised. This dependence does not lead to an infinite regress, however, for at a certain level these differences can be thema-

DEF.

Questioning back (Minneapolis: Winston Press, 1985) and J.-L. Marion, *Dieu sans l'être* (Paris: Fayard, 1982).

59 De Man, *Allegories of reading: figural language in Rousseau, Nietzsche, Rilke, and Proust* (New Haven: Yale University Press, 1979), p. x.

tised under the rubric of *trace*, *différance* or *archi-écriture* – words which name a mode of difference which is transcendental yet incapable of forming a firm ground. It is quite possible to define sin in terms of difference – as man asserting his difference from God – but to talk of a soul 'deconstructed by sin', as Allen does, is to argue that the soul depends for its identity upon the difference that constitutes sin; and that is definitely at odds with the fundamentalist theology espoused by Allen. What he means to say, I suspect, is that the human soul is *corrupted* by sin, a less impressive yet more accurate formulation.

Caputo's error is of a somewhat more sophisticated kind, and as his argument resembles mine it requires more detailed attention. His chief claim is that the deconstruction of Thomistic metaphysics will yield the mystical insights which are, he believes, the animating force of St Thomas's philosophical theology. Aquinas's texts, we are told, 'need to be deconstructed in the light of the experience of Being – of *esse subsistens* – to which they give way'.[60] *Esse subsistens* is, as Caputo reminds us, 'pure subsistent Being';[61] and the claim is that an experience of this pure Being is sufficient to require the deconstruction of St Thomas's discourse on God as *esse subsistens* which Caputo, agreeing with Heidegger, thinks to be metaphysical. This is surely at odds with how Derrida presents deconstruction, for he insists that 'there is no experience of *pure* presence, but only chains of differential marks'.[62] The root of the problem is that Caputo is confusing deconstruction with something else, as is evident from his definitions of the word. 'A retrieval or deconstruction is not a destruction or leveling but a dismantling of the surface apparatus of a thought in order to find its essential nerve, its animating centre' he claims, and elsewhere, 'To retrieve or deconstruct is, not to destroy, but to shake loose from a text its essential tendencies which the text itself conceals'.[63] Here Caputo identifies Heideggerian *Destruktion* with Derridean deconstruction. Now 'deconstruction' not only translates '*Destruktion*', it also draws upon the grammatical term 'deconstruction', in circulation long before *Of grammatology*, which means 'to

---

60 Caputo, *Heidegger and Aquinas*, p. 9.
61 Caputo, *Heidegger and Aquinas*, p. 3.
62 Derrida, *Margins of philosophy*, p. 318.
63 Caputo, *Heidegger and Aquinas*, p. 8. Cf. p. 247.

reveal the laws of literary composition'.[64] If we take the phenomenological and grammatical senses together, deconstruction is therefore an attempt to show how philosophical discourses are constructed. The difference between Heidegger's and Derrida's projects is that whereas Heidegger is often drawn, at least in part, to uncover a text's 'animating centre' Derrida calls all such desires into question, even Heidegger's; and this is an issue I shall explore in the final chapter.

One or two characteristic difficulties which arise from the misuse of the *concept* of deconstruction are worth discussion. Whilst it is quite true that no specific act of deconstruction can finally put the whole of onto-theology to rest, and will in fact remain – at least partly – within the closure of onto-theology, it is not accurate to say that the deconstruction of a tradition or a theory may proceed in the service of a presence. Thus when Magliola maintains that the declarations of the Council of Nicea deconstruct subordinationism, he gets into theological difficulties. The subordinationist heresy sets the Father above the Son while the Council maintains that the Father and the Son are co-equal and consubstantial. Yet if the Father–Son hierarchy were to be open to deconstruction, the Son would have to be a determined modification of the Father's condition of possibility – a view not held by the Church Fathers. Further, if the hierarchy were to be deconstructed, both Father and Son would be shown to depend upon a generalised version of the prior difference between Father and Son. And as this would imply that God is conditioned, it would run directly counter to the doctrines promulgated at Nicea and supported by Magliola. Similarly, when Caputo attempts to deconstruct what he sees as a hierarchic distinction between the God of metaphysics and the God of mystical faith, he forgets that deconstruction can begin in this instance only if the God of mystical faith is not conceived as presence. It makes no sense at all to claim that an experience of 'pure subsistent Being' precipitates the act of deconstruction, for it is the notions of 'purity' and 'presence' which are put in question by the act of deconstruction.

I began this chapter by arguing that what at first appears to be the natural and inevitable context of deconstruction is in fact

---

64 See Derrida, 'Letter to a Japanese friend', in *Derrida and differance*, ed. David Wood and Robert Bernasconi (Warwick: Parousia Press, 1985), pp. 1–3.

motivated by secularist assumptions, and that this context is called into question by the text of deconstruction. And I have brought this chapter to a conclusion by demonstrating that what seems, in a number of instances, to be a theological appropriation of deconstruction is little more than a misunderstanding of the word and the concept. Before passing to other matters, though, let us stand back and see what is common to these approaches. Each approach is troubled by an unacknowledged equivocation, for the word 'deconstruction' at once _describes_ a particular process of self-subversion within an interpretation of a text and _names_ the philosophical position which seeks to identify and trace this process. Now the problems that beset both approaches arise mainly from attempts to link deconstruction with atheism or theism. If we take theism to affirm God as a presence, it seems that deconstruction is already in the service of atheism. But the moment one articulates a positive atheism, that there is no God, we have the thematisation of the classical opposition between presence and absence which is precisely the critical object of the process of deconstruction. The confrontation of theology and deconstruction that has occupied us over these chapters has led us to the point where we can see the fundamental flaws involved in the thematic study of their combination. What is needed, it seems, is attention to structural problems. So we will now turn to the various assumptions and questions concerning structure that have been waiting in the wings while this confrontation has been staged.

3 | Metaphysics and theology

1   'Ground' and critique

All critiques exercise reason and question grounds, but only some seek to interrogate the ground of reason itself. At a certain level of generality the enterprise of offering a critique of reason is circular, since the very distinctions which permit the operation of critique are themselves conditioned by reason. Upon closer inspection, however, it becomes clear that the circle need not be vicious and that such a critique can be lodged. One needs, first of all, to distinguish between offering specific reasons to justify a particular position, as all philosophers do, and construing reason as a ground, such as in the Leibnizian principle of sufficient reason. And second, one needs to demonstrate that reason, thus defined, is blind to its condition of possibility. The question arises, though, just how far the critique is to be taken. For in specifying the condition of reason's possibility one also begins a process of supplying another ground, such as the will or being; and while this new ground may differ importantly from reason, its function as ground will remain unchallenged. We must ask, then, whether the object of a critique of reason is 'reason' or the more fundamental and redoubtable notion of 'ground' itself. Modern philosophy offers examples of both kinds of critique, and matters are complicated by the fact that the critique of ground often develops by way of a critique of reason. Such is the case with Nietzsche, and the concerns of this chapter may be brought into focus by a brief comparison and contrast between this mode of critique and the other mode, exemplified by Kant, which questions reason though not 'ground' as such.

It is this critique of ground, unbroached by Kant, which interested Nietzsche and which, in his last writings, he sought to affirm: in part by extending the bounds of the Kantian problem-

71

atic and in part by a trenchant critique of the critical philosophy. Kant is therefore taken to task on two principal issues, concerning what he chose to submit to critique and what he meant by 'critique'. Both criticisms ultimately revolve around the theological ambitions of Kant's project. The thrust of Nietzsche's first objection is that the rejection of the noumenal as a positive object of knowledge 'is only a theologian's success'.[1] Here Nietzsche draws attention to the grand purpose of Kant's programme; for the remarks on limits and parerga, the deduction of the Categories, and the fundamental distinction between thinking and knowing, are all directed to the one end: the reinstatement of faith in a universe hitherto constructed and, so Kant held, *mis*constructed in the name of knowledge. At one level of the text, as is well known, Kant openly acknowledges the theological implications of his epistemology, confessing that he found it necessary 'to deny *knowledge*, in order to make room for *faith*'.[2] This is not all Nietzsche has in mind, however. He detects a complicity between 'faith' and 'reason' which remains beneath the surface of Kant's text and which counts against Kant's explicit insistence that God must be thought only in the light of His self-revelation.

Endorsing the Kantian dictum that reason prescribes its laws to nature and does not derive them from nature, Nietzsche nonetheless insists that these laws have outlived their usefulness for man whose destiny it is to become the overman. The valorisation of reason is a particular way of mastering circumstances, one possible mode of interpretation that vies with others. It is a mastery which in turn has mastered us by presenting itself as an *a priori* state of affairs rather than as an interpretation. Reason now presents itself to us as both *de facto* and *de jure*. 'Rational thought is interpretation according to a scheme that we cannot throw off', Nietzsche contends, and its recalcitrance consists in its repeated success within history which has led to its gradual incorporation 'in language and in the grammatical categories', such that if we renounced it 'we would have to cease thinking'.[3] Thus from the claim that grammar conceals a meta-

---

1 Nietzsche, *The anti-Christ* § 10 (p. 121).
2 Immanuel Kant, *Critique of pure reason*, trans. Norman Kemp Smith (London: Macmillan, 1933), B xxx.
3 Nietzsche, *The will to power*, trans. Walter Kaufmann and R. J. Hollingdale, ed. Walter Kaufmann (NY: Vintage Books, 1968), § 522 (italics removed).

physical agenda it is, for Nietzsche, a short step to supply details, the most familiar of which is suggested in the lament, 'I fear we are not getting rid of God because we still believe in grammar'.[4] Because the Kantian critique never questions the value of reason for man in his historical situation it lacks the radicalism which Nietzsche deems necessary if critique is to be useful to man. Indeed, because Kant fails to question the inherited structure of thought he unwittingly preserves structures which encourage man to confuse what is merely named through grammatical exigency with what is true. Chief amongst these possible confusions is that between a *conception* of God (which may have had value for man at a particular historical period) and the view that there *is* a God: a timeless, unchangeable being who prescribes eternal truths. On this account the idea of God is not regulatory, as it is for Kant, but simply misleading. Whereas Kant questions the status of the concept of God, Nietzsche questions the status of the *concept* of the concept of God, and in this way develops a critique without adducing a firm ground.

This allows Nietzsche to introduce a second objection, that Kant's figure of reason as an 'appointed judge' unintentionally leads him to misconstrue the nature of immanent critique. If Kant's figure were the only one which could be called upon, the critique of reason would have to be conducted by reason itself; the bench becoming indistinguishable from the dock. One must therefore think 'immanent critique' otherwise, and for Nietzsche the solution lay in taking the *de jure* claim of reason in all seriousness: hence his appeal to the related figures of genealogy and the will to power. However, at least according to Nietzsche's claim, the will to power does not constitute itself as a ground; rather, like reason, it is an interpretation, albeit one with more use than reason for man in his present state. For Kant, then, the proper exercise of reason depends upon what can be experienced, while for Nietzsche reason has no foundation other than the play of the non-ground of interpretation. The one understands critique as establishing grounds while for the other critique dissolves grounds. That is, an immanent critique of reason itself was revealed by Nietzsche to be an interpretative possibility, and one which was desirable precisely because it would erase the theology inscribed within Kant's transcendental critique.

4 Nietzsche, *The twilight of the idols*, § 5 (p. 38).

The foregoing contrast between the Kantian transcendental critique and the Nietzschean immanent critique is a common theme in contemporary discussion of deconstruction, and one whose theological import is frequently underlined. Against Kant's recuperative critique, with its firm insistence upon a transcendental ground, is pitted the Nietzschean unbounded critique in which all grounds are seen as fictions, including its own tacit affirmation of the will to power; and Derrida's programme of deconstruction is thus viewed as the most sophisticated and thoroughgoing heir of this mode of immanent critique. Thus Richard Rorty, for one, tells us that Derrida 'is suggesting how things might look if we did not have Kantian philosophy built into the fabric of our intellectual life', that Derrida, like Nietzsche, recognises 'that the idea of method presupposes that of a privileged vocabulary . . . a vocabulary which lets us get what we want' and, hence, that he, along with Nietzsche and Heidegger, is 'forging new ways of speaking, not making surprising philosophical discoveries about old ones'.[5] On this account, deconstruction is to be aligned with Nietzsche (and thus atheism) and opposed to Kant (and thus theism); it is, in Rorty's terms, an 'abnormal' philosophy, deriving its power from a particular vocabulary, to be contrasted at every opportunity with the 'normal' philosophy represented by Kant.[6] Whereas 'normal' philosophy extols presence and self-identity, 'abnormal' philosophy, at least in Derrida's case, values absence and difference; the one develops by argument and the other by parodying argument or, if there are arguments, without faith that they can serve to establish eternal truths.

This view of deconstruction has an initial plausibility, but it is, I shall argue, quite mistaken. My contrary claim, to be worked out in part II, is that Derrida finds the Kantian and the Nietzschean modes of critique to be irreducibly entwined and that his mode of critique, deconstruction, seeks to reveal the systematic link between a text's ground and its non-ground. Deconstruction is accordingly a critique of 'ground' as such, though not an affirmation of groundlessness. Upon my reading,

5 Rorty, *Consequences of pragmatism* (Brighton: Harvester Press, 1982), p. 98 (italics removed) and p. 152; 'Deconstruction and circumvention', *Critical Inquiry*, 11 (1984), p. 9.
6 Rorty, 'Derrida on language, being, and abnormal philosophy', *The Journal of Philosophy*, 74 (1977), pp. 679–81.

deconstruction possesses no assertive power; it is, quite simply, a way of seeing how a particular edifice, a general theory or a specific text, is constituted and deconstituted. Like any critique, it seeks to reveal conditions of possibility; but, unlike most critiques, it purports to show that there can be no condition of possibility for a discourse of any explanatory power to be both consistent and complete: there will always be, Derrida maintains, certain propositions generated within that discourse which render it inconsistent or incomplete, thereby undermining its claim to offer a comprehensive and satisfactory account of phenomena. However, if deconstruction at once works with and displaces the Kantian and Nietzschean modes of critique, there remains an important question to answer. Can the Nietzschean critique of 'ground' be reconciled with the Kantian accommodation of religious faith?

In order to answer this question, we need to understand what Derrida means by 'onto-theology', his adopted word for all discourses which presuppose a ground. Drawing upon the conclusions of the preceding chapters, I shall argue that while 'onto-theology' exhausts the whole of metaphysics it does not cover all of theology. This leaves us with the theoretical possibility that there is such an area as 'non-metaphysical theology'; and in the final section I shall examine one or two maps of the area.

2 'Onto-theology'

'Onto-theology' was first used by Kant to designate that particular region of theology which tries to deduce God's existence by concepts with no appeal to experience. In recent years, however, the word's sense has been expanded by both Heidegger and Derrida so that it now includes the metaphysics Kant called into question and aspects of the critical philosophy itself. And yet despite these changes, the word still bears eloquent testimony to the fact that, in questions of religious faith at least, the philosophies of Heidegger and Derrida are compromised by the very Kantianism they interrogate.

In the *Critique of pure reason* Kant analyses theology into its constituent parts. The first division distinguishes rational from revealed theology. Rational theology is then broken into transcendental and natural theology which further divides into physico-theology and moral theology. Transcendental theology, in turn, is comprised of cosmo-theology and onto-theology, both of which try to apprehend God by means of transcendental concepts: *ens summum, ens originarium and ens entium.*[7] Thus in onto-theology God is defined in terms of being: first of all, as the *highest* being, endowed with every reality; then as the *original* being, underived from anything else; and ultimately as the *being* of all beings, the ground of all that is. In the *Lectures* Kant emphasises that these three predicates, taken together, are constitutive of what we mean by 'God': while we may add other predicates we must take these three to be absolutely fundamental. And if this is so, the question of the relation between theology and metaphysics appears to be settled. All discourse on God must be metaphysical. Thus Kant advises us to pass from the study of God's being to the study of God's kingdom, from theology to theodicy.

Let us, however, approach the problem from another angle. Rather than thinking of God as a particular kind of being, and therefore as a metaphysical entity, let us explore the possibility that it is metaphysics which compels us to regard God as a particular kind of being. We can begin by pressing into service Heidegger's analysis of metaphysics. For Heidegger, metaphysics arises from an unthought identification of two distinctions: Being and beings; and ground and the grounded. Metaphysics is that discourse which takes Being as the ground of beings. The strength of this idea of Being is such that it has dominated western thought from Plato to Nietzsche. Moreover, this situation could not have been otherwise; the epoch of the ontico-ontological distinction has been *sent* to man by Being. This is, to be sure, a puzzling claim, and as with a number of themes from Heidegger's later thought it resists neat resolution into proposition or metaphor. We can go some way towards clarifying it, though, by observing that 'epoch' is used here partly in the sense of 'era' but primarily, in the sense of '*epoché*' or 'moment of withholding'. In the epoch of onto-theology, Being reveals itself in beings but at the same time withholds

7 Kant, *Critique of pure reason*, A 631 B 659. A slightly different taxonomy is offered in his *Lectures on philosophical theology*, trans. Allen W. Wood and Gertrude M. Clark (Ithaca: Cornell University Press, 1978).

itself: 'As it reveals itself in beings, Being withdraws'.[8] The history of western thought is a *Seinsgeschick*, a history of the sendings of Being. This is not to be understood as fashioning intellectual history as a series of epistemological ruptures, such as one finds in Bachelard, Kuhn and, more problematically, in Foucault. The epochs of Being overlap each other in their historical sequence. Moreover, this sequence 'is not accidental, nor can it be calculated as necessary'.[9] Now if we accept this, two consequences follow. In the first place, it would seem that Kant has little choice in conceiving God as a metaphysical object; after all, Kant must fulfill the destiny of Being, and Being reveals itself in the ontico-ontological difference. Nevertheless, it is also possible to find evidence of another epoch of Being at work in Kant's text, an epoch in which God is not taken metaphysically. And in the second place, our attention must pass from the problem of how we conceive God to how we conceive the *conception* of God. Before we can embark for this passage, however, and before we agree to subscribe to Heidegger's *Seinsgeschick*, we need to focus more intently upon Heidegger's analysis of metaphysics as onto-theology.

In the *Metaphysics* Aristotle defines 'first philosophy' or metaphysics as the study of 'being *qua* being', that is, the being of beings.[10] Heidegger's central point is that there is a fundamental ambiguity in this definition, since the study of the being of beings can be at once a questioning of being *as such* or a questioning of beings *as a whole*. In the former case, the quest is for the essence of Being in general, the *on hē on*, and is thus known as 'ontology'. In the latter case, the quest is for the ground of beings as a whole, and as this highest ground is known in Greek as the *theion*, this enterprise is to be called 'theology'. This ambiguity cannot, however, be resolved into independent areas of investigation. In order to inquire about the highest ground we need also to inquire about the essence of being in general, thus making theology dependent upon ontology; and as theology accounts for the ground of ontology, once

8 Heidegger, *Early Greek thinking*, trans. D. F. Krell and F. A. Capuzzi (New York: Harper and Row, 1975), p. 26.
9 Heidegger, *On time and Being*, trans. J. Stambaugh (New York: Harper and Row, 1972), p. 9.
10 Aristotle, *The works of Aristotle*, Vol. VIII, *Metaphysica*, trans. W.D. Ross. Second edition. (Oxford: Clarendon Press, 1908), 1026a 32.

more the discourses are entwined. Hence, upon Heidegger's reading, metaphysics is at once ontology and theology; or, as he prefers to call it, 'onto-theology'.

It must be understood that Heidegger is not claiming that *some* metaphysics is theological but that metaphysics *as such* is theological. It is true that Heidegger's most detailed exposition of the onto-theological constitution of metaphysics is a reflection upon Hegel's *Science of logic* and that this book is peculiarly suited to this analysis. And we know that Hegel often presents his metaphysics in a quasi-religious vocabulary, claiming, for example, that the content of logic is nothing other than 'the exposition of God as he is in his eternal essence before the creation of nature and a finite mind' and that God 'has the absolutely undisputed right that the beginning be made with him'.[11] All this is part of Hegel's general insistence that 'philosophy is theology', the knowledge of God as *Geist*. Yet Heidegger is adamant in this essay on Hegel, as he is elsewhere, that metaphysics is *constituted* as onto-theological. And long before writing on this theme with specific reference to Hegel, he speaks of metaphysics in this way with respect to Leibniz, Schelling, Nietzsche and of course Aristotle.

Perhaps the most economical way of drawing out the implications of Heidegger's claim is by a comparison with Kant. The central distinction of the Kantian philosophy is between thinking and knowing. We become enmeshed in metaphysical illusions when we claim to *know* about God what we can only *think* regarding Him. The Heideggerian problematic is a repetition of the Kantian to the extent that it turns upon a similar distinction, between thinking and reasoning. Metaphysics, for Heidegger, is a discourse governed by reason considered as an *Ur-grund*, a firm foundation; yet it can be shown, he thinks, that reason is in fact an *Un-grund*, a necessary appearance of a firm foundation. One consequence of this, Heidegger argues, is that throughout the history of western metaphysics Being has been approached only by reason. Metaphysics, we recall, insists upon a difference (*Differenz*) between Being and beings in terms of ground and the grounded. Yet if this system is to be both complete and consistent, as reason demands, it requires something to be self-grounding; and this *causa sui*, Heidegger contends, is the God of

11 Hegel, *Science of logic*, pp. 50, 78.

metaphysics.[12] The entry of God into metaphysics is therefore inevitable; it is entailed by the very distinctions between 'ground' and 'grounded', 'Being' and 'beings'. However, while Heidegger rejects the God of metaphysics he most certainly does not reject the possibility of belief in God. Quite the contrary: 'The god-less thinking which must abandon the god of philosophy, god as *causa sui*, is thus perhaps closer to the divine God'.[13]

Kant and Heidegger agree, on the whole, that God can be thought and that this thinking must occur through an openness to revelation; but they disagree in that while Kant affirms that the God of metaphysics answers to what we *mean* by 'God', Heidegger stresses that this is definitely *not* what the faithful mean by 'God'. The root of this disagreement is that Heidegger's question 'What is metaphysics?' is prior to Kant's question 'What is the relation between metaphysics and theology?' Heidegger shows, conclusively I think, that the relation between metaphysics and theology is always already determined from *within* metaphysics. Another point of disagreement is that whereas Kant elucidates the relation between man and metaphysics in *a priori* terms, Heidegger does so by way of historicity. Metaphysics, for him, covers a vast era of human history: one whose end has already been marked, though not yet fully realised, in Nietzsche's claim 'God is dead'. Nietzsche is crucial for Heidegger partly because the inversion of Platonism one finds in *The will to power* brings metaphysics to its conclusion and partly because it is Nietzsche's account of nihilism which Heidegger takes as his prooftext in his reading of the history of metaphysics as the history of nihilism. 'What does nihilism mean?' asks Nietzsche, *'That the highest values devaluate themselves'*, then adds, 'The aim is lacking; "why?" finds no answer'.[14] It is this remark

---

12 In describing the God of metaphysics as the *causa sui* Heidegger seems to be thinking in particular of the opening statement of Spinoza's *Ethics*: 'By cause of itself I understand that whose essence involves existence, or that whose nature cannot be conceived unless existing' (Benedict de Spinoza, *Ethics*, ed. J. Gutmann (New York: Hafner Pub. Co., 1949), Part I def. 1). Also relevant is Hegel's remark, 'The actual Concept effects itself; it is the *cause* of itself', *Encyclopedia of philosophy*, trans. Gustav Emil Mueller. 1817 edition. (New York: Philosophical Library, 1959), §112. More generally, however, he has in mind the tradition of God as the unmoved mover, as elaborated by Aristotle and Aquinas.

13 Heidegger, *Identity and difference*, p. 72.

14 Nietzsche, *The will to power*, §2 (p. 9). Emphasis in original. Quoted and discussed by Heidegger in *Nietzsche*, Vol. IV *Nihilism*, esp. Ch. 2 but *passim*.

which becomes the leitmotif of Heidegger's elucidation of nihilism.

Upon Heidegger's reading, the question of value is grounded in the question of Being: a value, he argues, is what is valid; and to be valid is the manner in which value as value *is*. Furthermore, the notion of 'value' entails the notion of hierarchy. '"Values" are *accessible* and capable of being a standard of measure', Heidegger writes, 'only where things such as values are esteemed and where one value is ranked above or below another'.[15] If we take these points in tandem we arrive at the view that the God who enters metaphysics at its inception, the *causa sui*, must be the highest value. Within metaphysics, God is lauded as the original being, the highest being and the being of beings; yet, for Heidegger, 'When one proclaims "God" the altogether "highest value", this is a degradation of God's essence'.[16] Metaphysics is nihilism in that this highest value is devalued in the epoch from Plato to Nietzsche. 'Nihilism', as Heidegger succinctly puts it, 'is that historical process whereby the dominance of the "transcendent" becomes null and void, so that all being loses its worth and meaning', the end of which is given in Nietzsche's 'God is dead'.[17] It follows that 'God is dead' is not a formula of unbelief but rather a statement about the highest ground (*theion*) and indeed one that remains within metaphysics as a theological statement.[18] Thus, 'nihilism in Nietzsche's sense in no way coincides with the situation conceived merely negatively, that the Christian god of biblical revelation can no longer be believed in'.[19] Regardless of his intentions, what Nietzsche offers is a critique of theology, of accounts of the highest ground, not a critique of faith.

For Heidegger there may be a God who can be apprehended solely by faith, and therefore he is committed to the possibility of two theologies, one which forms part of onto-theology and one which does not. Thus when specifying the characteristics of onto-theology Heidegger observes that 'we must remember that the word and concept "theology" did not first grow in the

15 Heidegger, *Nietzsche*, Vol. IV, p. 16.
16 Heidegger, 'Letter on humanism', in *Basic writings*, ed. and introd. David Farrell Krell (London: Routledge and Kegan Paul, 1978), p. 228.
17 Heidegger, *Nietzsche*, Vol. IV, p. 4.
18 Heidegger, *Nietzsche*, Vol. IV, p. 210.
19 Heidegger, *The question concerning technology*, p. 63.

framework and service of an ecclesiastical system of faith, but within philosophy'.[20] Odd as it may seem, Heidegger is following tradition. 'Theology', Aquinas tells us, 'is twofold: *one* in which divine things are considered not so much as the subject of the science but as the principles of its subject, and such is that theology which the philosophers sought after and which by another name is called "metaphysics"; the *other* which considers divine things on their own account as the very subject of its science, and this is that theology which is communicated in Sacred Scripture'.[21] Moreover, Heidegger is quick to reject the view that metaphysics becomes onto-theological only with the Alexandrian synthesis of metaphysics and scripture.[22] The question we must ask, though, is how are these theologies related, for Heidegger does not hold the epoch of the ontico-ontological distinction to be uniform and homogeneous.

In his published writings at least, Heidegger does not enquire how the Christian thought of God may trouble philosophy; he concentrates exclusively upon the thought of Being. In analyses of philosophers as diverse as Aristotle, Leibniz and Hegel he finds instances where the ontico-ontological distinction is silently questioned from within, but solely with respect to Being, never God. Interestingly enough, Heidegger's 1919 lecture course on Meister Eckhart at Freiburg did not address Eckhart's view of God but his account of Being. As the title of the course suggests, Heidegger's concern was with 'The philosophical foundations of medieval mysticism'. When he does discuss God – or, increasingly in the later works, the sacred and the gods – Heidegger attends to the poets: Angelus Silesius, Rilke and, above all, Hölderlin. There is, after all, a gulf between thought and faith. A distinction is drawn between Christendom, 'the historical, world-political phenomenon of the Church and its claim to power within the shaping of Western humanity and its modern culture', in which philosophy plays a lead role, and 'the Christianity of New Testament faith'.[23] Heidegger insists that

20 Heidegger, *Schelling's treatise*, p. 50.
21 Quoted from Aquinas's commentary on Boethius' *De Trinitate* by James F. Anderson, *An introduction to the metaphysics of St Thomas Aquinas* (Chicago: Henry Regency Co., 1969), p. 104.
22 See, for example, Heidegger's 'The way back into the ground of metaphysics', in *Existentialism from Dostoevsky to Sartre*, ed. Walter Kaufman. Rev. and expanded edition (New York: New America Library, 1975), p. 275.
23 Heidegger, *The question concerning technology*, p. 63.

there *is* a tension between them, that the quest for a meta-physical foundation for faith 'conceals and distorts' that faith;[24] but nowhere does he offer an analysis of this tension.

As Heidegger insists time and time again, he is a philosopher, not a theologian. More arresting than such denials, though, is the one remark on how he would write a theology. 'If I were still writing a theology – I am sometimes tempted to do just that – the expression "Being" should not figure in it . . . There is nothing to be done here with Being'.[25] By now we need not stress the point that Derrida is not a theologian, so it is all the more worthy of our attention that he remarks how his work can be read as a *translation* of this very observation by Heidegger.[26] A careful reading of the writers in question will reveal that Derrida at once sharpens and extends Heidegger's idea of onto-theology, and that this is done on two fronts: by distinguishing between the axiomatic and axiological elements of onto-theology; and by clarifying the structural and the genetic determinants of onto-theology. We shall discuss each in turn, then consider if Derrida's translation of the Heideggerian theme of a non-metaphysical theology might be of more use to us than the original.

The constant target of deconstruction, I have argued, is total-isation. Some content has already been given to this notion in the preceding chapters and I shall examine it in more detail in part II. We need now, however, to study 'totalisation' from a slightly different perspective, from that of axiomatics. The epoch of onto-theology can be viewed, Derrida tells us, as an assem-blage of various systems, each of which is based upon a small number of axioms or *archai*. Taken by itself this is a familiar thesis. In any formal system there will be various *archai* which

24 Heidegger, *Being and time*, trans. John Macquarrie and Edward Robinson (Oxford: Blackwell, 1973), p. 30.
25 The remark in full and in the original is as follows: 'Certains d'entre vous peut-être que je sors de la théologie, que je lui garde un veil amour, et que j'y entends même quelque chose. Si j'entreprenais d'écrire une théologie, à quoi bien souvent je me sens incliné, alors en elle c'est le mot être, qui ne saurait intervenir. La foi n'a pas besoin de la pensée de l'être'. Heidegger, *The piety of thinking*, trans. and eds. James G. Hart and John C. Maraldo (Bloomington, IN: Indiana University Press, 1976), p. 184. In the body of this chapter I have quoted the translation of Derrida's quotation of the text by John P. Leavey. See Derrida's discussion of this passage in 'Comment ne pas parler', *Psyché: inventions de l'autre* (Paris: Galilée, 1987), pp. 590–92 and in *De l'esprit: Heidegger et la question* (Paris: Galilée, 1987), pp. 12–14.
26 Derrida, 'Letter to John P. Leavey', *Derrida and biblical studies*, p. 61.

compete for the role of the most indispensable: the principle of non-contradiction and the principle of identity are perhaps the strongest contenders. Less familiar, yet more controversial, is the claim which Heidegger and Derrida both advance that these formal and apparently empty principles are themselves grounded in metaphysics. Upon Derrida's reckoning, the *archai* are in fact held to be moments of irreducible presence. Instances abound: *'eidos'* (Plato), *'ousia'* (Aristotle), *'esse'* (Aquinas), 'clear and distinct ideas' (Descartes), 'sense impressions' (Hume), *'Geist'* (Hegel), 'logical simples' (Russell), 'pre-reflective intentionality' (Husserl) and, more problematically, 'Being' (Heidegger). With Plato, for instance, the account of Being as *eidos* is entirely unrevisable; it is the fixed centre of the system, the governing principle of its structure and the sole element which escapes structurality. From this one grounded element, Derrida contends, it is possible to generate a system which, in its internal arrangement, lays claim to being both consistent and complete.

The phrase 'consistent and complete' as applied to a formal system recalls Gödel's 1931 paper on formally undecidable propositions.[27] Derrida insists that he is drawing nothing more than an analogy between formal and philosophical systems and that, in this spirit, he wishes to apply certain of Gödel's conclusions about formal systems to philosophical systems.[28] We must be careful not to let this analogy efface what is, perhaps, Derrida's more compelling semi-formal critique of philosophical systems. This critique will concern us in the following chapter, and we will examine the status of this analogy with Gödel's theorem in chapter 5. In the meantime, we need a preliminary account of Gödel's results. What Gödel shows is that an arithmetical system of any richness is capable of generating at least one proposition which must be considered true within the system but which cannot be proven within that system. Quite clearly, if the system were to be complete this proposition would have to be proven within the system; but if this were done, the system would be inconsistent. The upshot of Gödel's paper is that no system, as described, can be both complete and consistent; and this is generally taken to be an extremely strong case that no

27 Kurt Gödel, 'On formally undecidable propositions of *Principia mathematica* and Related Systems', in *From Frege to Gödel*, ed. J. van Heijenoort, (Cambridge, MA: Harvard University Press, 1977).
28 See Derrida, *Writing*, p. 162; *Positions*, p. 43; and *Dissemination*, p. 219.

arithmetical system can be complete. If formal and philosophical systems are analogous, the result would be that a philosophical system would generate at least one proposition which is structurally undecidable within that system. And this is what Derrida claims, even going so far as to remark that 'there is something like an axiom of incompletion in the structure of the scene of writing'.[29] In other words, no philosophical text can be totalised by an *archè*; regardless of what hermeneutic is applied to it, there will always be an undecidable word generated by the operation of the hermeneutic upon the text: '*supplément*', '*hymen*', '*parergon*' or whatever.

However, as is evident from our discussion of metaphysics as nihilism, philosophical systems are governed axiologically as well as axiomatically: the founding moment of presence is understood as a *value*. In a manner which is more straightforward than Heidegger's, Derrida analyses onto-theology in these terms and simultaneously advances his critique along these two lines. Like Heidegger, Derrida formulates metaphysics by way of a hierarchy of values:

> All metaphysicians, from Plato to Rousseau, Descartes to Husserl have proceeded in this way, conceiving good to be before evil, the positive before the negative, the pure before the impure, the simple before the complex, the essential before the accidental, the imitated before the imitation, etc. And this is not just *one* metaphysical gesture among others, it is *the* metaphysical exigency, that which has been the most constant, most profound and most potent.[30]

As we know, Heidegger takes the Nietzschean inversion of Platonism to be a metaphysical gesture, indeed the final gesture of metaphysics, because it remains entirely within the field of concepts generated by Platonism. The Heideggerian response to metaphysics is not to invert its founding values but to step back into the groundless ground of metaphysics, the *Austrag*, and from here to re-think the other possibilities inherent in Being.

After our earlier discussion of metaphysics as determined by 'fall' it comes as no surprise to find that Derrida has no complaint against the Nietzschean–Heideggerian account of metaphysics

29 Derrida, *The post card*, trans. Alan Bass (Chicago: University of Chicago Press, 1987), p. 313.
30 Derrida, 'Limited inc', trans. S. Weber, *Glyph*, 2 (1977), p. 236.

as nihilism, a fall from the highest to the lowest values. But the relation between Derrida, Nietzsche and Heidegger is a good deal more subtle than this might suggest. Derrida's tactic is to take both the Nietzschean inversion and the Heideggerian *reculer pour mieux sauter* at one and the same time. 'To deconstruct the opposition, first of all, is to overturn the hierarchy at a given moment', Derrida informs us; then with a backwards glance to Heidegger, 'To overlook this phase of overturning is to forget the conflictual and sub-ordinating structure of opposition. Therefore one might proceed too quickly to a *neutralization* that in *practice* would leave the previous field untouched'.[31] Agreeing with Heidegger about Nietzsche, Derrida then tells us that 'to remain in this phase is still to operate on the terrain of and from within the deconstructed system'. Our task is also, and at the same time, to mark 'the interval between inversion, which brings low what was high, and the irruptive emergence of a new "concept", a concept that can no longer be, and never could be, included in the previous regime'.[32] This new 'concept' is held to be not so much other *than* metaphysics as the other *of* metaphysics, a site or perhaps non-site that remains unthought by metaphysics, in which metaphysics is inscribed, and from which it may be questioned. And this 'other' to which metaphysics remains blind is, of course, that mode of radical alterity which is not defined with reference to a prior notion of identity – what we have learnt to call, amongst other names, *'différance'*.

It may be objected that Derrida's *'différance'* is little more than a renaming of a movement already at work within Heidegger's discourse. And as I am arguing that Derrida improves the Heideggerian account and critique of metaphysics, this objection deserves a hearing. In a discussion with Henri Ronse, Derrida acknowledges a debt to Heidegger: that, at one level at least, *différance* 'would name provisionally this unfolding of difference, in particular, but not only, or first of all, of the ontico-ontological difference'.[33] Certainly this squares with what Heidegger says about this difference:

> The 'differentiation' [*Unterscheidung*] is more appropriately identified by the word *difference* [*Differenz*], in which it is intimated that beings and Being are somehow set apart from each

31 Derrida, *Positions*, p. 41.   32 Derrida, *Positions*, p. 42.
33 Derrida, *Positions*, p. 10.

other, separated, and nonetheless connected to each other, indeed of themselves, and not simply on the basis of an 'act' of 'differentiation'. Differentiation as 'difference' means that a *settlement* [Austrag] between Being and beings exists. We shall not say from where and in what way the settlement comes about.[34]

The *Austrag*, then, is that which opens up the difference between Being and beings; and if we take this difference to be the space in which metaphysics is elaborated, it is the *Austrag* which is responsible for the sending of metaphysics. Indeed, it would seem that the *Austrag* is responsible for every sending and concealing of Being: 'the onto-theological constitution of metaphysics has its origin in the perdurance [*Austrag*] that begins the history of metaphysics, governs all its epochs, and yet remains everywhere concealed as perdurance [*Austrag*], and thus forgotten in an oblivion which escapes even itself'.[35]

If we agree to all of this, we are committed to the view that the God of metaphysics, the *causa sui*, is sent by the *Austrag*, as will be, perhaps, the divine God of whom Heidegger writes in such reverent tones. It is at this stage that Christians will object to the idea that God can be *sent* by anything. And one does not have to be religious to ask, with some justification, what is the status of this *Austrag* and of Heidegger's knowledge of it. To restrict ourselves to the first question, it is never made explicit by Heidegger whether the *Austrag* performs an ontological or an epistemological role. Does the *Austrag* somehow constrain God to appear to us in one way and then in another? Or is it rather a matter of how *we* come to think about *Him*? It is in the wake of these questions that we must judge the Heideggerian notion of *Austrag* against the Derridean notion of *différance*. We can agree that '*différance*' is, at least in part, a translation of '*Austrag*' but our attention is compelled by what is at once lost and gained in translation, not to mention the other quite distinct senses of Derrida's word. And from what we have already encountered, we can also agree that while both *Austrag* and *différance* are to be understood as conditions of possibility, Derrida's word commits

34 Heidegger, *Nietzsche*, Vol. IV, p. 155. '*Austrag*' has been commonly translated as 'settlement' and 'perdurance', but the most evocative translation is Caputo's 'dif-ference'. For a particularly lucid account of the *Austrag*, to which I am indebted, see his *Heidegger and Aquinas*, pp. 148–60.
35 Heidegger, *Identity and difference*, p. 68.

us to far less than does Heidegger's; after all, Derrida demonstrates with regards to particular texts that the appeal to presence depends upon an unacknowledged reliance upon *différance*.
But before we can go any further we need to understand the
second way in which Derrida sharpens the Heideggerian
account and critique of metaphysics, his distinction between
genesis and structure.

We can take as our starting-point the following passage from
Heidegger's 1940 lectures on Nietzsche:

> the name *metaphysics* means nothing other than knowledge of
> the Being of beings, which is distinguished by apriority and
> which is conceived by Plato as *idea*. Therefore, *meta-physics* [*sic*]
> *begins* with Plato's interpretation of Being as idea. For all sub-
> sequent times, it shapes the essence of Western philosophy,
> *whose history, from Plato to Nietzsche, is the history of metaphysics*.
> And because metaphysics begins with the interpretation of
> Being as 'idea', and because that interpretation sets the stan-
> dard, all philosophy since Plato is 'idealism' in the strict sense
> of the word: Being is sought in the idea, in the idea-like and the
> ideal. With respect to the founder of metaphysics we can
> therefore say that all Western philosophy is Platonism. *Meta-
> physics, idealism, and Platonism* mean essentially the same thing.
> They remain determinative even where countermovements
> and reversals come into vogue. In the history of the West,
> Plato has become the proto-typical philosopher. Nietzsche did
> not merely *designate* his own philosophy as the reversal of
> Platonism. Nietzsche's thinking *was* and *is* everywhere a single
> and often very discordant dialogue with Plato.[36]

It seems a simple matter to draw a line between where Derrida
and Heidegger are in agreement in this passage and where they
differ; but the line is far from straight. In the first place, both
agree that 'metaphysics', 'idealism' and 'Platonism' are co-
ordinate concepts, and both agree that these concepts pervade
western thought. Yet whereas Heidegger specifies this epoch as
running from Plato to Nietzsche inclusive, Derrida has it extend
from Parmenides to Heidegger, with Nietzsche as the very
figure who calls its characteristic concerns most vividly into
question. While Heidegger's entire programme is to be understood as a critique of the metaphysics of presence, he nonetheless finds himself caught up in a thematics of presence. While he

36 Heidegger, *Nietzsche*, Vol. IV, p. 164.

rejects the idea that Being *is* presence, he still regards Being as *Anwesen*, a coming-into-presence. In the second place, while Heidegger thinks it possible to step outside metaphysics Derrida rejects this possibility as yet another ruse of metaphysics and instead talks of the closure of this epoch, which is to say, in effect, that metaphysics has been convicted in principle but cannot be banished once and for all. Indeed, upon Derrida's understanding, it is metaphysics which allows us to distinguish between the *de jure* and the *de facto* in the first place.

The main difference between Heidegger and Derrida, then, is that while Heidegger thinks it possible to step beyond onto-theology, Derrida argues that all such attempts are entangled in the metaphysics they seek to leave behind. The step beyond (*le pas au-delà*) always turns out to be a step *not* beyond (*un pas au-delà*), as Derrida maintains with respect to Freud, Nietzsche and Blanchot as well as Heidegger. It is time to probe this point and thereby put some pressure upon Heidegger's use of 'onto-theology'. To begin with, Heidegger's view of the history of philosophy as congruent with the history of metaphysics stems from his early commitment to phenomenology. Husserl hailed phenomenology, in both its eidetic and transcendental modes, as a fresh way of philosophising, one that avoided all unnecessary involvement with the history of philosophy. At the same time, though, Husserl believed firmly in the spiritual heritage of European thought and in the need for the philosopher to acknowledge and work within that heritage. 'Our task', he tells us, 'is to make comprehensible the *teleology* in the historical becoming of philosophy', by attempting 'to elicit and understand the *unity* running through all the [philosophical] projects of history that oppose one another and work together in their changing forms'.[37]

Nothing could sound more Hegelian than this passage. Yet whereas the Hegelian system unifies all past philosophies in its disclosure of Spirit as absolute ground, Husserl sees the unity of various philosophical projects in methodological terms, as the scientific *quest* for a firm ground. Far from anything like Hegel's 'Cunning of reason', the teleology invoked here is the con-

37 Edmund Husserl, *The crisis of European sciences and transcendental phenomenology*, trans. and introd. D. Carr (Evanston: Northwestern University Press, 1970), p. 70.

vergence of 'ground' and 'subjectivity', which Husserl claims to find in the historical sequence of Descartes, Kant and himself – a passage from the axiomatics of the *cogito* to the doctrine of transcendental subjectivity. Phenomenology, we are elsewhere assured, 'does no violence to the problem-motives that inwardly drive the old tradition into the wrong line of inquiry and the wrong method'. Moreover, Husserl distinguishes cleanly between 'naïve metaphysics' and 'metaphysics as such', making it quite explicit that phenomenology has no objection to the latter.[38] Metaphysics, for Husserl as for Hegel, is a question of the origin, the foundation, the ground. When he proposes a critique of metaphysics it is a critique of those discourses which have failed to lay proper grounds, never a critique of 'ground' as such. Whatever other aims it has, phenomenology above all seeks to ground speculation in pre-reflective and pre-theoretical intentionality; it is this quest which makes phenomenology a 'first philosophy', a metaphysics, even when it criticises previous systems for their metaphysics. Although Husserl is, to be sure, involved with both a structural inquiry (a description of eidetic structures) and a genetic inquiry (an account of the provenance and ground of such structures), it is important to recognise that he regards metaphysics only in genetic terms. For Husserl, the difference between naïve and good metaphysics is determined according to if the inquiry is ungrounded or grounded; either way, however, metaphysics is taken genetically. Now while both Heidegger and Derrida endorse Husserl's aim of offering a critique of metaphysics, neither accepts the distinction between 'naïve' metaphysics and metaphysics 'as such'. *All* metaphysics is metaphysics as such, they say, and subject to critique. Even despite this difference, though, Heidegger is still in agreement with Husserl; for while Heidegger's elucidation of metaphysics is neither simply historical nor simply conceptual, it remains entirely genetic, as a tradition of thought arising from a founding concept – Being as idea. Derrida is perfectly happy to agree that metaphysics as such is a matter of genesis, whether historical or conceptual. Unlike Heidegger and Husserl, however, he *also* considers it structurally, as instituted and endlessly repeated in and by the concept 'sign'.

38 Husserl, *Cartesian meditations*, trans. D. Cairns (The Hague: Martinus Nijhoff, 1977), p. 156.

Which means that for Derrida a critique of metaphysics must develop simultaneously along other, genetic and structural, lines. 'To concern oneself with the founding concepts of the entire history of philosophy', Derrida remarks (with Heidegger in mind), 'is probably the most daring way of making the beginnings of a step outside philosophy'.[39] But if metaphysics is written into the structure of the sign, and is therefore presupposed in all discourse, the most cogent critique of the founding concepts of metaphysics will remain trammelled in metaphysics. On the face of it, we need to be able to use critique without thereby being committed to metaphysics, to realise the possibility of auto-critique that abides within discourse whilst not falling prey to Nietzsche's criticisms of the Kantian notion of 'critique'. In brief, we must seek to conserve 'all these old concepts ... while here and there denouncing their limits, treating them as tools which can still be used'.[40] This second path can be pursued only as the result of a structural critique, such as we find in Derrida's analysis of the metaphysical conception of the sign. In this critique, it will be remembered, 'sign' is shown to depend structurally upon a generalised version of that which it devalues. The signifier is to be used as a tool in dismantling the sign's metaphysics. This is, to be sure, a powerful metaphor; but it may be stated more precisely. It is not so much the signifier which is the tool here as it is the *difference* between signified and signifier, and the signifier is characterised, within metaphysics, by way of this difference.

Following Hegel, Derrida argues that 'difference' remains a metaphysical concept insofar as it derives from 'identity'. And here the signified is seen as self-identical whereas the signifier is characterised by difference, since it gains its identity through repetition over empirical differences yet admits different significations in different contexts. As we saw in the first chapter, the signified can never be presented purely and simply; it is divided internally in its origin, and thus may be said to differ from itself: it can gain identity though never *self*-identity. What is unthought within metaphysics, then, is that signified and signifier gain their identity from a mode of difference that does not derive from a predetermined notion of identity; and this, of course, is what Derrida calls '*différance*'. It is plain, I think, that this struc-

39 Derrida, *Writing*, p. 284.   40 Derrida, *Writing*, p. 284.

tural critique comes in response to the claim that the concepts in question exist in a natural and inevitable relationship. And this is the case with the relation between 'signified' and 'signifier'. Equally plain, however, is the genetic critique's reliance on the possibility of a structural critique. If this were *not* possible, the founding structure would be natural and inevitable. So Derrida's aim is to manage a genetic and a structural critique. Deconstruction demonstrates that the two are mutually dependent and illustrates the practice of using both at the same time. It is the deployment of this doubled mode of critique, a 'dislodged and dislodging writing' as Derrida puts it, which marks the closure of onto-theology.[41]

This is not to say, of course, that Heidegger is not aware of the need to borrow the syntax and lexicon of metaphysics when submitting it to critique. In *The question of Being*, for example, one finds Heidegger crossing out 'Being' so that the word is legible but its traditional associations are suspended.[42] Derridean deconstruction is a dialogue with and a departure from Heideggerian *Destruktion*, and this departure can be observed in the passage from 'Being' to 'sign' as the point of incision for a critique of onto-theology. Heidegger never spells out why, if the ontico-ontological difference is *sent* to us by Being, it is so wrong to think Being in relation to beings, but Derrida establishes that metaphysics inheres in the distinction between signified and signifier; that this account of the sign is, on its own terms, unstable; and that there is always a rapport between metaphysics and what is held to lie outside metaphysics. As we have already discussed the first two points in the first chapter, we shall turn to the third, taking our bearings from Derrida's remarks upon the sign.

Derrida is keener in the formulation of his problem than Heidegger, and moreover his formulation has a substantially wider scope. As we know, Derrida takes the distinction between presence and representation to institute and govern the whole of western thought. More particularly, he views metaphysics from the perspective of the distinction between the intelligible and the sensible: for since Plato, he contends, the intelligible has been

41 Derrida, *Positions*, p. 42.
42 Heidegger, *The question of Being*, trans. and introd. W. Kluback and J. T. Wilde (London: Vision Press, 1959), p. 81.

construed as presence (self-presence, presence in time, presence to a subject, or whatever) while the sensible is taken to be the representation of that presence. Formulated in this fashion, the sign is metaphysical, both with respect to a referent and in its internal constitution: in the first place, it is taken to represent a presence – a sign is always a sign *of* something; and in the second, the signified is regarded as the intelligible content of the sign whereas the signifier is by definition a sensible mark, a phoneme or a grapheme. Without any immediate loss of clarity, Derrida is able to resolve the text of western thought, what he calls the 'general text', into a number of distinctions which ultimately merge with that between presence and representation.[43] If metaphysics is to be read as constituted by the distinction between the intelligible and the sensible, the same is to be said of epistemology with respect to the distinction between the simple and the complex. Similarly, theology arises from the distinction between the transcendent and the immanent; mysticism from that between immediacy and mediation; and so on. Such distinctions can easily be multiplied, cutting across all generic divisions. Thus we have distinctions between identity and difference, reason and non-reason, the original and the derivative, the *archè* and the an-*archè*, the literal and the figural, and – to conclude with the one for which Derrida is perhaps best known – between speech and writing.

So while Derrida accepts the description of metaphysics as onto-theology he does not take this to be the sole description of metaphysics or even the most telling. In fact many of these distinctions find a place under the description of metaphysics as 'logocentrism', an overdetermined word whose specific meanings must be drawn out. On one level, 'logocentrism' signifies any attempt to determine a unique master-word which could serve as a firm foundation, a ground, for speculation; and Derrida claims that all philosophy is logocentric in this sense. On a straightforward linguistic level, *Logos* means both 'reason' and 'speech', and Derrida takes any appeal to a natural order of reason, prior to all linguistic determination, to be logocentric. More controversial is Derrida's other claim that the valorisation of speech over writing is of a piece with these characteristics of metaphysics. Finally, the word signifies Christ as the divine

43 See, for example, *Positions*, p. 44 and pp. 59–60.

Logos and recalls the doctrine, first formulated by Justin Martyr, of the *Logos spermatikos*. Thus when Derrida asserts that 'God and the *logos* are one'[44] he is asserting that Christianity, reason and the quest for grounds have been complicit from St Paul to Heidegger; and once more the three are linked by the structure of the sign. The structure of the sign would therefore seem to be metaphysical, theological and Christological: the *Logos* is a 'passage from the infinite to the finite, from the finite to the infinite', the archetype of the sign.[45] Or more pointedly: the intelligible signified, the *Logos*, is incarnated in the sensible signifier.

Are we to conclude from this that all theology is to be taken as metaphysics? I do not think so. The object of Derrida's critique is the uncritical equation of 'God' and 'full presence' which he finds at work in Christian theology and particularly in the doctrines concerning Jesus as the Christ. And if this is so, Derrida like Heidegger is offering a critique of theology and not a critique of faith. Thus he can agree with Moses Mendelsohn that the God of Judaism 'does not manifest himself, he is not truth for the Jews, total presence or parousia'.[46] It is the concepts of 'truth', 'total presence' and 'parousia' that are called into question, not the concept 'God' as such. Nor is Judaism the only religion to put pressure upon metaphysics: Derrida happily admits that before they were assimilated into Greek culture both Judaism and Christianity were indeed the 'other' of philosophy. 'And one can argue', he continues, 'that these original, heterogeneous elements of Judaism and Christianity were never completely eradicated by Western metaphysics. They perdue throughout the centuries, threatening and unsettling the assured "identities" of Western philosophy.'[47] Far from being an *object* of deconstruction, Christian theology – in some of its elements at least – is part of a *process* of deconstruction.

This reading of deconstruction puts me at odds with many readers of Derrida's texts, whether religious or not. I still need to temper the foregoing formula, though, and the best way to do this is to show what Derrida's refinement of the Heideggerian doctrine of metaphysics as onto-theology means for theology.

44 Derrida, *Glas*, p. 77a.   45 Derrida, *Glas*, p. 31a.
46 Derrida, *Glas*, p. 51a.
47 Derrida, 'Deconstruction and the other', p. 117.

We shall therefore confine ourselves to five main points. (1) First of all, Derrida demonstrates that it is far more difficult to disentangle oneself from metaphysics than Heidegger or Kant would have us believe. If metaphysics inheres in the structure of the sign, then the *language* of theology will always be complicit with metaphysics. And to the extent to which theology is constrained by this metaphysics to place God within the ontico-ontological difference, it will use 'God' as an *archè*, a means of totalisation, and thus the *desire* for totalisation, a positive determinant of metaphysics, will be inscribed within theology. (2) Unlike Heidegger's thought, especially his later thought, Derrida makes little use of a religious or quasi-religious vocabulary; and though it may appear paradoxical this is, perhaps, of greater use to theology than the often tantalising remarks offered by Heidegger. For if there is any theological programme to be deduced from Heidegger and grafted on to any current theology, it comes down to a form of quietism. Heidegger offers the possibility of a divine God being revealed to us, though one that is far removed from the God of biblical revelation, and about whom we cannot say anything at all. The burden is upon Heidegger to describe what sort of revelation would count as a revelation of God rather than Being, and nowhere does he offer such a description.

Nor does Derrida, but he does offer something of far greater benefit to theology than Heideggerian quietism. (3) Where Heidegger is unclear if the *Austrag*'s sending of Being is to be understood ontologically or epistemologically, Derrida is plain that *différance* is the enabling condition for all discourses, totalisable or not. Whilst it is doubtless true that Derrida seeks to situate epistemology with respect to *différance*, it is also true that he makes no claims about anything other than the *status* of our knowledge and truth claims. *Différance* may block the way to a totalised ontology, but it is not concerned with questions of what there is in the universe and what conditions its coming into presence. (4) Despite those who try to give *différance* some sort of quasi-divine status, it is merely a transcendental principle; we can see how in his analysis of 'sign' Derrida passes from phenomenal difference to transcendental *différance*. If people talk of this or that as sent by *différance*, we know full well, as we do not with Heidegger, that a metaphor is being employed. Indeed, while we may take *différance* to mark the 'other' of metaphysics, we have no right to specify this 'other' in any exclusive thematic sense. Thus Rorty and others are wrong to read deconstruction as a debate solely or even primarily between 'philosophy' and 'literature'; there is no reason why it cannot also be taken as a debate between 'philosophy' and 'theology'. (5) Finally, although Heidegger does not picture onto-theology as an homogeneous unity of thought, Derrida's emphasis upon texts over Being allows us to be more precise about how and where to find points within the classical texts of our tradition from which metaphysics is questioned. These points are not, strictly speaking, wholly within metaphysics since they must make some reference to the 'other' of metaphysics in order to call it into question. If we allow that this 'other' can be theological, we can find particular movements within the texts of Christian theology which call the claims of onto-theology into question; and the movement I wish to keep in sight, and to which part III is devoted, is negative theology.

I began this section by talking of a hidden genealogy relating Heidegger and Derrida to Kant. It is a genealogy which we shall trace as this study proceeds, but we are now in a position to discern its larger branches. Both Heidegger and Derrida stand squarely in the Kantian heritage of critique of metaphysics. Whereas Kant sees metaphysics arising from the trespass of pure reason over assigned limits, Heidegger sees it as arising from a *failure* to trespass over those limits, and Derrida sees metaphysics as both conditioned and called into question by its trespassing over its own assigned limits, specifically the limits announced in the metaphysical conception of the sign. Kant's critique of pure reason leads him to adopt a negative theology; yet unlike most negative theologians Kant does not use this in dialectical tension with a positive theology as such but with an ethics. We have, in fine, a theology which lets God reveal Himself as God but which allows only a moral life as a human response to this revelation. Unlike Kant, however, Heidegger and Derrida stress that it is *metaphysics* which makes us look for God within the ontico-ontological distinction. Both reject ethics as an adjunct of metaphysics. What is left, then, is negative theology. For Heidegger this results in a theological quietism in which we are told to be still, to listen to the poets and wait for the divine God to be revealed. Derrida, however, fastens more firmly upon the Kant of the antinomies, and in construing metaphysics structurally and genetically, argues that discourse performs an auto-critique. It does not follow from this that deconstruction is a mode of negative theology; but it does supply us with a rather more secure position from which to inquire about negative theology's relation to language, and that will be of assistance to us in reading not only Pseudo-Dionysius and Meister Eckhart but also Kant and Heidegger.

3 Non-metaphysical theologies

Let us return to our guiding question: how are metaphysics and theology related?

Our central concern has been the notion of 'onto-theology' and, more particularly, a fundamental difference between its Kantian and Heideggerian senses. For Kant the content of onto-theology is determined by what God *is*, a particular kind of being whose essence is the Being of being; it follows that God must be a metaphysical entity and thus beyond the realm of possible knowledge. Kant assumes that the identification of 'God' and 'Being' precedes the discourse on being as such – metaphysics – and it is precisely this assumption which we have called into question. Agreeing with Heidegger, I have argued that it is the onto-theological constitution of metaphysics which determines the concept of God. If Kant asks us to be cautious in using the concept 'God', Heidegger leads us to question the very idea of the concept 'God', asking whether the God who is generated by the constitution of metaphysics is what people *mean* by 'God', and his answer is that it is not. At a certain level of generality, both Kant and Heidegger propose a non-metaphysical theology, one in which God can be thought yet not known. They disagree, though, in that for Kant God can only be thought in the context of His self-revelation while for Heidegger it is God who is revealed by the *Austrag*. We already have, it seems, different kinds of non-metaphysical theologies, one broadly Christian and one which is less easy to assimilate to Christianity, as the number of attempts to do so testifies.

But if we agree with Heidegger that 'God' aids and abets metaphysics must we also agree with his theology rather than, say, Kant's? Our study of the Derridean displacement of the *Austrag* by *différance* leads us to answer no. Besides, it is increasingly evident that the description 'non-metaphysical theology' covers a diverse corpus of texts and approaches to texts, so before we can proceed we need to be a good deal clearer about what sorts of non-metaphysical theology there are and where we stand with regards to them. To begin with, we may take as a benchmark of metaphysical theology Etienne Gilson's provocative remark that 'He Who is the God of the philosophers is HE WHO IS, the God of Abraham, of Isaac, and of Jacob'.[48] So, by 'metaphysical theology' we shall understand any discourse in which the God of metaphysics, the *causa sui*, is completely identified with the God of faith. This leaves us with two principal ways in which a theology can be non-metaphysical: by claiming a decisive rift between the God of metaphysics and the God of faith; and by elaborating a theology which works between them.

We have already discussed the first way in some detail with regards to Heidegger. As the case of Heidegger reminds us, not all non-metaphysical theologies are self-evidently Christian. And we should also remember that those Christian theologies which do seem 'non-metaphysical' may not all fulfil this description in the same way or to the same degree. There are theologies which claim, implicitly or explicitly, to be wholly non-metaphysical, but which nonetheless find themselves entangled in metaphysics. And there are other theologies, perhaps the majority, which may appear thoroughly metaphysical but which are questioned from within by non-metaphysical elements. We shall restrict our attention for the time being to this first group. Given our allowance of heterogeneity, it is an easy matter to list some names: St Paul, Tertullian, St Augustine, Luther, Pascal, Kierkegaard and Barth.

Consider Tertullian. Nothing could be more obvious than Tertullian's wish to distinguish theology from philosophy; indeed, it is Tertullian who set Athens and Jerusalem to stand for philosophy and theology. 'What indeed has Athens to do with Jerusalem?' he fulminates, 'What concord is there between the Academy and the Church? what between heretics and Christians?'[49] It seems that by 'philosophy' Tertullian wishes us to

48 Etienne Gilson, *God and philosophy* (New Haven: Yale University Press, 1941), p. 144.
49 Tertullian, *Prescription against heretics*, Ante-Nicene Christian Library, Vol. XV. *The witings of Tertullian* (Edinburgh: T. and T. Clark, 1870. Vol. 2 Ch. viii (p. 9).

understand 'Greek philosophy' and by 'theology' something like 'faith in scripture'. Now 'philosophy' and 'theology' do not designate changeless fields of discourse; so we can be more precise by distinguishing Tertullian's contrast from Philo's: for whereas Philo reads 'philosophy' and 'theology' as 'concept' and 'scripture', Tertullian takes 'philosophy' in a wider sense to mean both natural and speculative philosophy. On the one hand Thales, Anaximines, Anaximander and others are condemned for deifying the constitutive elements of the world; on the other hand, speculative philosophers are castigated for believing themselves able to solve problems which lie outside the limits of human knowledge. In either case heresy is held to be instigated by philosophy, and either way faith is distinguished from reason – its sole object and sustenance being God's revelation of Himself in both His Word and word. Needless to say, Tertullian will have nothing to do with the allegorical hermeneutic: we are to believe in the literal word of scripture, and any tensions between the Old and New Testaments are to be resolved by means of typology. Accommodations of faith to reason, such as one finds in Docetism, therefore meet with immediate rejection. Thus the reply to Marcion: 'The Son of God was crucified; I am not ashamed because man must needs be ashamed [of it]. And the Son of God died; it is by all means to be believed, because it is absurd [*ineptum*]. And He was buried, and rose again; the fact is certain, because it is impossible'.[50] Whether we take this to be a *sacrificium intellectus* or a spirited plea to limit human *hubris*, the point remains that Tertullian patently wants to keep reason and faith, philosophy and theology, at the greatest possible distance from each other.

If one accepts the Heidegger–Derrida account of philosophy as metaphysics, though, it is not hard to show that there is a philosophical discourse at work within Tertullian's text. Tertullian readily employs all manner of concepts inaugurated by Greek philosophers, and nowhere is this more evident than in his account of God. 'All men's common sense will accept', Tertullian assures us, 'that God is the supremely great, firmly

---

50 Tertullian, *On the flesh of Christ*, in *The writings of Tertullian*, Vol. 2, pp. 173–74. Cf. Søren Kierkegaard, 'What now is the absurd? The absurd is that the eternal truth has come into being in time, that God has come into being. . .', *Concluding unscientific postscript*, trans. D. F. Swenson and W. Lowrie (Princeton: Princeton University Press, 1968), p. 188.

established in eternity, unbegotten, uncreated, without beginning and without end'.[51] So, God is the original being, the
highest being, and the ground of all that is – the very predicates
which establish the discourse of onto-theology. It might be
objected that Tertullian is employing philosophical discourse
only to defeat Marcion on his own ground, and that he could talk
of God in a pure biblical language. This assumes that it is
possible to distinguish between philosophical and biblical language, and as I have already suggested, this cannot be done.
Both philosophical and biblical languages are complex entities
with various strata, and there can be no single line drawn to
separate one from the other. One may not *intend* to make a
metaphysical commitment in talking about the 'real presence',
say, but upon Derrida's analysis such a commitment is nonetheless made by virtue of the fact that both 'real' and 'presence' are
grounding concepts of philosophy. Moreover, the objection
assumes that metaphysics is a response to construing God in a
particular way, whereas it is our contention that metaphysics
precedes 'God', leading us to imagine God as a particular kind of
being – the original, the highest, and the ground of beings.

One might accept these arguments and still remain un-
convinced of the claim that one cannot develop a purely non-
metaphysical theology. There are two main lines – call them (1)
and (2) – that one could adopt.

(1) First of all, one could say that Tertullian's error lies precisely in his attempt to elaborate a doctrine of God, that Christianity has to do with believing in God and living a good life, not
with speculating upon the nature of God. Kant and Heidegger
play variations on this theme, but the most extreme is Wittgenstein's. 'Christianity is not a doctrine, not, I mean, a theory
about what has happened and will happen to the human soul',
he contends, 'but a description of something that actually takes
place in human life'.[52] Doubtless no one would disagree that
Christian faith is in major part a matter of personal experience;
but if one takes *no* account of the doctrines of the Trinity, the
incarnation, the resurrection, and so forth, it is hard to know
what Wittgenstein could mean by 'Christianity'. If we press

51 Tertullian, *Adversus Marcionem*, ed. and trans. Ernest Evens (Oxford: Clarendon Press, 1972), Vol. I, Sec. 3.2.
52 Ludwig Wittgenstein, *Culture and value*, ed. G. H. Von Wright and N.
Nyman. Second edition. (Oxford: Blackwell, 1980), p. 28e.

Wittgenstein on this point we get a confusing response. We are told in Rilkean tones that 'one of the things Christianity says is that sound doctrines are all useless. That you have to change your *life*'.[53] Christianity involves radical conversion, to be sure, but how would one know in what way to change one's life if it were not for some doctrinal content? Furthermore, if doctrine helps one to change one's life for the better it cannot be useless; and no doctrine is likely to persuade one to change one's life unless it is thought to be (in some sense) sound. Wittgenstein could rightly argue that there is no positive link between the Christian faith and *totalised* doctrines. But he is wrong to suggest that there is a pure form of Christianity untouched by doctrine and unmotivated by a will to totalise.

At least in the English-speaking world, the phrase 'non-metaphysical theology' signifies a network of arguments drawn largely from Wittgenstein and elaborated by, amongst others, Hare, MacIntyre, Miles and Ramsey. While we cannot do justice to the variety of views and arguments represented here, we do need to explain why, upon our assumptions, this theology is not non-metaphysical; and the best place to begin is with Wittgenstein's remarks on Christian faith:

> A proof of God's existence ought really to be something by means of which one could convince oneself that God exists. But I think what *believers* who have furnished such proofs have wanted to do is give their 'belief' an intellectual analysis and foundation, although they themselves would never have come to believe as a result of such proofs. Perhaps one could 'convince someone that God exists' by means of a certain kind of upbringing, by shaping his life in such and such a way.[54]

We see here the beginning of what was to become the familiar explanation of religious faith as a *blik*. The word is R. M. Hare's and signifies any deep conviction which is not susceptible to verification or falsification.[55] Moreover, a *blik* does not constitute an explanation, as it is precisely that by which we decide what will or will not count as an explanation. Quite clearly, Wittgenstein claims that Christian belief is a conviction of this kind, the

53 Wittgenstein, *Culture and value*, p. 53e. Cf. p. 83e.
54 Wittgenstein, *Culture and value*, p. 85e.
55 See R. M. Hare, 'Theology and falsification' in *New essays in philosophical theology*, eds. A. Flew and A. MacIntyre (London: SCM Press, 1955), pp. 99–103.

locus classicus of which would be St Anselm's ontological proof of God's existence, set in the context of a prayer. Anselm and Wittgenstein agree that faith is in quest of understanding. However, while Anselm thinks his proof can convince the atheist that God does exist, Wittgenstein takes the acquisition of religious faith solely as the development of a set of *bliks*.

This view must be set against the positivist critique of metaphysics, according to which metaphysics consists of statements which are, strictly speaking, meaningless in that they do not admit of verification (as Ayer requires) or falsification (as Popper requires). It is evident that if one measures meaning by verification or falsification, all theological statements are also meaningless. There are no facts to which one can point which could establish or refute a statement such as 'God is a loving Father'. If one accepts the general thrust of the positivist critique of metaphysics and still wishes to elaborate a theology, it is plainly necessary to develop a non-metaphysical theology, one in which the categories of verification and falsification have no role to play. And this is precisely what the *blik* theory provides us with, an account of religious faith in which verification and falsification are preceded by that which cannot be verified or falsified. The Wittgensteinian account of faith gives content, then, to the idea of a non-metaphysical theology. But is this particular attempt to determine a non-metaphysical theology successful? Given our account of metaphysics, the answer must be no. Even if we set aside the familiar difficulties involved in formalising the principles of verification and falsification, there are reasons why the positivist critique of metaphysics will not do. In the first place, it assumes that a line can be boldly drawn between metaphysics and non-metaphysics, which is itself a metaphysical gesture. And second, positivism remains metaphysical in its quest for an *archè*, an absolute epistemological starting-point, whether this be in a 'protocol' sentence or the principle of verification itself.

There is, however, an entirely different way of trying to excise metaphysics from theology, and since it leads us to the border land between (1) and (2) we would do well to attend to it here. It is sometimes held that certain mystical texts develop a theology which makes no metaphysical claims. It is easy enough to gather a wealth of remarks by mystics which denigrate philosophy. St Teresa of Avila, for instance, seems almost to repeat Tertullian

101

word for word when, writing of one of her experiences, she claims that 'The less I understand this, the more I believe it and the greater is the devotion it arouses in me'.[56] Philosophy becomes an *ancilla theologiæ* whose services can be dispensed with, for anyone 'who has got as far as reading theology must not descend and read philosophy'.[57] But the argument for mysticism as non-metaphysical does not rely so much upon what mystics think of philosophy as on how commentators understand mysticism. Caputo, for instance, maintains that Aquinas's purported mystical experience before his death is 'the story of a "step back" out of metaphysics' and that the mystical kernel of Aquinas's thought can be discerned by 'a deconstructive reading of St Thomas's metaphysics'.[58]

Several points are immediately called for. First, we have already seen that Caputo is engaged with Heideggerian *Destruktion*, not Derridean deconstruction; and the discussion earlier in this chapter details the differences between these modes of critique. Second, we have raised a number of objections to the view that it is possible to 'step back' out of metaphysics. And third, we have demonstrated the superiority of *différance* over the *Austrag* as an account of the 'ground' of metaphysics. Keeping these points in mind, we can probe Caputo's case in more detail. It may be resolved into the following questions: Can deconstruction uncover a mystical kernel of a text? and What relation obtains between mysticism and metaphysics? With regards to the first question, our discussion leads us to conclude that while it is possible to claim that deconstruction seeks to find the 'other' of metaphysics, it is far from self-evident that this 'other' can be readily identified with 'mysticism'. Caputo follows a certain philosophical reading of mysticism as pure, immediate union with the Godhead, notions which are themselves targets of deconstruction. This is not to say that the category of the mystical is of no use to us – quite the contrary. But it does imply that Caputo's sense of this category or, if you like, non-category, entails apparent contradictions. This leads us to the second and somewhat more vexed question. Because it can certainly be

56 St Teresa of Avila, *Spiritual relations*, p. 351. (All references to St Teresa are to the particular text as collected in *The complete works of St Teresa of Jesus*, trans. E. Allison Peers (London: Sheed and Ward, 1978).)
57 St Teresa, *Book called way of perfection*, in *Complete works*, p. 156.
58 Caputo, *Heidegger and Aquinas*, p. 254 and p. 12.

argued that, with the possible exception of the Pseudo-Dionysius, mystics are not so much concerned with *knowing* God as with *loving* Him; and while Derrida can see epistemological questions cooperating with metaphysics, it is unlikely that he will also see falling in love as a metaphysical state of affairs.

Yet the situation is not quite this simple. There can be no strict division between 'knowing' and 'loving' with regards to mystical experience. St Teresa may be right to affirm that 'the important thing is not to think much, but to love much', but this is a matter of priority not of exclusive prescription.[59] Furthermore, even though mystical experience is more concerned with loving than with knowing, it bespeaks a relation between the two. The mystic loves God because he or she already knows something of Him: love is in quest of knowledge, and knowledge leads to a deepening of love. If this is so, mystical experience would seem to have a troubled relationship with metaphysics, one that needs broad and fine clarification. Part of the problem is to do with the scope of 'mysticism', since the word ranges over a kind of experience, a hermeneutic (the allegorical hermeneutic) and a mode of theologising, namely negative theology. Now these three work in a complex and covert economy, and it is one of the aims of this study to shed some light upon how this economy works. Most philosophical study of the area has been concentrated upon experiential mysticism; but we shall focus upon negative theology and the allegorical hermeneutic, and our reasons for doing so constitute our account of the second main way in which a non-metaphysical theology could be developed.

(2) What is most persuasive about Derrida's refinement of the Heideggerian account of onto-theology is his argument that metaphysics is inscribed within the structure of language, and so there can be no direct rapport between what is 'within' metaphysics and what is 'without'. The deconstruction of metaphysics is accomplished in showing that the ground of a metaphysical discourse is linked systematically to a non-ground, held to be *prior* to the ground. In other words, the *archè* is shown to be related to an an-*archè*. Thus the difference between signified and signifier, for example, is metaphysical in that it can be understood only with respect to a prior notion of self-identity; while the deconstruction of the metaphysical conception of the sign is

59 St Teresa, *Interior castle*, in *Complete works*, p. 233.

given in the demonstration that *both* 'self-identity' *and* 'difference' have as their condition of possibility a mode of difference which is not defined with respect to a prior notion of self-identity. A non-metaphysical theology would accordingly be one which would show that metaphysics obliges us to take God as a ground; it would uncover a sense in which God could be apprehended as a non-ground; and it would show that the conceptions are systematically related.

Positive theology is linked to onto-theology: both are discourses motivated by appeals to full presence. The God of the philosophers, the *causa sui*, may not be reducible to the God of positive theology but nor are they irreducible. We shall use 'positive theology' to denote those onto-theological discourses which *explicitly* orient themselves to God, however imagined. And it is in this sense that we may say that, whatever else they are, Pseudo-Dionysius and Kant are also positive theologians. What one finds in these – as in all – positive theologies is a supplement of negative theology; it is needed to check that our discourse about God is, in fact, about *God* and not just about human images of God. According to our definitions, those theologies are metaphysical which claim that this supplement is merely added to a positive theology, that positive theology is prior to negative theology. What I wish to argue, though, is that this supplementation takes place at the origin and ground of theology, that origin and ground are themselves supplements. Negative theology is a supplement which is, strictly speaking, prior to all the statements of positive theology. To use the vocabulary steadily developed over part I, negative theology performs the deconstruction of positive theology. In doing so, negative theology reveals a non-metaphysical theology at work within positive ideology. But it is, I shall argue, incapable of isolating non-metaphysical from positive theology.

II | Examination

It is equally deadly for a mind to have a system or to have none. Therefore it will have to decide to combine both.

Friedrich Schlegel

4 | The status of deconstruction

1 Problems of definition

While Derrida allows metaphysics to have a far wider scope than any other philosopher, even Heidegger, he also claims to have recognised a region which is other than metaphysics, in which it is inscribed, and from which it can be analysed. This is not to say that this region is located entirely outside or beyond metaphysics, for deconstruction is concerned to mark limits, not ends. We can look at this situation from opposing sides. From the one viewpoint, metaphysics has neither a simple exterior nor a pure interior; the utopia of pure grammatology and the equable realm of idealism are equally foreign places to Derrida. Yet it can also be seen that any critique of metaphysics must maintain a tacit relationship with what it interrogates: the 'other' of metaphysics cannot be 'wholly other'. And thus arises the question of the status of deconstruction. I have already used deconstruction to uncover several difficulties with metaphysical theology and to suggest how, in general terms, we can develop a coherent non-metaphysical theology. But before we make use of these conclusions it seems we must take a step back and enquire more thoroughly as to the relation between metaphysics and deconstruction. I shall therefore once more pose the question, 'What is deconstruction?'

Strictly speaking, we should be wary of using the singular at this stage of our enquiry, for it is by no means self-evident that 'deconstruction' is univocal. I have observed how various commentators have misused the word 'deconstruction' or misconstrued the concept 'deconstruction', and part of the problem is that Derrida allows a certain elasticity to the word. Deconstruction, he once remarked to Lucien Goldmann, 'is simply a question of (and this is a necessity of criticism in the

107

classical sense of the word) being alert to the implications, to the historical sedimentation of the language which we use'.[1] That was in 1966, and in 1979 one finds the similarly straightforward observation that to deconstruct is 'to take apart an edifice in order to see how it is constituted or deconstituted'.[2] This sounds very much like a classical account of critique, a view from which Derrida only departs when observing that what is new in deconstruction is that it gives rise to the 'internal auto-critique of philosophy'.[3] Elsewhere, however, one finds Derrida insisting that deconstruction 'is not *neutral*. It *intervenes*', that 'because deconstruction interferes with solid structures, "material" institutions, and not only with discourses or signifying representations . . . it is always distinct from an analysis or a "critique"'; or, still more pointedly, that 'deconstruction is deconstruction of dogmatic critique'.[4]

This apparent looseness of expression can be explained without too much special pleading. While Derrida put the word 'deconstruction' into circulation, it is not his favoured description of *all* his various enterprises. In the late sixties 'deconstruction' was one word amongst many others – including *'différance'*, 'grammatology', 'trace' and 'dissemination' – with which he was working. However, the alacrity with which Derrida was taken up, especially by literary critics on the east coast of America, required that his work be labelled by a catchword, and that came to be 'deconstruction'. Derrida was caught up with this popularising movement himself and, knowingly or unknowingly, contributed to its consolidation, and this gives rise to a tension in his vocabulary. Not every strategy which captures his attention fits nicely under the heading 'deconstruction', as the word is used, say, in *Of grammatology*, yet conversely the word has become a privileged term for explaining whatever Derrida does,

1 Derrida, 'Discussion' in *The structuralist controversy*, p. 271.
2 Derrida *et al.*, *The ear of the other*, ed. Christie V. McDonald and trans. Peggy Kamuf and Avital Ronell (New York: Schocken Books, 1985), pp. 86–87; Derrida remarks here that this is a classic operation, though what is *not* classical about it is its object, namely the history of western philosophy.
3 Derrida, 'Où commence et comment finit un corps enseignant', in *Politiques de la philosophie*, ed. Dominique Grisoni, (Paris: Bernard Granet, 1976), p. 64.
4 Derrida, *Positions*, p. 93 and *The truth in painting*, trans. Geoff Bennington and Ian McLeod (Chicago: University of Chicago Press, 1987), p. 19. Elsewhere Derrida remarks, 'deconstruction is neither an *analysis* nor a *critique*', 'Letter to a Japanese friend', p. 4.

and is, moreover, a word he now feels obliged to use. The consequence, in short, is that 'deconstruction' has become thoroughly overdetermined; it must be approached with circumspection.

We have seen that the hermeneutic model of interpretation can be read as an allegory of Adam's fall. Interestingly enough, one of Derrida's most winning accounts of deconstruction is an allegory of mankind's second fall as dramatised in the story of the tower of Babel. Upon Derrida's reading of Genesis 11: 1–9, God is the deconstructor of the tower of Babel. 'He interrupts a construction', Derrida observes, then adds, 'The deconstruction of the tower of Babel, moreover, gives a good idea what deconstruction is: an unfinished edifice whose half-completed structures are visible, letting one guess at the scaffolding behind them'.[5] It would be useful to see how Derrida reads this story as an allegory of deconstruction. The story itself is well known: the Shemites fear that they may be 'scattered abroad upon the face of the whole earth' and so they desire to organise themselves into the one city and to have the one proper name. God observes their actions and, as the story is conventionally read, chastises the people for their hubris in wishing to build 'a tower, whose top may reach unto heaven'. God confuses their language and thereby realises the people's fear: 'So the Lord scattered them abroad from thence upon the face of all the earth: and they left off to build the city'.

The Shemites overstep the proper limits assigned to man by God, and – as with Adam – their trespass of the sign has consequences in direct opposition to their desired end: far from consolidating their self-identity, their action brings difference into their midst. Once more we have a fall, and once more the fall has linguistic ramifications. As Derrida observes, 'shem' means 'name',[6] so in building a tower that reaches into heaven the Shemites wish to impose not just their language but more particularly their proper name upon the entire universe; and they do so, it seems, from a fear of losing their self-identity. When God interrupts their construction and confuses their language, He merely realises the difference they have attempted to

5 Derrida, et al., *The ear of the other*, p. 102. Also see Derrida's essay 'Des tours de Babel' in *Difference in translation* ed. Joseph F. Graham (Ithaca: Cornell University Press, 1985), pp. 165–77.
6 Derrida, et al., *The ear of the other*, p. 100.

suppress. God's deconstruction produces a dispersal, what Derrida amusingly calls a 'disshemination'. And thus ends Derrida's reading.

I argued in part I that Derrida wishes to question the status of both genetic and structural explanations, and this allegory goes some way towards refining this view. The tower is pictured, above all, as a *construction*: it is built at a particular time and in a particular place, and it has a specific structure. On the one hand, then, deconstruction is concerned to show that no matter how abstract a theory appears, how much it seems to be a question of connections between ideas, it can be traced back through historical periods. Deconstruction is therefore genealogical. Which is not to say that it commits the genetic fallacy: for it is precisely the explanatory force of 'origin' that is held to be problematic. And on the other hand, deconstruction seeks to demonstrate that any attempt to unify earth and heaven by means of the *one* structure – to explain the material in terms of the ideal or *vice versa* – will inevitably result in structurally undecidable statements which count against the explanatory force of the theory. We can further refine this account by distinguishing between four levels of Derrida's exegesis: (1) the philosophical; (2) the meta-philosophical; (3) the psychoanalytic; and (4) the political.

(1) To begin with, deconstruction is a first-order thesis about the relative priority of identity and difference. It is a criticism of what Derrida calls 'the metaphysics of the proper'. We know that 'shem' means 'name', and Derrida reads the bestowing of a proper name as a desire for identity. He argues that this desire is always already inhabited by the structure of writing which is, for him, a synecdoche for pure negative difference. For example, one meaning of 'proper' is 'literal meaning', and it is Derrida's contention that what seems to be a text's literal meaning is always already divided between the literal and the tropological. More generally, deconstruction is a criticism of the totalising claims of all hermeneutics. Just as the Shemites seek to comprehend the universe in terms of their one name but end up scattered across the earth, so the hermeneutic attempt to comprehend a sign system results in not one interpretation but two conflicting and irreducible interpretations, that is, not identity but difference. Moreover, just as the tower is not destroyed in the Genesis story, so the deconstruction of a metaphysical dis-

course is in no way a destruction of it. Derrida attempts to show that any attempt to totalise a text can be seen to depend transcendentally upon a generalised form of the differences it proposes to subsume. This is the classical element of critique at work in deconstruction.

(2) For Derrida as for Heidegger, any discourse is metaphysical which seeks to ground speculation in an *archè*: Cartesian 'clear and distinct ideas', Humean 'sense-impressions', Russellian 'logical atoms', and so forth. In each case, Derrida avers, we have a construction, erected upon a particular foundation, which attempts to totalise an entire textual field; and this makes each of these metaphysical discourses analogous to the tower of Babel. No theory whose foundation is held to be an *archè* can hope to account for the whole of a text solely in terms of that *archè*. Even so, Derrida adds, all philosophical systems are ultimately based upon one *archè* or another, and it follows that each philosophical system will inevitably break down, that all philosophical systems are built both *out of* and *upon* the ruins of prior philosophical foundations. Metaphysical theories arise only to fall short of their ambition by dint of that ambition.

There is another way in which this allegory situates deconstruction as a meta-philosophy, however, and that is because, like Heidegger, Derrida understands philosophy to be 'the fixation of a certain concept and project of translation'.[7] Derrida's formulation is admirably clear:

> What does philosophy say? What does the philosopher say when he is being a philosopher? He says: What matters is truth or meaning, and since meaning is before or beyond language, it follows that it is translatable. Meaning has the commanding role, and consequently one must be able to fix its univocality or, in any case, to master its plurivocality. If this plurivocality can be mastered, then translation, understood as the transport of a semantic content into another signifying form, is possible. There is no philosophy unless translation in this latter sense is possible.[8]

7 Derrida, *et al.*, *The ear of the other*, p. 120. Cf. Derrida's earlier remark that there is 'a violent difficulty in the transference of a nonphilosopheme into a philosopheme. With the problem of translation we will thus be dealing with nothing less than the problem of the very passage into philosophy', *Dissemination*, p. 72. Cf. Heidegger, *Poetry, language, thought*, trans. and introd. Albert Hofstadter (New York: Harper Colophon, 1975), p. 23.
8 Derrida *et al.*, *The ear of the other*, p. 120.

Philosophy as translation, then: Whitehead and Russell's desire in the *Principia mathematica* to devise a new Adamic language into which our ordinary fallen language could be translated; and G. E. Moore, for whom philosophy was at root the translation of unclear into clear statements. One may well wonder whether people such as Tarski and Quine emerge as philosophers on this account; after all, Tarski does not hold truth to abide *behind* language, and Quine offers a decisive critique of propositions. I shall postpone problems of scope to the next chapter, though, and attend to Derrida's point which I take as directly related to the doubling of the sign. For example, if *'le supplément'* means both 'addition' and 'replacement' in Rousseau's text, any attempt to erect a unified construct – a philosophical discourse – upon the text will find itself caught in a double-bind; since *'supplément'* at once invites and forbids translation by virtue of its undecidability. Now Derrida tells us there will always be a word, phrase or movement similar to *'supplément'* in any text. Once we are persuaded of this (and only a great deal of scrupulous close reading can persuade us), and once we accept Derrida's description of philosophy as metaphysics, it certainly follows that all philosophical constructs are built upon shaky ground.

(3) While this meta-philosophical saga makes use of the traditional lexicon of philosophy, it also accords a privilege to the categories of Freudian psychoanalysis. Spivak rightly stresses that 'Derrida does not look at psychoanalysis as a particular or "regional" discipline, but as a way of reading'; and here the psychological conflicts revealed in the Genesis narrative are transferred and repeated in the allegory itself.[9] Expositions of deconstruction almost invariably talk of the *desire* of onto-theology or of deconstruction; one is just as frequently informed of the *repression* of differences in onto-theology; and Derrida generally maintains that if differences are repressed this will result in their unexpected appearance elsewhere. In short, Derrida appeals to the Freudian doctrine that there is always a displacement from latent to manifest content. If we were to examine Derrida's employment of psychoanalytic categories in more detail, we would find various other Freudian concepts pressed into service. We could note his use of the dream-work's transmutation of words into things in his treatment of the

9 Spivak, 'Translator's preface', *Of grammatology*, p. xxxviii.

shapes of words and syllables; his use of the repetition compulsion on those occasions when he argues that any interpretation of the text has been anticipated by the text itself – rhetorically, thematically or in terms of its narrative structure – and is therefore a repetition. And we could easily trace this tendency to ascribe psychological attributes to the text back to that *point d'appui* of contemporary French thought, Kojève's lectures on Hegel's *Phenomenology of mind*, especially the discussion of the Lord and Bondsman.

(4) If Derrida calls upon the vocabulary of psychoanalysis to develop his critique of metaphysics, he makes even more show of political rhetoric. What he seems to object to most strenuously in the Genesis story is the Shemites' attempt to claim universal applicability for their particular language; and if the Shemites stand for philosophers, Derrida seems to take metaphysics as an ideology. More generally, one can point to the political rhetoric with which Derrida discusses the operations of deconstruction. In one frequently cited passage we hear that metaphysics is 'a violent hierarchy', that one of its terms 'governs the other . . . or has the upper hand', that we must bring 'low what was high' and that metaphysics is a 'regime'.[10] Indeed if, as I shall argue, Derrida's main point is that the condition of possibility of an interpretation is also and at the same time its condition of impossibility for totalising a text, his thought is largely analogous with, indeed derived from, a familiar political thesis. I have in mind Rousseau's view that 'the flaws which make social institutions necessary are the same as make the abuse of them unavoidable'.[11]

If we take these four points together we have what seems to be a satisfactory account of deconstruction. Yet there are various criticisms that can be levelled at the theory as stated. It will surely be objected, by someone like G. E. Moore, that while some philosophers, most notably idealists, do attempt to explain the whole of reality, many others set about discussing just one aspect of it.[12] While Derrida's theory might well apply to Plato

10 Derrida, *Positions*, pp. 41-42.
11 J.-J. Rousseau, 'A discourse on the origin of inequality', in *The social contract and discourses*, trans. G. D. H. Cole (London: J. M. Dent and Sons, 1973), p. 99.
12 See, for example, G. E. Moore, *Some main problems of philosophy* (London: George Allen and Unwin, 1953), p. 24.

and Hegel, it does not obviously apply to analytic philosophers from Moore to Davidson who tend to tackle problems in piecemeal fashion. It must be remembered, though, that Derrida does not argue that all discourses are metaphysical in the same way or to the same extent. An analytic philosopher such as J. L. Austin contributes a great deal to the deconstructive enterprise (much as he would have disliked it in some respects) yet never fully frees himself from certain metaphysical commitments, as becomes clear in his treatment of etoiliated speech acts. Having accepted that reply, one might point to what appear to be flaws in the allegory. The position that the deconstructor is assigned in the allegory seems not to square with Derrida's general insistence that there can be no Archemedian point outside the text. And given Derrida's case against foundationalism what allegorical role, one wonders, could be attached to the ground on which the tower is built? Objections could be multiplied but to no real purpose; no allegory can be completely consistent in its details. Besides, there is a more damaging objection that can be raised. For although there are problems with the theory as stated, the main problem seems to stem from stating the theory at all.

Derrida characterises the hermeneutic model of interpretation as an allegory of Adam's fall. If this is so, deconstruction is not opposed to hermeneutics; it is the demonstration that the hermeneutic model is itself unstable. There is no difficulty in taking hermeneutics as the allegory of a narrative; after all, allegory is the privileged hermeneutic mode by virtue of its attempted mastery of textual differences. But there is a difficulty in offering an allegorical explanation of deconstruction, since it is that very model of interpretation which deconstruction sets out to question. The difficulty does not arise accidentally, because deconstruction just happens to be presented here as the allegory of a biblical text. It stems, rather, from the fact that Derrida puts into question not one mode of representation or one theory of representation but the idea of representation *as such:* and if this is so the difficulty will recur whenever one attempts to define 'deconstruction'. With this in mind, we can return to (1)–(4) above and see how deconstruction gives tacit credence to what is under critique. For example, the terms Derrida draws from Freudian psychoanalysis are themselves open to deconstruction in certain contexts. Similarly, metaphysics can never be said, without qualification, to be an ideology, since the distinction between the *de facto* and the *de jure* which is needed to define 'ideology', is itself sanctioned by metaphysics.[13]

In order to free ourselves from what may seem a dizzying series of *mises en abîmes* we must now heed a question whose importance we have noted but which we have had to keep waiting. We know that deconstruction is directed against the distinction between presence and sign upon which 'representation' relies, but what sort of force is thus directed? Does deconstruction seek to *argue* against 'representation', pointing out by more or less agreed rules of argumentation that any theory of representation relies upon premises which undercut its claims? Or does it eschew classical 'critique' and seek, instead, to *discredit* the framework in which metaphysics works and which it seems to require for its own workings? Christopher Norris answers the first question in the affirmative, maintaining that 'Derrida *argues*, and moreover argues "rigorously"'.[14] Others, however, answer the second question in the affirmative, yet disagree amongst themselves as well as with Norris. There are those in this group, such as T. K. Seung, who take a decidedly negative estimation of deconstruction, construing it as 'irrationalism . . . intellectual anarchy . . . shallow tricks in obscurantism and shady gimmicks for specious arguments'.[15] And there are those, such as Richard Rorty, for whom this amounts to a positive point. Deconstruction, he contends, derives its power from its vocabulary, not from any assembly of arguments we could reasonably call a 'critique'.[16] For Rorty, deconstruction is a Nietzschean (or groundless) – not a Kantian (grounded) – mode of criticism. Contrary to Norris, Seung and Rorty, my claim is that Derrida understands both modes of criticism, the grounded and the groundless, to be irreducibly entwined. That is, deconstruction is a matter of *both* critique *and* vocabulary.

13 I am indebted here as elsewhere in this chapter to V. Descombes's rigorous analysis of Derrida's thought in *Modern French philosophy*, trans. L. Scott-Fox and J. M. Harding (Cambridge: Cambridge University Press, 1980), esp. p. 137.

14 Christopher Norris, *The contest of faculties* (London: Methuen, 1985), p. 219. See also his discussion on pp. 18, 44.

15 T. K. Seung, *Structuralism and hermeneutics* (New York: Columbia University Press, 1982), p. xii. Seung returns to the point on p. 274 when we are told that 'Derrida's critique of logocentrism turns out to be a series of specious arguments'.

16 See, for example, Rorty, *Consequences of pragmatism*, pp. 93–97 and pp. 140–41.

Let us look again at deconstruction as critique. We can quickly reach the central issue by distinguishing different ways of perceiving deconstruction. The claim that deconstruction is a critique relies upon deconstruction's ability to show that what appears to be a monistic whole is in fact always already *doubled*. And second, deconstruction seems always to be in the process of *doubling* itself, thereby making problematic what we mean by 'deconstruction'. I have explicated the first claim in the opening chapter; my present task, therefore, is to work out the relation between these claims. To this end, I recall what have become our three fundamental points: Derrida takes 'philosophy' as it is understood in the Cartesian-Husserlian tradition as 'an all-embracing science grounded on an absolute foundation', in Husserl's words;[17] he seeks to locate the 'other' of philosophy, the vantage-point from which metaphysics can be interrogated; and it is impossible to locate a point *wholly* outside metaphysics. Now a powerful critique of a powerful system will ruin the system entirely or be incorporated into it to modify the system and further strengthen it. Moore's criticisms of Bradley's idealism, for example, effectively brought that system to ruin; yet Kant's criticisms of idealism were incorporated by Hegel to give rise to a more vigorous idealism as explicated in the *Encyclopedia of the philosophical sciences*. Deconstruction does not fit into either of these modes of critique, though, for it seeks to offer a critique not just of this or that philosophical position but of philosophising as such. Needless to say, perhaps, the very activity of offering a critique gives rise to a position which is, by definition, within philosophy. So Derrida has to negotiate a double-bind: an effective critique of 'philosophy' will confirm what is submitted to critique; but unless the critique tacitly assumes what it questions, it will not be recognised as a critique in the first place.

In a dialogue with Levinas, Derrida gives some credence to *feigning* the language-game of philosophy: he will use philosophical language but in full awareness that he is playing a game.[18] The tactic here is one of intention, and as Derrida argues that intention cannot fix a text's meaning, he cannot then argue, from the premise of intentional duplicity, that it can determine his text as other than philosophy. Derrida is committed, though,

17 Husserl, *Cartesian meditations*, p. 152.   18 Derrida, *Writing*, p. 89.

116

to the view that deconstruction must reveal itself 'only under the species of the non-species';[19] and this provides him with a more powerful principal strategy. Here, deconstruction consists in perpetually combining what has become normative under its rubric with another – hitherto unknown – element. Thus we have deconstruction as critique (classical in its form though not in what it submits to critique); then Derrida insists that deconstruction is *both* a critique of metaphysics *and* a critique of the institutions in which that discourse is practised – and that this removes deconstruction from a classical notion of 'critique'. A theory of supplementation, deconstruction is itself always open to be supplemented: it cannot be formalised without remainder.

We have isolated two elements which are peculiar to deconstruction as critique: its ability to show that what seems to be a monistic whole is always already doubled, and its tendency to double itself. The first determines the success of deconstruction as critique, while the second is a critical response to that success, one that stems from the scope of what is submitted to critique. Deconstruction is not a methodology; it can only be defined by the practices done in its name. But while this sets our questioning within a visible horizon, we are still some way from accounting for deconstruction as a matter of both critique and vocabulary. We need to examine how a whole can be always already doubled, and how a critique can always be in the process of doubling itself.

2 Interpretations of interpretation

I take as my point of orientation a short yet highly influential passage from Derrida's early essay 'Structure, sign and play in the discourse of the human sciences'. It is possibly the most frequently cited passage of Derrida as well as the source of the most common misconceptions about the methods and aims of deconstruction. Derrida contrasts two ways of regarding interpretation: one is turned 'toward the lost or impossible presence of the absent origin' and is characterised as the 'saddened, *negative*, nostalgic, guilty, Rousseauistic side of the thinking of play' while the other is the 'Nietzschean *affirmation*, that is the

---

19 Derrida, *Writing*, p. 293.

joyous affirmation of the play of the world and of the innocence of becoming, the affirmation of a world of signs without fault, without truth, and without origin which is offered to an active interpretation'. The most often quoted passage, though, is this:

> There are thus two interpretations of interpretation, of structure, of sign, of play. The one seeks to decipher, dreams of deciphering a truth or an origin which escapes play and the order of the sign, and which lives the necessity of interpretation as an exile. The other, which is no longer turned toward the origin, affirms play and tries to pass beyond man and humanism, the name of man being the name of that being who, throughout the history of metaphysics or of onto-theology – in other words, throughout his entire history – has dreamed of full presence, the reassuring foundation, the origin and the end of play.[20]

Note that while Derrida associates these modes of interpretation with Rousseau and Nietzsche, he could just as easily use the standard contrast between Kant and Nietzsche. Either way, the general contrast he wishes to draw is between grounded and ungrounded interpretations.

The Nietzschean mode of interpretation is plainly the inverse of the Rousseauistic, for the one values the play of signs over presence while the other extols the determining power of presence over signs. And it appears as though Derrida is enjoining us to favour the Nietzschean mode over the Rousseauistic. Certainly this is what a large number of commentators, both sympathetic and unsympathetic, take Derrida to say; and various dubious conclusions are drawn from this. It is time to hear what the critics have to say. Wayne Booth, for one, attempts to sum up Derrida's position wholly in terms of play: 'Jacques Derrida', he claims, 'seeks a "free play" amounting to a "methodical craziness", to produce a "dissemination" of texts that, endless and treacherous and terrifying, liberates us to an *errance joyeuse*'.[21] James Hans seems to agree with Booth's description but does propose an argument. He holds that the second interpretive mode, which he calls 'freeplay', is 'apparently the alternative to our previous ways of structuring the world' and that deconstruction's provenance is freeplay. He therefore takes

20 Derrida, *Writing*, p. 292.
21 Wayne Booth, *Critical understanding* (Chicago: University of Chicago Press, 1979), p. 216.

Derrida to assert that 'there is no center but only freeplay'.[22] After setting up the case he argues that the alternative between 'center' and 'freeplay' is facile and that deconstruction 'has not escaped the metaphysic but merely turned it on its head'.[23] Hans takes the 'alternative', as he puts it, between the modes of interpretation as the basis of an immanent critique of deconstruction. Denis Donoghue, however, simply remarks that 'Derrida favours' the second mode of interpretation and, from here, proceeds to suggest that unless Derrida forges a link between play and force, deconstruction will render all human enterprises fundamentally trivial.[24] Donoghue agrees with Hans that deconstruction is to be identified with the second mode of interpretation, but from this assumption, he develops an external critique of deconstruction based upon humanist grounds.

Mark C. Taylor divides the interpretative modes into 'Logocentrism's interpretation of interpretation' and 'Deconstruction's interpretation of interpretation', and while he does not discuss Rousseau he does equate Nietzsche's position with Derrida's. So it is no surprise to find deconstruction identified with the thematics of God's death. 'What if the presence of the logos is a fanciful dream that is a function of desire rather than experience?', he asks, 'What if there is no firm foundation, no secure anchor, no abiding truth? What, in other words, if God is dead?'[25] Here Taylor's 'in other words' does not serve to sharpen his previous rhetorical questions but translates them into another, less stable,

22 J. S. Hans, 'Derrida and freeplay', *Modern Language Notes*, 94 (1979), pp. 809–10. Hans repeats his contention that Derrida offers us an alternative between the two interpretations of interpretation in a later article when he maintains, once more with regards to this particular passage, that 'one can move in only two directions according to Derrida'. See 'Hermeneutics, play, deconstruction', *Philosophy Today*, 24 (1980), p. 301.

23 Hans, 'Derrida and freeplay', p. 818.

24 Denis Donoghue, *Ferocious alphabets* (London: Faber and Faber, 1981), pp. 165–66. Other commentators who align Derrida with the second interpretation of interpretation include the following: F. V. Bogel, 'Deconstructive criticism: the logic of Derrida's différance', *Centrum: working papers of the Minnesota Center for Advanced Studies in Language, Style, and Literary Theory,* No. 6 (1978), pp. 55, 57; S. Mitchell, 'Post-structuralism, empiricism and interpretation', in *The need for interpretation*, ed. S. Mitchell and M. Rosen (London: Athlone Press, 1983), p. 63; and D. C. Hoy, *The critical circle* (Berkeley: University of California Press, 1978), p. 83.

25 M. C. Taylor, 'Deconstruction: what's the difference?', *Soundings: An Interdisciplinary Journal*, 66 (1983), p. 396.

frame of reference, one that can be read variously in metaphysical, epistemological, theological or ethical terms. Taylor's exact meaning need not concern us here; the point at issue is merely that he aligns deconstruction with Nietzsche and, more specifically, with one of Nietzsche's views. Unlike Taylor, Gregory Ulmer's discussion of the passage in question addresses both Rousseau and Nietzsche; yet, like Taylor, Ulmer steers Derrida towards Nietzsche, both of whom, in his view, have assigned themselves 'the task of undoing Rousseau's eighteenth century'.[26] A contrast is quickly established, this time between 'logocentrism' and 'grammatology'. Rousseau's logocentrism is held to be a 'theological view' by which Ulmer understands that it is 'based on notions of an immanent God, and of self-consciousness as the guarantee of identity' while grammatology, 'in contrast, is a theory of language that corresponds to a world *without God*'.[27] Notice how Ulmer passes from Derrida's distinction between the two interpretations of interpretation to a distinction between Rousseau's natural theism, as indicated in the *Profession of faith*, and Nietzsche's doctrine of God's death. Although Ulmer sees deconstruction as upsetting certainty and dogmatism, he has no doubt that deconstruction shows Nietzsche's views 'already present in Rousseau's texts' and mentions nothing about what of Rousseau's views may be present in Nietzsche's or Derrida's texts.[28] For him, deconstruction proceeds thematically and only in the one direction. Once more, deconstruction merges with Nietzsche and, even more specifically, with the doctrine of God's death.

And so we have several arguments based on this familiar passage: one that develops an immanent critique of deconstruction; another that points the way to an external critique; and two that align deconstruction with the view that God is dead. None of the arguments is particularly impressive. In various ways all of them are misled by 'free play' which, far from licensing anarchy, indicates – as Derrida puts it – 'that the structure of the machine, or the springs, are not so tight, so that you can just try to dislocate [*sic*]'.[29] 'Free play', it seems, is neither completely

26 G.L. Ulmer, 'Jacques Derrida and Paul de Man on/in Rousseau's faults', *The Eighteenth Century*, 20 (1979), p. 165.
27 Ulmer, 'Jacques Derrida. . .', p. 167.
28 Ulmer, 'Jacques Derrida. . .', p.172.
29 I. Salusinszky, *Criticism in society* (London: Methuen, 1987), p. 20.

free nor all that playful. Like 'free verse', it has constraints of its own. Whatever their limitations, these arguments are part of what I shall call the 'common reading' of deconstruction. If we stand back and survey these arguments, we can isolate four antitheses which, taken together, map out the possible variations of this common reading: decipherment/play; Rousseau/ Nietzsche; logocentrism/deconstruction; and theism/atheism.

When any of these distinctions are uncritically conflated – as they variously are by the commentators quoted above – it is easy to see how deconstruction can be associated with a doctrine of hermeneutic anarchy, one or more of a number of Nietzsche's ideas, atheism, or indeed all of the foregoing. Yet such identifications are not convincing. After all, deconstruction cannot be reduced to the second mode of interpretation, and we need to weigh the status of the couple 'Rousseau–Nietzsche' before we can confidently transpose any particular claims made by either writer onto the mode of interpretation he represents. If deconstruction is more than 'Nietzschean' free play, what is it?

It will be recalled that James Hans argues that freeplay is 'apparently the alternative to our previous ways of structuring the world'. But does Derrida provide us with an *alternative* between Rousseau and Nietzsche? This is how Derrida concludes his comments, a passage cited far less often than the one with which we commenced our discussion:

> For my part, although these two interpretations must acknowledge and accentuate their difference and define their irreducibility, I do not believe that today there is any question of *choosing* – in the first place because here we are in a region (let us say, provisionally, a region of historicity) where the category of choice seems particularly trivial; and in the second, because we must first try to conceive of the common ground, and the *différance* of this irreducible difference.[30]

On the face of it, Derrida addresses regional politics and is concerned with what we may or may not take to be a viable choice in a particular historical situation. Yet he also raises an epistemological question: what are the conditions of possibility for choices in general?

Derrida insists that the two interpretations are irreducible; and this is certainly the case, for the Nietzschean account, as framed,

30 Derrida, *Writing*, p. 293.

is an inversion of the Rousseauistic. It is also claimed that there is something which underwrites this 'irreducible difference', its *différance*, and that this disallows our choosing between the Rousseauistic and the Nietzschean theories of interpretation. If this is so, it is evident that Derrida cannot be urging the interpretations of interpretation as *alternatives* between which we must choose; he seems more concerned to elaborate why we *cannot* choose between them. A closer inspection of the passage reveals that, contrary to the commentators' view of the matter, there are not two but *three* interpretations of interpretation: two first-order interpretations (Rousseau's and Nietzsche's) and one second-order interpretation, Derrida's. Whereas Rousseau's theory assumes a ground, and Nietzsche's is an affirmation of groundlessness, Derrida's theory establishes the relationship between apparently 'grounded' and 'groundless' theories of interpretation. This does not yield a secure meta-philosophical position, however, for Derrida's vantage-point – *différance* – turns out to be that which at once structures and destructures all positions. 'Such a play, *différance*, is thus no longer simply a concept', Derrida tells us, 'but rather the possibility of conceptuality'.[31] So it would seem that Derrida's claim is not that we should support one sort of interpretation over another but that the condition of possibility of the Rousseauistic interpretation also enables the Nietzschean interpretation.

The most economical way of drawing out what is at issue here requires us to turn to the concluding pages of 'Plato's pharmacy' where we find the following remarkable account of *différance*:

> The disappearance of truth as presence, the withdrawal of the present origin of presence, is the condition of all (manifestation of) truth. Nontruth is the truth. Nonpresence is presence. Differance, the disappearance of any original presence, is *at once* the condition of possibility *and* the condition of impossibility of truth. At once. 'At once' means that the being-present (*on*) in its truth, in the presence of its identity and in the identity of its presence, *is doubled* as soon as it appears, as soon as it presents itself. It *appears, in its essence, as* the possibility of its own most proper non-truth, of its pseudo-truth reflected in the icon, the phantasm, or the simulacrum. What is is not what it is, identical and identical to itself, unique, unless it *adds to itself* the possibility of being *repeated* as such. And its identity is

31 Derrida, *Margins of philosophy*, p. 11.

hollowed out by that addition, withdraws itself in the supplement that presents it.[32]

Despite the density and paradoxical flair of this passage, its
general lines are clear. I have already explicated the main argument developed here, with specific regard to the relation
between a presence and a sign, in the opening chapter. It will be
remembered that the sign always works with two modes of
repetition. The one, sanctioned by metaphysics, allows for the
sign to repeat its originating presence; but the other, a structural
trait of the sign, concerns its repetition outside its original
context. Now when the sign is so repeated, what it signifies will
be modified by the chance new context. In being subject to the
second mode of repetition, the sign must fail to perform its first
and primary mode to the extent to which it does not signify the
presence purely and simply. But as this accident is a *structural*
possibility of the sign it is, we are bound to say, essential to the
sign. The second mode of repetition is a supplement to the first;
it is, however, a dangerous supplement in that in supplying the
part it supplants the whole, dislodging the first mode's grip on
signification. It does not follow, of course, that the second mode
of repetition now holds sway, since what is put into question is
precisely the ability of either mode to govern. We do not have an
undivided origin of signification, governed by a presence, but an
origin which is itself already doubled by dint of the nature of the
sign.

It is an easy matter to apply the foregoing argument about
signs to interpretations. For within metaphysics the function of
an interpretation is to repeat the text's proper meaning. If this is
so, we must agree that an interpretation is a *sign* of a text, and
therefore a specific instance of the argument we have rehearsed.
Just as the origin of signification is always already doubled,
so too with the origin of interpretation. We shall call the
two interpretations of any given text the 'proper' and 'non-
proper' respectively, thereby keeping in mind Derrida's notion
of 'the metaphysics of the proper'. A proper interpretation will
therefore repeat a text's proper or *determinate* meaning. What
counts as a 'determinate meaning' will of course depend upon
one's theory of meaning. Along one possible axis, one may set
both 'authorial intention' (Hirsch) and 'literary language'

32 Derrida, *Dissemination*, p. 168.

(Shklovsky); in each case, though, an underived origin, an *archè*, must be assumed at some stage of the theory. However, the sign's structure is its condition of possibility for being repeated, and hence for non-proper significations to occur. The condition of possibility for the proper interpretation, it seems, also enables a non-proper interpretation. The proper interpretation lays claim to repeat the text's meaning purely and simply, but this claim is contested by its condition of possibility. The proper interpretation cannot *totalise* the text: its condition of possibility disables all attempts to totalise the text. Formulated in various ways and used in various contexts, this is Derrida's central contention.[33]

We can go further. If no animating presence can be signified as it is, we can never rightly say that we have a sign of a presence. The presence can never present itself; it will always withdraw behind signification, not to the first degree (as in 'sign of a presence') but always to the second degree (as in 'sign of a sign'). Now if, within metaphysics, a sign is held to differ from and defer its animating presence, all the concept of 'sign of a sign' leaves us with is a process of difference and deferment; and this, as we know, is what Derrida calls *différance* or *la trace* or *archi-écriture*. Not that *différance* can ever occur in and for itself: it is a condition of possibility, to be sure, though not a Kantian *a priori* condition of possibility. Before *différance* can come into play we need a text which asserts a metaphysical state of affairs, such as, for example, that 'presence' is to be naturally valued over 'sign'. In other words, *différance* is transcendental but does not constitute a transcendental ground; it is always revealed in any text, though never revealed as such because there is no such thing as

---

33 To gain an idea of the frequency with which Derrida uses this formulation consider the following quotations: 'The condition of possibility for these effects is simultaneously, once again, the condition of their impossibility, of the impossibility of their rigorous purity', *Margins of philosophy*, p. 328; 'Their possibility is their impossibility', *Speech and phenomena*, p. 101; 'The rebus signature, the metonymic or anagrammatic signature, these are the condition of possibility and impossibility', *Signsponge* p. 64; 'So time, an element of degree, marks at once the possibility and the impossibility of frivolity', *The archæology of the frivolous: reading Condillac*, trans. John P. Leavey, Jr (Pittsburgh: Duquesne University Press, 1980), p. 132; 'Differance produces what it forbids, makes possible the very thing that it makes impossible', *Of grammatology*, p.143; 'This axiom of non-closure or non-fulfillment enfolds within itself the condition for the possibility and the impossibility of taxonomy', 'The law of genre', trans. A. Ronell, *Glyph*, 7 (1980), p. 212.

'différance as such'. To rewrite Heidegger's apothegm: As it reveals itself in differences, *différance* withdraws.

So the proper and non-proper interpretations are irreducible; and the existence of the non-proper interpretation contests the claim of the proper interpretation to totalise the text. We can give more content to these modes of interpretation by turning to a particularly astute and elegant passage by Michel Foucault. To interpret or comment, Foucault tells us,

> is to admit by definition an excess of the signified over the signifier; a necessary, unformulated remainder of thought that language has left in the shade – a remainder that is the very essence of that thought, driven outside its secret – but to comment also presupposes that this unspoken element slumbers within speech *(parole)*, and that, by a superabundance proper to the signifier, one may, in questioning it, give voice to a content that was not explicitly signified.[34]

The proper interpretation ascribes priority to the signified over the signifier; it seeks to locate the essence of what is literally signified. The non-proper interpretation values the signifier over the signified. One way it can do so is by using the signifier to uncover what is latently signified; if the latent meaning is determinate, we have a hermeneutics of suspicion. Another way is to use the signifier with the intention of disseminating rather than recovering meaning, and here we do not have, strictly speaking, a hermeneutics at all. According to our assumptions, in which all hermeneutics, whether of faith or of suspicion, are 'proper' interpretations in that they eventually recur to an *archè*, it follows that only disseminative interpretations are non-proper.

We have already observed that the non-proper mode of interpretation is the inverse of the proper; and we can make this quite exact by using the formulæ S/s and s/S in which 'S' stands for 'signified' and 's' for 'signifier'. There is no difficulty in regarding S/s as metaphysical, in Derrida's sense of the word; but can we agree with the common reading of deconstruction which claims that s/S is non-metaphysical? We cannot – at least not if we agree with Heidegger and Derrida that an inversion of a metaphysical hierarchy remains immanently within metaphysics. According to Heidegger, the epoch of metaphysics

34 Michel Foucault, *The birth of the clinic*, trans. A. M. Sheridan Smith (New York: Vintage Books, 1975), p. xvi.

extends from Plato to the inversion of Platonism as found in Nietzsche. It little matters at present if we agree that Nietzsche does in fact merely invert Platonism; all we need agree upon is that the model which Derrida proposes regards *both* the proper *and* the non-proper interpretation as metaphysical: whether Nietzsche represents non-proper interpretation is another question. Deconstruction has two movements – a phase of inversion and a phase of displacement – and this doubling is not to be found in non-proper interpretation. So we cannot identify deconstruction with non-proper interpretation, as the common reading of deconstruction invites us to do. Nor can we unproblematically identify deconstruction with atheism. We have seen how Derrida regards the sign S/s as 'theological', with the signified forever 'turned toward the word and the face of God';[35] but Derrida also takes the inverted configuration, s/S, as 'atheistic'.[36] And if deconstruction is an operation on both S/s and s/S it cannot be solely theistic or atheistic. Deconstruction's relation to theology must be thought otherwise.

It would seem, therefore, that deconstruction is a metaphilosophical position; but to accept this at face value would be to forget that the exemplary texts of deconstruction are scrupulously close readings of other texts. Is it possible that deconstruction can be an interpretative practice as well as a theory of interpretation? And if deconstruction *is* an interpretative practice, does this not contradict the conclusion we have just reached, that deconstruction is not a mode of non-proper interpretation? Before anything else, we need to ask what sort of interpretative practice deconstruction is; and a salient example can be found in *Of grammatology*. As we know, one of Rousseau's crucial words, *'le supplément'*, can mean both 'addition' and 'replacement'. When Rousseau figures writing as a *supplément* to speech his intention is to characterise it as an unnecessary addition; speech is complete within itself, and writing can serve only to introduce unnatural difficulties and misunderstandings. There is, however, another layer of Rousseau's text in which writing is held to be a *supplément* in the other sense. For Rousseau is perfectly clear that only by writing (and thereby shunning the presence of natural, living speech) can he present himself as he really is. Here, writing is a replacement for speech.

35 Derrida, *Of grammatology*, p. 13.   36 Derrida, *Dissemination*, p. 54.

As with writing so with masturbation: Rousseau at once takes masturbation as an addition to normal sexual practice and as a convenient replacement; it is, as he says, 'a dangerous supplement'. So upon close examination what appears to be the one text by Rousseau can be opened up into two texts, using *'supplément'* as a hinge. These texts are irreducible but not opposed; indeed, Rousseau cannot argue that speech and writing are opposed, for he has maintained that writing is *both* an addition to *and* a replacement for speech.

We would be missing the point, I think, if we took Derrida's essay to be nothing more than an *interpretation* of Rousseau's text. For while Derrida would not wish to quarrel with the epistemological point that his remarks on interpretation are themselves interpretations, not facts, it does not seem to me that Derrida is offering anything like a first-order interpretation of Rousseau's text. Throughout Derrida's analysis our attention is directed to the workings of the signifier *'le supplément'* and not to matters of description, theme or evaluation such as one normally finds in readings of Rousseau. What we have, I would suggest, is Derrida using Rousseau's text against the tradition of Rousseau interpretation. And this tradition becomes the object of criticism by virtue of its tendency to totalise Rousseau's text in the very oppositions – nature/culture, presence/absence, and so forth – that his text can be shown to subvert.

If we turn from Derrida's reading of Rousseau to his remarks upon the two interpretations of interpretation, the Rousseauistic and the Nietzschean, we find the same emphasis. Even though we pass from a close reading of a particular text to a meta-philosophical point, the critical object remains the same – totalisation – and so there is no contradiction between the views that deconstruction is a textual practice and a meta-philosophical theory. Whether discussing a text or a theory of textual interpretation, Derrida's point is constant: there are always 'Two texts, two hands, two visions, two ways of listening. Together simultaneously and separately'.[37]

We can dismiss any conflation of the distinction between logocentrism and deconstruction with distinctions between Rousseau and Nietzsche, proper and non-proper interpretations or theism and atheism. More generally, the relationship between

---

37 Derrida, *Margins of philosophy*, p. 65.

metaphysics and deconstruction is more subtle than the common reading of deconstruction suggests. Our focus in this section has been on the first two of the four points by which we characterised deconstruction; and we have established, *contra* Rorty, that deconstruction is, at least in part, a mode of argumentative critique. The question of the status of deconstruction's vocabulary will be taken up in the following section, and this will involve us in a discussion of the remaining two points.

3   Erasure and palæonymy

'What is is not what it is', Derrida insists, 'unless it *adds to itself* the possibility of being *repeated* as such'.[38] Now what is true of the critical objects of deconstruction must also be true of deconstruction itself. That is, deconstruction gains *its* identity by being repeated outside its originary context (Derrida's critique of genetic phenomenology) in other, chance contexts; and it is precisely because the element of chance is a structural trait of the sign (or any group of signs) that we cannot rigidly fix the identity of deconstruction. We may say of it what Derrida says of Condillac's method of analysis, 'it is already no longer there when we naively believe we have captured it in a wide-mesh net'.[39]

The parallel between Condillac's 'analysis' and Derrida's 'deconstruction' is worth pursuing a little further. In his *Essay on the origin of human knowledge*, Condillac distinguishes between two kinds of metaphysics.[40] The first, instituted by Aristotle, is a discourse upon grounds and upon the highest ground (*theion*); it is a metaphysics of essences and causes, a 'first philosophy', and its aim is to explain what is hidden. Condillac, however, elaborates a second kind of metaphysics, one concerned with phenomena and relations, which he proposes to call 'analysis'. Whereas Aristotelian first philosophy works by establishing a set of *archai*, Condillac's method of analysis proposes itself as a discourse upon the *archè* – an archeology – and it will therefore reflect upon the status of the *archai*. The true science of origins, analysis will retrace the genesis of first philosophy; and its impulse for so doing is, as Derrida neatly puts it, that first philosophy 'has

38 Derrida, *Dissemination*, p. 168.   39 Derrida, *Archæology*, p. 63.
40 Etienne Bonnot de Condillac, *An essay on the origin of human knowledge*, trans. Thomas Nugent (Gainesville, FL: Scholars' Facsimiles and Reprints, 1971), p. 2.

consisted of bad linguistic use coupled with a bad philosophy of language'.[41]

Analysis will seek to account for, or re-mark, the defects of the language of metaphysics. To do so, it requires a new language of greater formal precision, one which will supply the old language with what it lacks. In re-tracing the ways in which these defects arise, that is, in accounting for particular lapses in a general theory, the new discourse of analysis must itself develop general principles which, once formalised, comprehend the old discourse in its totality. Analysis does not cure metaphysics but discovers what can be seen, after the fact, as the *ground* of metaphysics, the condition of possibility to which it has remained blind. Analysis can therefore claim to have the greater explanatory force, since it re-marks not only the defects of the prior theory but also the theory as such; it supplants the old in the act of supplying it with what it cannot itself supply. This new discourse is a calculus; it must of necessity appear more artificial than the language of the old metaphysics; yet it shows itself, through specific analyses, to be capable of ascertaining the natural provenance of that metaphysics. And in this very demonstration the calculus lays hold of what seems, within the old language, nevertheless to precede language, the realm of the metaphysical itself. In sum, the calculus proves itself to be a metaphysics despite its claim to be a critique of metaphysics.

We have here, as Derrida observes, 'a theory of the general conditions for the upsurge of a theory'.[42] And this is exactly what Derrida himself wishes to establish, but with one important difference: unlike Condillac, Derrida desires a critique of metaphysics that is not itself metaphysical. He proposes to retrace the stages of Condillac's theory and to supplement and supplant it with his own without, in this process, supplying a *ground*. In other words, whereas Condillac's 'new science' is an Adamic venture, passing back beyond Babel 'to give ideas their names',[43] deconstruction is the demonstration that Babel *precedes* Adam's naming day in Eden. Derrida must therefore *retrace* Condillac's account of retracing and supplying/supplanting, then *supply it* with what it lacks – an account of the

41 Derrida, *Archæology*, p. 36.   42 Derrida, *Archæology*, p. 63.
43 Derrida, *Archæology*, p. 33.

difference which will supplant it while *not* providing a new ground. This calls for a detailed explanation.

Condillac's first stage of retracing is entirely immanent, and elements external to the theory in question appear only in the second stage; yet even here there must be, as Condillac says, a 'quantity of connection' between what supplies and what requires supplementation.[44] If this condition is to be met, though, we cannot say that there is a rigorous distinction between what is within the prior theory and what is outside it, for the supplement must be at once within and outside the theory. And the same holds for Derrida's reading of Condillac's theory: it must locate what is needed to be supplied from outside the theory from within that theory. In addition, both writers' first moves are concerned with what is present and known – a previously established theory – while their second moves concern what appears, within the given theory, to be absent and unknown. So there is an analogy between Condillac's analysis and Derrida's deconstruction; in fact, it is the notion of 'analogy' which is fundamental to each.

It would be useful to begin with Condillac's use of 'analogy' which is somewhat different from the more familiar Aristotelian usages. For we do not have, with Condillac, an analogy between elements which are present and known but, rather, an analogy between what is present and known and what is, at first, absent and unknown. Perhaps the situation is best expressed by Duchamp's observation that 'since a three-dimensional object casts a two-dimensional shadow, we should be able to imagine the unknown four-dimensional object whose shadow we are'.[45] This is not an analogy of proportion, which locates a difference of degree, nor is it – strictly speaking – an analogy of proportionality, since although it does specify a difference of kind this difference can be discerned only after the fact. The point of the analogy, as Duchamp's example shows, is to link the known and the unknown, and thereby to situate what is known in a wider, imaginative context. Analogy, here, consists in a generalising after the fact and requires – as the notion of people being shadows suggests – a metaphoric transfer of predicates from one

44 Derrida, *Archæology*, p. 72f.
45 Quoted by Octavio Paz, *Alternating current*, trans. Helen R. Lane (London: Wildwood House, 1974), p. 66.

subject to another. The drawing of such an analogy can thus be seen to be equivalent to Condillac's analytic method of retracing the present and known and supplementing it with what is, within the prior theory, absent and unknown. Similarly, there must be a 'quantity of connection' between the poles of the analogy for it to be an analogy; and this, for Condillac, decides the truth or the non-truth of the analogy. 'Truth' is a matter of quantity of connection.

It is here that Derrida detects a gap in Condillac's reasoning. He does not contest the introduction of 'truth' and 'non-truth' – they are necessary effects of the theory – only Condillac's claim to master thereby the operation of the analytic method. 'But since mastery', he objects, 'in order to be what it is, must take possession of what it is not, of nothing then, to be sure it is never itself' from which he concludes that 'Mastery, *if there is any*, does not exist'.[46] A puzzling remark, this can be cashed out as follows. Mastery can only be a mastery over that which is present and known. Within Condillac's theory, though, this condition never obtains: there is always one element which is absent and unknown, so by his own presuppositions Condillac cannot master his method. But if the analytic method claims superiority over 'first philosophy' by virtue of its ability to give ideas their 'true names', there is an aporia at the heart of Condillac's theory; for the analytic method at once claims to give true names and subverts the possibility of our knowing if they are true or non-true. The ground of analysis – truth – can therefore be said to differ from itself. Thus Derrida's re-reading of Condillac supplies the analytic method with what it lacks, an account of why this difference arises. But as difference is shown to occur in what Condillac proposes as the *ground* of the theory, we have already passed from supplementing the theory from outside to supplanting it apparently from within. We have seen how analysis is prior to metaphysics; by the same reasoning, we must admit that deconstruction is prior to both analysis and metaphysics.

First philosophy establishes a number of *archai* as its grounds, while Condillac's critique of metaphysics is directed not to the question of ground as such but to whether Aristotle's *archai* are the *right* grounds. By contrast, Derrida's critique of Condillac

46 Derrida, *Archæology*, p. 78.

does not seek to establish a new and better ground. Yet it would be a mistake to conclude from this that Derrida holds there to be *no* grounds, that there are only 'an-*archai*'. Derrida does not replace the *archè* with the an-*archè* : he demonstrates that the *archè* is always already related to an an-*archè*. If we give credence to Condillac's unusual notion of 'analogy', what is absent and unknown is accounted for as a *lack* within what is present and known: it is not 'wholly other' for it is what is missed within the theory in question and, moreover, negatively implied by that theory's *archai*. This is not an affirmation of groundlessness – anarchy – but a meta-philosophical remark about the nature of grounds.

The point can be sharpened by a brief contrast. In the *Posterior analytics* Aristotle argues that not all knowledge is demonstrable, for the knowledge of the *archai* comes not by demonstration. Indeed, these *archai* are known better than what is deduced from them, which implies that the basis of rational knowledge is not itself rational knowledge but something still more certain, *nous*.[47] For Aristotle *nous* (or 'intuition') is accordingly the transcendental *ground* of reason which is itself non-rational though not, of course, irrational. Following Kant and Heidegger, Derrida distinguishes between 'thought' and 'reason'; he observes that '"Thought" requires *both* the principle of reason and what is beyond the principle of reason, the *arkhe* and anarchy'.[48] This, after all, is not an attack against reason or a systematic doubting of reason's claim upon us; but it is a questioning of the limits of reason from the viewpoint of the nature of reason, and its upshot is that a ground can be posited only if we acknowledge that it must be linked to a non-ground. Whether Derrida fastens upon 'reason', 'truth', '*archè*' or 'ground', his point is the same: a discourse's condition of possibility is also, and at the same time, its condition of impossibility for being totalised.

Which brings us to the question of vocabulary. As we know, Condillac wishes to conserve the name 'metaphysics' for the analytic method even though he rejects metaphysics as first

---

47 Aristotle, *Analytica posteriora* in *The works of Aristotle*, ed. W.D. Ross, Vol. 1 (London: Oxford University Press, 1928), Book 1, Ch. 3, 72b18 and Book 2, Ch. 19, 100b 5f.
48 Derrida, 'The principle of reason: the university in the eyes of its pupils', trans. Catherine Porter and Edward P. Morris, *Diacritics*, 13 (1983), pp. 18–19.

philosophy; and this is because, in his view, analysis includes and surpasses Aristotelian metaphysics. This same tactic – 'palæonymy', the science of old names – is used extensively by Derrida. Within metaphysics, for example, identity is held to be prior to difference; but the deconstruction of this hierarchy reveals that both identity and difference, as defined within metaphysics, are in fact conditioned by a form of pure negative difference – *différance* – so that both identity and difference can be said to be determined modifications of *différance*. Similarly, with the hierarchic division between speech and writing, both phenomenal speech and script are shown to depend transcendentally upon a generalised form of script, what Derrida calls '*archi-écriture*'. Rather than talk about devaluation we could choose to talk about repression, as is suggested by the word 'hierarchy', and this is the basis for Derrida's use of political and psychoanalytical vocabularies. The same point can be made with reference to either discourse, so I will concentrate upon Derrida's employment of a political vocabulary.

The use of a political vocabulary in metaphysics and epistemology is as old as philosophy itself. Writing to Dionysius, king of Syracuse, Plato draws an analogy between the first principle (*archè*) and the king.[49] And thus begins a tradition. In the *Treatise* Hume views reason as a queen 'in possession of the throne, prescribing laws, and imposing maxims, with an absolute sway and authority', while reason's enemy, scepticism, 'is oblig'd to take shelter under her protection, and by making use of rational arguments to prove the fallaciousness and imbecility of reason, produces, in a manner, a patent under her hand and seal'.[50] Notice that there is no *reason* offered by Hume why reason has possession of the throne; philosophy is frankly presented as a monarchy, and reason's enemy must accept the grounds established by the monarchy. At first glance Derrida's problem seems to turn upon this dilemma: 'The unsurpassable, unique, and imperial grandeur of the order of reason, that which makes it not just another actual order or structure . . . is that one cannot speak out against it except by being for it, that one can protest it only

49 Plato, 'Letter II' 312e in E. Hamilton and H. Cairns, eds. *The collected dialogues of Plato: including the letters* (Princeton, N.J.: Princeton University Press, 1963).
50 David Hume, *A treatise of human nature*, ed. L. A. Selby-Bigge, 2nd. ed. (Oxford: Clarendon Press, 1978), p. 186.

from within it'.[51] Heidegger provides us with a radical solution to the problem. 'Has reason constituted itself to be the ruler of philosophy?' he enquires, 'If so, by what right?'[52] The question of rights raised here cuts very deep, suggesting that there is an authority prior to reason. And for Heidegger there is – the thought of Being. The sceptic must presuppose, at least provisionally, the ground of reason; but Heidegger adduces the ground in which reason is itself grounded. The true ruler of philosophy, for Heidegger, is not reason but Being, a groundless ground, an an-*archè*.

Derrida differs markedly from both Hume and Heidegger. Whereas Hume's sceptic can question reason only from within reason's realm, and Heidegger's thinker attempts to 'step back' outside metaphysics, Derrida positions himself at a point at once within and without the realm of philosophy. It is *within* philosophy in that the critique begins from what is devalued or suppressed by metaphysics – the phenomena of script, play and difference, for example – and it is *without* metaphysics in that the critique works from the enabling condition for metaphysics: the transcendentals *archi-écriture*, *jeu* and *différance*. Deconstruction as critique is doubled, then, in that it works at the same time from two realms: the phenomenal and the transcendental. To translate this into political terms, philosophy may present itself as a monarchy – with reason as the monarch, appealing only to natural rights – but can do so only by suppressing a contender to the throne, namely that which arises from the monarch's 'other', the an-*archè*. A critique of philosophy must necessarily be political, as philosophy itself is always a political state of affairs.

We cannot separate Derrida's use of political metaphors from his mode of critique, for the political metaphor is inscribed within the history of philosophy and within what Derrida takes philosophy to be: a discourse upon the *archè* to the exclusion of the an-*archè*. Palæonymy may be a strategy in the political sense – it responds to a situation which is political because it is always already a question of domination – but, as our account of Derrida's reading of Condillac shows, it is also a strategy in the sense that it is part of an argument. Whether a matter of politics

51 Derrida, *Writing*, p. 36.
52 Heidegger, *What is philosophy?* trans. and introd. W. Kluback and J. T. Wilde (New York: Twayne Publishers, 1958), p. 25.

or argumentation, it is plain that Derrida derives strategic benefit from giving the name of the phenomena which is devalued within metaphysics to the transcendental which conditions metaphysics. And this is part of a larger problem, arising from the extraordinary extension which 'metaphysics' is allowed to have.

It is time to return to the relation between 'presence' and 'sign'. We have seen how Derrida uses the structural peculiarities of the sign to launch a critique of presence, specifically of that which is signified in and of itself – the *archè* or the 'transcendental signified'. As Derrida well realises, however, 'as soon as one seeks to demonstrate . . . that the play of signification henceforth has no limit, one must reject even the concept and word "sign" itself – which is precisely what cannot be done'.[53] It is impossible to use the word or concept *sign* without thereby making a commitment to metaphysics. Not only does 'sign' *mean* 'sign of a presence' but even if one works with the Saussurian bivalent sign, one finds the instituting distinction of metaphysics, that between the intelligible and the sensible, repeated in the distinction between the signified and the signifier, the very structure of the sign. Even though deconstruction may launch its critique from the 'other' of metaphysics, the critique of metaphysics seems unable to free itself from a complicity with metaphysics. Deconstruction's problem, it seems, is a problem about vocabulary or, at any rate, about the relation between vocabulary and argument. For even though Derrida provides us with a persuasive *argument* against metaphysical totalisation, the stating of the argument requires a vocabulary which would seem to call into question the efficacy of the argument.

All this can be taken as a problem of translation. Philosophy, for Derrida, is a certain practice of translation, 'the transport of a semantic content into another signifying form'.[54] And yet there is something of great importance to philosophy that remains forever untranslatable – the proper name. Condillac objected that Aristotle failed to give ideas their proper names, and that was the task he assigned himself in developing the method of analysis. However it is considered, from the point of view of Aristotelian 'first philosophy' or Condillac's 'analysis',

53 Derrida, *Writing*, p. 281.   54 Derrida, *et al.*, *The ear of the other*, p. 120.

metaphysics is an Adamic enterprise in that it seeks to recover the proper names of ideas, the names which were given before the fall *into* language and the fall *of* language. When Derrida names the transcendentals which condition metaphysics, though, he does not seek to ascribe proper names. *'Différance'*, *'Archi-écriture'*, and so forth, are names (or, better, nicknames) drawn from a system whose instituting claims are called into question; the choices are governed by considerations of critical strategy, not of institution. Moreover, it is Derrida's claim that the border between proper and common names shifts, that proper names can take on lexical attributes and get caught up in a signifying system. We have then a claim – directed *against* philosophy – that the proper is always already related to the non-proper. The claim is framed *by* the language of philosophy though it is not, strictly speaking, *in* the language of philosophy; for to be within philosophy is, upon Derrida's account, not to contest the primacy of the proper.

If this is so, we are led to admit that Derrida uses the language of philosophy against itself. When Husserl uses the word 'sign', for instance, it is used philosophically; but when Derrida uses the same word to undo Husserl's semiology it is not simply used philosophically. Insofar as 'sign' or 'difference' is a determined modification of what conditions metaphysics it cannot be philosophical; yet insofar as the word is always already framed by metaphysics it remains metaphysical. To use 'sign' in this way is to use it under erasure (*sous rature*), and to draw our attention to the peculiar status of such words, Derrida, following a convention established by Heidegger, crosses out the words as they are written.[55] We may link together palæonymy and erasure in the following way: crossing *over* from the phenomenal to the transcendental involves a provisional crossing *out* of a word's metaphysical commitment.

This brings me to the end of my discussion of Derrida's use of vocabulary as well as to the more general discussion of the status of deconstruction. My conclusions are these. First of all, we can reject Rorty's claim that deconstruction is entirely a matter of vocabulary and involves no argumentation whatsover. As my analysis of Derrida's reading of Condillac demonstrates, the

---

55 See Heidegger, *The question of Being*, p. 81f. and Derrida, *Of grammatology*, p. 19 and p. 60.

question of vocabulary arises as a result of an argument about the status of the *archai*. It is not true to claim, as Rorty does, that Derrida '[does] not *have* arguments or theses'.[56] Nor is Norris entirely correct to read deconstruction as argumentative critique; the question of vocabulary is inextricably bound up with the strategy of deconstruction. Related to this is my second conclusion, that deconstruction is not a celebration of groundlessness. Derrida shows that any *archè* is always already related to an an-*archè*; and this is a meta-philosophical remark about the nature of philosophical systems, not an apologia for irrationalism and anarchy. And finally, I can state quite exactly the status of deconstruction with regards to metaphysics: the condition of possibility for metaphysics also enables the deconstruction of metaphysics. Or in rather less cumbersome terms: deconstruction acts as an originary *supplément* to metaphysics, supplying it with what it lacks only to supplant it.

56 Rorty, *Consequences of pragmatism*, p. 93.

5 | Questions of scope

Introduction

However much readers of Derrida may disagree, there is no dispute about one point: that Derrida takes apparently clear binary oppositions and seeks to demonstrate that they are neither oppositions nor clear. One place where arguments do arise, though, is over the question whether Derrida's concern is critical or ideological. If the former, deconstruction consists in showing that the apparent opposition between, say, identity and difference is in fact a mode of difference, not an opposition. If the latter, deconstruction also demonstrates that a philosophical tradition of affirming the priority of identity is contested, within history, by a minor tradition which affirms the priority of difference. So far my discussion of Derrida has focussed upon criticism rather than ideology, arguing that appeals to a genetic origin and to a structural centre are equally open to deconstruction. I have pointed out Derrida's reliance upon the Heideggerian–Nietzschean account of the history of philosophy as the history of nihilism; but I have not yet considered Derrida's ideological stake in the history of philosophy.

Indeed, my examination of the status of deconstruction has tended to foreclose questions that might arise concerning its scope. *Différance* is not merely the name of a particular concept but also the condition of possibility for conceptuality as such. Thus the scope of deconstruction is unlimited: it operates in all texts – philosophical, theological, literary or whatever – as well as in all the various positions in any given dispute. A cursory reading of Derrida confirms this view. He points with the one hand to thinkers such as Plato and Hegel who elaborate the central themes of metaphysics with exemplary power; and, with the other hand, to writers such as Husserl and Heidegger who

138

put pressure upon these themes and try to free themselves from metaphysics. Yet Derrida does not condemn the traditional texts of metaphysics or celebrate the attacks against them. There are, to be sure, essays in which Derrida takes a venerable meta-physical text and shows that the text's arguments are subverted by a certain layer of the text itself. However, there are also essays in which he shows that all those modern attempts to step outside the tradition of presence turn out to be entangled in the very concepts they challenge. Phenomenology, structuralism, 'ordinary language' philosophy, Freudian and Lacanian psycho-analysis: all are shown to be in fee to the notions of presence they claim to reject.

Nevertheless, there still appears to be a hidden agenda in what is submitted to deconstruction. For while Derrida admits that no text can stand wholly outside metaphysics (from which it follows that all texts are open to deconstruction) there are privi-leged texts which Derrida does not deconstruct but which are variously invoked in the deconstruction of other texts. I touched upon this issue in the second chapter, but it is time for a more thorough discussion. At a quite general level, Derrida sets literary against philosophical language: Mallarmé and Genet are used to unsettle Hegel; Poe is shown to undo Lacan; Husserl plays the straight man to Joyce; and so on. Similarly, Derrida plays off the tradition of Jewish textuality against Christian theology. Despite an early hesitation, the texts of Marx, and – more particularly – the Leninist reading of Marx, are exempted from critical interrogation. Moreover, elements of Marxist rhetoric are written into Derrida's descriptions of deconstruc-tion. And finally, while Nietzsche is invoked on occasion by way of criticising Heidegger, at no time – not even in *Spurs* – is Nietzsche himself brought under deconstructive scrutiny. To be sure, Derrida offers *readings* of passages by Nietzsche, but this is a different matter from *deconstructing* Nietzsche's claims. And the same may be said of Derrida's treatment of Artaud, Blanchot, Celan, Jabès, Kafka, Mallarmé, Ponge and Sollers: in fact, all the novelists and poets he admires.

There are two distinct problems here. First, it must be recog-nised that deconstruction is not exhausted by Derrida's deployment of it. Derrida does engage in playful ('affirmative' is his favoured word) readings of texts apart from his strict de-constructive critiques. He is sympathetic to 'open Marxism', and

139

he is Jewish. It may be that deconstruction can be used to promote political and cultural ends, but this is not to say that in accepting the deconstructive critique of metaphysics one is thereby committed to Derrida's particular views or his literary taste. Second, Derrida is often less than clear whether those writers who affirm difference over identity are pointing the way to a critique of 'value' as specified within metaphysics or promoting a different, and perhaps better, set of values. In other words, are we to prize Nietzsche because his interpretation of interpretation has a *tactical* value or because it is a *better* interpretation of interpretation?

These problems invite us to question the scope of deconstruction. A number of Derrida's points have already been examined; now we shall see if it is possible to connect them in a new way. To begin with, we shall examine Derrida's well-known distinction between Rousseau and Nietzsche. Derrida's Nietzsche is seen to subvert Rousseau, but is it possible to find another Nietzsche who is subverted by Rousseau? In other words, does deconstruction work in only *one* direction or can it work simultaneously in *two*? This is not a matter of questioning the structural asymmetry of deconstruction but the way in which it has been thematised. Deconstruction is commonly portrayed as presupposing a distinction between philosophy and literature. Is this the only distinction that can be used? If not, what happens if we work with other distinctions? And finally, what does Derrida mean by the phrase 'general text', and just how general is it?

1 'Oppositions': Rousseau and Nietzsche

Derrida's interest in apparent binary oppositions stems partly from the work of structuralists such as Lévi-Strauss, and partly from Nietzsche. 'The fundamental faith of the metaphysicians is *the faith in antithetical values*', Nietzsche tells us,[1] a remark which leads Derrida to view structuralism as one more instance of metaphysics. Overlooked, as often as not, is the variety of conceptual oppositions to which Derrida attends, and the question of what relations we may legitimately draw between them. Derrida often talks about the 'complicity' or 'systematic solidarity' between certain oppositions, and these are phrases whose

---

1 Nietzsche, *Beyond good and evil*, §2, p. 16.

weight in Derrida's general argument we shall have to determine and whose usefulness we shall have to assess. But before we do so, it is important to recognise the range of oppositions Derrida discusses and judge the degree of precision which it is reasonable to expect of his analyses.

Although the opposition between Rousseau and Nietzsche is frequently taken to institute Derrida's use of binary oppositions, it is preceded by another, and perhaps more influential, opposition between Husserl and Joyce. Both writers wish to isolate a pure historicity, but their strategies are widely divergent. Husserl attempts to reduce empirical history to a pure historicity by reducing empirical language to a strict univocality or at least a manageable polysemy. Only if a text is *readable* – univocal or at the least comprehensible in its plurivocality – can it be transmitted, and thus form part of an historical tradition. If Husserl works towards an idea of linguistic underdetermination, Joyce works with the idea of linguistic overdetermination. By maximising semantics over syntactics, Joyce attempts to call up, quite unpredictably, the historical resonances sedimented within each word, indeed within each syllable.[2] The contrast here is itself overdetermined, since it can easily be read as operating between different strategies of grasping historicity, between philosophy and literature, and between univocality and dissemination. We are reminded, too, that Husserl seeks to establish a natural, ideal language – an Adamic tongue – while Joyce is clearly a writer of the Fall: not only of the first trespass of the sign, the Fall of Adam, but also of its second trespass, the deconstruction of Babel, the fall of the signified into chains of signification. In *Finnegans wake*, according to Derrida, Joyce 'repeats and mobilizes and babelizes the (asymptotic) totality of the equivocal, he makes this his theme and his operation';[3] and here Derrida could well be speaking of *Glas* as well as sections of *The post card* and *The truth in painting*.

There is, though, yet another opposition which precedes that between Rousseau and Nietzsche. In Derrida's 1964 essay on Edmund Jabès one reads:

2 Derrida draws the distinction in his *Edmund Husserl's The origin of geometry*, trans. and introd. John P. Leavey, Jr. (Stony Brook, NY: Nicholas Hays, 1978), pp. 102–3.
3 Derrida, 'Two words for Joyce', in *Post-structuralist Joyce*, ed. Derek Attridge and Daniel Ferrer (Cambridge: Cambridge University Press, 1984) p. 149.

> In the beginning is hermeneutics. But the *shared* necessity of exegesis, the interpretive imperative, is interpreted differently by the rabbi and the poet. The difference between the horizon of the original text and exegetic writing makes the difference between the rabbi and the poet irreducible. Forever unable to reunite with each other, yet so close to each other, how could they ever regain the *realm*? The original opening of interpretation essentially signifies that there will always be rabbis and poets. And two interpretations of interpretation.[4]

The rabbi, here, represents a mode of interpretation which seeks to recover literal meaning, while the poet affirms the endless play of interpretation. So we have three variations on the one theme: Husserl/Joyce; rabbi/poet; and Rousseau/Nietzsche.

The philosophers mentioned indicate quite sweeping approaches to interpretation. There is nothing peculiarly Rousseauistic about the emphasis upon 'deciphering a truth', and it is evident from Derrida's general remarks upon interpretation that this first type may be called Platonic or Hegelian or, in short, 'philosophical'. It is also important to recognise that each of these oppositions is a matter of *bricolage* rather than of engineering. The opposition between Husserl and Joyce is formulated in an essay on Husserl; that between the rabbi and the poet in an essay on Jabès's prose-poems on the Jew and *écriture*; and that between Rousseau and Nietzsche in an essay on Lévi-Strauss's latent Rousseauism. We could take the first opposition, between Husserl and Joyce, to denote a distinction between philosophy and literature; but this does not quite fit with the third opposition, as both Rousseau and Nietzsche are pre-eminently 'literary' philosophers. Similarly, we could take the second opposition, between the rabbi and the poet, to bespeak a general opposition between theology and literature; but this hardly squares with Derrida's more general distinction between the Book and the text, with its unmistakable reference to Christianity and Judaism.

Further, one can point to Derrida's less overt yet nonetheless important opposition between Parmenides and Heraclitus. Once more the opposition is thoroughly overdetermined, suggesting 'being/non-being', 'one/many', not to mention a rigid *choice* between the ways of 'is' and 'is not' and the undifferentiated *play*

4 Derrida, *Writing*, p. 67.

of becoming. Such oppositions abound in Derrida's work: between presence and sign, the intelligible and the sensible, the *archè* and the an-*archè*, the name of the father and the name of the mother, and so forth. But one does not need to multiply examples to make what are by now obvious points: Derrida uses a wide variety of oppositions – between one genre and another, one synecdoche and another, one individual and another – and the scope of these oppositions cannot be neatly delimited. Derrida's model of the text is informed by its root metaphor of 'textile'. The oppositions constitute a fabric's woof and warp; their function is formal rather than substantive, and substantive relays between different oppositions are therefore not to be countenanced. It may be, for example, that Derrida does satis- factorily demonstrate a convergence between signified/signifier and intelligible/sensible, but it does not follow that one can pass, as is so often done, from Rousseau/Nietzsche to philosophy/ deconstruction or, for that matter, to theism/atheism. Phil- osophy as metaphysics may form a system, and a system may, as Kant says, 'exhibit the connection of its parts in conformity with a single principle', but this is not to say that the system's mode of connection is single or simple.[5] I turn now from this general consideration of Derrida's oppositions to a specific dis- cussion of the opposition between Rousseau and Nietzsche.

The first thing one notices here is the alacrity with which commentators pass illicitly from 'Rousseau/Nietzsche' to 'meta- physics/deconstruction', and thus – by identifying 'deconstruc- tion' with 'Derrida' – equate Derrida's views with Nietzsche's. In short, the assumption, perhaps most directly phrased by Rorty, that Derrida merely 'continues along a line laid down by Nietzsche' is seldom questioned.[6] Three questions are relevant: (1) Do Nietzsche and Derrida in fact hold the views ascribed to them? (2) Upon what points are Nietzsche and Derrida in agree- ment? and (3) Does Derrida hold these shared views as a con- sequence of deconstruction or upon other grounds?

5 Kant, *Critique of pure reason*, A 645. Derrida's view that philosophy as meta- physics is an absolute system is drawn from Heidegger's 'Sketches for a history of Being as metaphysics', in his *The end of philosophy*, trans. Joan Stambaugh (London: Souvenir Press, 1975), p. 57.
6 Rorty, 'Deconstruction and circumvention', *Critical Inquiry*, 11 (1984), p. 2. There are many instances of this view. Ramen Seldon, for one, suggests that *The will to power* is 'the fountainhead of deconstructive logic'. See his *Criticism and objectivity* (London: George Allen and Unwin, 1984), p. 8.

(1) There is no doubt, I think, that Nietzsche and Derrida are often criticised for holding views which are in fact rejected by either or both of them. Gerald Graff, for one, takes Derrida to argue the pluralistic thesis that in 'the absence of any appeal to . . . a coercive reality to which the plurality of interpretations can be referred, all perspectives become equally valid'.[7] Nietzsche's central theory of the need to surpass 'man', and his condemnation of the 'herd mentality' remove him from any suspicion of pluralism. And Derrida does not hesitate on the matter: 'I am not a pluralist', he says, 'and I would never say that every interpretation is equal'.[8] T. K. Seung, for another, first assumes that Derrida's account of interpretation is to be identified with Nietzsche's, then, when he finds differences between them, criticises Derrida for going 'against the Nietzschean spirit of free play'.[9] Carl Raschke may observe that 'Deconstruction is the dance of death upon the tomb of God';[10] but Derrida is positive that, as far as he is concerned, deconstruction is *not* to be identified with a thematics of God's death. As he says, 'It is that conceptuality and that problematics that must be deconstructed'.[11]

(2) Speaking of Valéry's relation to Nietzsche, Derrida also – and perhaps incidentally – supplies us with a fair description of what is common to himself and Nietzsche:

> the systematic mistrust as concerns the entirety of metaphysics, the formal vision of philosophical discourse, the concept of the philosopher–artist, the rhetorical and philological questions put to the history of philosophy, the suspiciousness concerning the values of truth ('a well-applied convention'), of meaning and of Being, of the 'meaning of Being', the attention to the economic phenomena of force and of the difference of forces, etc.[12]

(3) One can distinguish between deconstruction as critique and as ideology. As critique, deconstruction asserts nothing; it shows how any text resists complete formalisation by producing

7 Graff, *Literature against itself* (Chicago: University of Chicago Press, 1979), p. 39.
8 James Kearns and Ken Newton, 'An interview with Jacques Derrida', *Literary Review*, 14 (1980), p. 21.
9 Seung, *Structuralism and hermeneutics*, p. 254.
10 Raschke, 'The deconstruction of God', in *Deconstruction and theology*, p. 28.
11 Derrida, *Of grammatology*, p. 68.
12 Derrida, *Margins of philosophy*, p. 305. Cf. *Writing*, p. 280 and *Of grammatology*, p. 19.

a supplement. It can therefore be applied to any theory, regardless of its ideological content, which claims to be both consistent and to offer (or be able to offer) a complete account of textual phenomena. But since it *is* a critique, deconstruction can be pressed into the service of particular aims which *do* have assertive power, and at all events Derrida does use deconstruction to support positions to which he gives at least tacit credence on independent grounds. These include a number of political objectives: a belief, for example, in the viability of a form of 'open Marxism'. Now Derrida's ideological convictions, while they are worth keeping in sight, need not detain us here. They may be *consequences* of the employment of his critique, but they are not necessary *ends* of that critique. As with all critiques, deconstruction can be turned against positions which it has been used to support, and it therefore does not commit one to particular political or religious positions. The patristic critique of rabbinical hermeneutics, with its emphasis upon the spirit rather than the letter, helped to establish the view that the Jewish scriptures prefigured the Christian revelation. The same hermeneutical principle was later used by Freud to demystify the doctrines it once supported when used by the Fathers: 'spirit' and 'letter' thus become, for Freud, latent and manifest content. And indeed it is part of Derrida's programme, in demonstrating that speech depends upon a prior notion of script, to call into question the authority of the spirit/letter distinction and thus to press into service the original Rabbinic emphasis upon the letter. In precisely the same way, deconstruction can be used to unsettle certain layers of Derrida's texts.

In pointing to the devolution of critique, I do not mean to suggest that deconstruction can be used to support any given position or that it has no agenda of its own. Derridean deconstruction comprises several first- and second-order positions, and its salient feature is that these second-order positions call into question the stability of the first-order positions. It is in this relation between first- and second-order positions that we see the point of closest contact between Nietzsche and Derrida. For Nietzsche is a non-cognitivist in meta-philosophy yet nonetheless argues strongly for a wide variety of philosophical positions; and Derrida is a nihilist (in the Nietzschean sense) in meta-philosophy, yet also holds a number of philosophical views, only some of which are derived from Nietzsche. If this is

145

so, Derrida may continue 'along a line laid down by Nietzsche', as Rorty says, but not quite in the simple linear sense in which this phrase is usually taken.

Derrida's characterisation of Rousseau and Nietzsche on interpretation is certainly open to question, as it is far from self-evident that Nietzsche's theory of interpretation celebrates 'the *innocence* of becoming'.[13] After all, Nietzsche's is a theory of the will to power and this necessarily involves struggles between strong and weak interpretations, victories and losses, which could hardly be considered innocent.[14] Derrida is most likely thinking of Nietzsche's well-known comment on Heraclitus: 'In this world only play, play as artists and children engage in it, exhibits coming-to-be and passing away, structuring and destroying, without any moral additive, in forever equal innocence'.[15] The word 'innocence' is not the antonym of 'guilt' or 'experience', only one of Nietzsche's synonyms for 'amoral'. An ethical thesis, then, yet also an epistemological thesis. Make no mistake, Nietzsche thinks that some positions are more moral than others, and that we can reason about these positions; but as a non-cognitivist in meta-ethics he denies the possibility that there is an *absolute* moral truth to reality. Similarly, while Nietzsche affirms the possibility of 'infinite interpretations' as a meta-philosophical thesis he also thinks that some interpretations are more persuasive or more useful, and (at least on occasion) more *sound*, than others. Play, consequently, is a matter of meta-ethics and meta-philosophy, and this to some extent limits the freedom of the play that Nietzsche can in fact affirm.

In fact if one continues to probe this opposition one soon finds that the link between Rousseau/Nietzsche and decipherment/play is far from strong. There is more agreement between Rousseau and Nietzsche over interpretation and specific moral issues than is generally acknowledged. Both writers adopt a genealogical approach to interpretation. We cannot prize the method of Nietzsche's *Genealogy of morals*, say, without valuing the method of Rousseau's *Essay on the origin of lan-*

13 Derrida, *Writing*, p. 292. My emphasis.
14 Samuel Weber develops this point in 'Closure and exclusion', pp. 35–36. I am indebted to his analysis.
15 Nietzsche, *Philosophy in the tragic age of the Greeks*, trans. and introd. Marianne Cowan (South Bend, IN: Gateway Editions, 1962), p. 62.

guages or *Discourse on the origins of inequality*, since both writers employ a hermeneutic of suspicion, searching for an explanation which is concealed within what seems natural and inevitable. Also, Rousseau and Nietzsche agree that western culture has evolved into a slave morality; and this is essential to both writers' diagnostic discussion of western morality. It is the basis of Rousseau's elevation of nature over culture and of Nietzsche's theory of the *Übermensch*. However, it might be objected, Derrida's contrast is not founded upon a scholarly examination of both writers' complete works: it answers to Nietzsche's reading of Rousseau. It is true that Nietzsche's texts are peppered with comments upon Rousseau, and it also seems to be true that Nietzsche had read only a small number of Rousseau's works. Let us see what happens if we construe 'Rousseau/Nietzsche' in line with this assumption.

How does Nietzsche picture Rousseau? In the early essay 'Schopenhauer as educator' Nietzsche maintains that there are three irreducible images of man which have been set up by the modern age: Rousseau's, Goethe's and Schopenhauer's. Whereas Rousseau's image 'possesses the greatest fire' and promotes 'violent revolutions', Goethe's, although it stems from Rousseau's, is finally of 'the contemplative man in the grand style', and one can be sure, Nietzsche confides, that with Goethean man 'no "order" will be overthrown'.[16] The favoured image, that of Schopenhaurean man, differs from both prior images but is clearly closer to the former than to the latter. Schopenhaurean man is 'in his knowledge full of blazing, consuming fire and far removed from the cold and contemptible neutrality of the so-called scientific man'.[17] If the portrait of Rousseau is positive when compared with that of Goethe in the 1874 essay, the situation is completely reversed by 1889, the date of *Twilight of the idols*. Here Nietzsche fulminates against Rousseau, calling him an 'abortion recumbent on the threshold of the new age' by dint of his desire for a 'return to nature'. 'I hate Rousseau even in the Revolution', Nietzsche continues, and 'what I hate is its Rousseauesque *morality*', Rousseau's purported endorsement of 'everything shallow and mediocre' in

16 Nietzsche, *Untimely meditations*, trans. R. J. Hollingdale and introd. J. P. Stern (Cambridge: Cambridge University Press, 1983), pp. 151–52.
17 Nietzsche, *Untimely meditations*, p. 153.

the name of revolution.[18] Goethe, however, is praised as the virtual embodiment of the will to power; he is pictured as 'a man of tolerance, not out of *weakness*, but out of strength, because he knows how to employ to his advantage what would destroy an average nature; a man to whom nothing is forbidden, except it be *weakness*, whether that weakness be called vice or virtue'; and, finally, Goethe is favourably compared with Nietzsche's ultimate image of affirmation, Dionysos.[19]

Nietzsche's mature view of Rousseau is brought sharply into focus by Hollingdale's observation that, for Nietzsche, 'Rousseau's "back to nature" means back to the animals, back to passion *uncontrolled*'.[20] This view of Rousseau is certainly at odds with Derrida's Rousseau who represents order and the nostalgic desire for a stable origin. Upon Nietzsche's reading, Rousseau's nostalgia for a purely natural state is associated with a *lack* of control and *condemned* for this very lack. Nor does the difficulty stop here: if Nietzsche is to condemn Rousseau for, amongst other things, a lack of control, he must be confident that his own position exhibits control. And if this is true, we must qualify the view that Nietzsche unreservedly affirms free play. I wish to suggest that this is the case, then trace one or two of the consequences.

While Nietzsche does not offer us a coherent system of thought, there are particular themes which constellate in his writings – the apparent opposition between Apollo and Dionysos, for example. As is well known, the opposition is first formulated in *The birth of tragedy* of 1872 in which 'Apollo' stands for the force that creates form and is itself in creative tension with 'Dionysos', the spontaneous overflow of energy. And although the distinction is not invoked so much by name in Nietzsche's middle period, the *terms* of the distinction – 'force', 'form', and so on – appear with an almost predictable regularity, structuring his response to a variety of problems. Hollingdale's contention that after *Thus spake Zarathustra* Nietzsche recognises only 'one force in the human constitution, the will to power' and that he calls this phenomenon by the single name of Dionysos,

18 Nietzsche, 'Expeditions of an untimely man' § 48, in *Twilight of the idols and the anti-Christ*, pp. 101–2.
19 Nietzsche, 'Expeditions of an untimely man' § 49, p. 103.
20 R. J. Hollingdale, trans. *Twilight of the idols and the anti-Christ*, p. 206.

begs the question.[21] The will to power, far from being a unitary force, is an economy of conflicting forces, within the one individual as much as between individuals. This is seen most clearly in Nietzsche's emphasis that one must *harness* forces, that is, subject them to some kind of order. 'The "great man" is great owing to the free play and scope of his desires', observes Nietzsche in 1887, 'and to the yet greater power that knows how to press these magnificent monsters into service'.[22] And in the following year Nietzsche once more invokes the distinction between Apollo and Dionysos, the former standing for 'freedom under the law' and the latter 'ecstatic affirmation'.[23] It is evident that Nietzsche attaches equal value to both elements.

So Derrida's characterisation of Rousseau and Nietzsche in terms of centre/play is based only upon Nietzsche's meta-philosophical views; but this correlation breaks down if we take stock of their respective philosophical views. In that case, the apparent difference *between* Rousseau and Nietzsche turns out to be a difference *within* Nietzsche. So we can trust Derrida's characterisation only if we agree to a strict distinction between philosophy and meta-philosophy. And this is an assurance that we cannot give. Meta-philosophical theses have no special marks to distinguish them from philosophical theses: paradoxical though it may seem, meta-philosophy is no more than a branch of philosophy. In addition, Derrida's entire programme is directed against the hierarchical order that is part and parcel of the traditional distinction between meta-philosophy and philosophy.

This conclusion does not affect Derrida's main point – that the interpretations of interpretation are irreducible – but it should make us careful when attributing scope and status to Derrida's oppositions. In the first place, they are used to make a *critical* point: that the agent of totalisation is always already doubled. Also Derrida often uses oppositions as *heuristic* devices, enabling both him and us to get our bearings with regards to a text, problem or tradition. And further, these oppositions play a *tactical* role in Derrida's discourse; when they are found in or implied by a text they provide a point of incision for deconstruc-

21 Hollingdale, trans. *Twilight of the idols and the anti-Christ*, p. 198.
22 Nietzsche, *The will to power*, § 933. Cf. § 928.
23 Nietzsche, *The will to power*, § 1050. Kaufmann observes in a footnote to this remark that 'neither element [Apollo, Dionysos] is given preference'.

tive analysis. With these distinctions in mind, let us once more focus upon the apparent opposition between Rousseau and Nietzsche. That this distinction has a definite heuristic value is evident by the amount of clarifying commentary it has spawned upon both interpretation as such and the specific authors concerned, and Paul de Man's *Allegories of reading* is a good example of this. Of particular moment is the apparent tension between the opposition's critical and tactical values. We are invited to see that *both* interpretations of interpretation, Rousseau's and Nietzsche's, are conditioned transcendentally by *différance*. Yet we are also invited to value Nietzsche, by virtue of the commerce between his affirmation of phenomenal difference and the knowledge of transcendental *différance*.

The question that must concern us, then, is this: if we are committed to the critical points of deconstruction, to what extent must we throw in our lot with Derrida's strategies?

2 Allegory and irony

At the beginning of what is doubtless the most accessible and reliable guide to Derrida's thought, Jonathan Culler observes 'I will not attempt to discuss the relationship of Derridian deconstruction to the work of Hegel, Nietzsche, Husserl and Heidegger'.[24] Culler follows this with an extended account of how deconstruction has been and should be applied to literary criticism. While Culler presents deconstruction as a literary phenomenon, he nonetheless maintains that 'a distinction between literature and philosophy is essential to deconstruction's power of intervention'.[25] This view is challenged by Richard Rorty who, by way of queering the distinction between literature and philosophy, finds that he has to draw a distinction between two different sorts of deconstruction. The first species refers to 'the philosophical projects of Jacques Derrida', where 'breaking down the distinction between philosophy and literature is essential'.[26] The second species of deconstruction is 'a method of reading texts', as practised not by Derrida but by literary critics; and here, Rorty tells us, there is need for a distinction between philosophy and literature.

24 Culler, *On deconstruction*, p. 85 n. 1.   25 Culler, p. 149.
26 Rorty, 'Deconstruction and circumvention', p. 2.

Interestingly enough, Rorty has reintroduced the distinction in the very act of rejecting it: the two modes of deconstruction he defines are 'philosophical' and 'literary'. This counts against Rorty's conclusion, but it also reminds us how recalcitrant this distinction is. And so it is no surprise to find that, of all the oppositions invoked with regards to deconstruction, the most common is that between philosophy and literature. I want to say something about this particular distinction, and why it is necessary; then I shall probe another opposition with which this seems to intersect, that between allegory and irony.

To begin with, it would be useful to take a closer look at what Rorty takes the distinction between philosophy and literature to mean. He offers two glosses: a 'contrast between the representational and the non-representational,' or the literal and the metaphorical'.[27] The first reduces to a distinction between that which conceives itself governed by a presence and that which does not; while the second aligns philosophy with the proper use of language and literature with the non-proper. The first gloss is less helpful to us than the second. For while no one would argue that literature is not conditioned by tropes, many would insist that certain texts are also representational. It cannot be denied that Zola, for example, uses a range of tropes – especially metonymy and hyperbole – but the claim of naturalist fiction is that it *does* represent the empirical world. We shall therefore take the distinction between philosophy and literature to be that between proper and non-proper use of language.

Upon Rorty's account, Derrida argues that philosophy is one literary genre amongst others, that the instituting distinctions of philosophy – between time and space, the sensible and the intelligible, subject and object, and so on – are, in effect, 'just a few extra tropes'.[28] It is not hard to find *prima facie* evidence for this claim: 'the task', Derrida tells us, 'is to consider philosophy also as a "particular literary genre"'.[29] As is often the case with Derrida's apparently authoritative statements, this remark is embedded in a commentary upon another writer – here, Paul Valéry – and the extent to which Derrida subscribes to this view is far from evident. Suppose he does agree with Valéry: what is said is that philosophy is to be considered *also* as a 'particular

27 Rorty, p. 3.   28 Rorty, p. 19.
29 Derrida, *Margins of philosophy*, p. 293.

151

literary genre', which means that philosophy is not reducible to literature. And this should not be unexpected: we have already seen that one of Derrida's main points is that it is impossible for any discourse wholly to escape philosophical determinations. Even if we adopt the extreme position of trying to read Hegel's *Phenomenology* as a *Bildungsroman* we cannot prevent it from making philosophical claims. Rorty's Derrida resembles the Quine who rejects the distinction between the analytic and the synthetic, understanding all statements as synthetic and hence revisable. Yet while there are some similarities between the Harvard and the Ecole philosophers, this is not one of them: Derrida situates himself critically and tactically with respect to boundaries; Quine erases them.

It is appropriate, then, that Derrida should accent the question of literary *genre* rather than literary language. At a general level, he is concerned to demonstrate that what seem to be distinct genres participate in each other; and there is no conceptual difficulty with this as regards literary genres. There may be passages in particular texts which participate in quite different genres at the one time – 'autobiography' and 'epic', say – and this may unsettle a tradition of reading Dante's *Commedia*. Even more unsettling, though, is the attempt to read philosophy as a literary genre. For in whatever age it is practised, philosophy views itself not just as a discourse on the truth (which is only one of its concerns) but as a discourse which *tells the truth*. Philosophers may develop accounts of categories but not genres: the former is a matter of concepts; the latter, words. For philosophers, Derrida insists, truth is before or behind language; and genre is a matter of linguistic arrangement and convention. One way of clarifying the distinction between literature and philosophy is by saying that whereas a literary text admits belonging to one or more genres, a philosophical text denies that, *qua* philosophy, it participates in any genre at all. This is not to say, of course, that certain literary texts make no claim to speak truly about the human condition. Truth claims are one of the effects of all texts, regardless of genre and – in some instances of experimental writing – despite protestations to the contrary. Philosophy cannot rid itself of all tropes (and to that extent is literary), while literature cannot prevent itself from making philosophical claims. There *are* philosophers who have wished

152

to blur the distinction between philosophy and literature, but Derrida is not amongst them.[30] For Derrida, the two discourses are thoroughly entwined, each helping to define the other in an irresolvable dialectic, preventing the possibility of what Rorty thinks Derrida is advocating, 'a seamless, undifferentiated "general text"'.[31]

On the basis of the untenable view that philosophy is *only* a literary genre, Rorty develops his account of the history of philosophy. 'Hegel invented a literary genre which lacked any trace of argumentation', we are told, and Nietzsche, Heidegger and Derrida are held to stand squarely in this tradition.[32] So we have a division between neo-Kantian *normal* philosophy, in which people argue along agreed lines about agreed problems, and Hegelian and post-Hegelian *abnormal* philosophy, in which philosophy is one literary genre amongst others – a genre of commentary on past philosophical texts. Rorty has a number of sources for this view, but the most important are Harold Bloom and Thomas Kuhn. Just as Bloom considers English literary history as a Freudian family romance, in which the ephebe poet must overcome the deadening influence of the father text, so Rorty takes philosophical history, of the abnormal sort, as 'what one writes after reading Plato, Kant, Hegel, Nietzsche, Freud. . .'[33] Similarly, whereas normal philosophy is like Kuhn's normal inquiry, abnormal philosophy is like Kuhn's abnormal inquiry. 'Abnormal inquiry – called "revolutionary" when it works and "kooky" when it does not – requires only genius' Rorty tell us.[34] A more helpful formulation would be that the aims of abnormal inquiry are discernible only after the fact; but Rorty's polemic intent is patent when he identifies 'abnormal philosophy' with 'Continental philosophy'.

---

30 Derrida remarks that 'one could reconsider all the pairs of opposites on which philosophy is constructed and on which our discourse lives, *not in order to see opposition erase itself* but to see what indicates that each of the terms must appear as the différance of the other. . .', *Margins of philosophy*, p. 17 (my emphasis). Cf. Wittgenstein's '. . .philosophy ought really to be written only as a *poetic composition*', *Culture and value*, p. 12e.

31 Rorty, 'Deconstruction and circumvention', p. 3.

32 Rorty, *Consequences of pragmatism*, p. 147.

33 Rorty, 'Derrida on language, Being, and abnormal philosophy', *The Journal of Philosophy*, 74 (1977), p. 680.

34 'Derrida on language', p. 679.

If I disagree with Rorty's premises, it would seem unlikely that I would agree with his conclusion that Derrida is an 'abnormal' philosopher. Yet this is just where I do agree with Rorty, for different reasons. Deconstruction is an abnormal philosophy, but in Gödel's sense of 'abnormal', not Kuhn's. In chapter 3 we noted that Derrida draws analogies between his account of undecidable elements and Gödel's theorem on formally undecidable propositions. Gödel's theorem tells us that there are propositions which, while they cannot be *proven* with respect to a given axiomatic system, must be admitted to be *true* within that system. If this is so, a system cannot be both complete and consistent: to be complete it would need to be able to prove all possible theorems which follow from its axioms; yet there will always be at least one theorem which can be proven only at the cost of inconsistency. And since incompleteness is to be valued over inconsistency, we must conclude that no system can be complete. So we have a proposition p which is formally undecidable with respect to a system S. Hence it follows that S can be extended by adding p or the negation of p. If we choose to add p, then S is extended in a normal direction; if not p, then in an abnormal direction.

Derrida's contention is that formal and philosophical systems are analogous. No text, he argues, can be translated into philosophical language without remainder; there will always be a supplement which resists formalisation. Recall the *Phaedrus*: Socrates' statement that writing is a *pharmakon* harbours a double signification; it can mean *both* that writing is a poison *and* that writing is a remedy, and its meaning cannot be decided within the terms of Plato's discourse. Normal philosophy – the tradition of metaphysics as onto-theology – adds on to the system of Platonic metaphysics the proposition that writing is a poison. And what makes Derrida a practitioner of abnormal philosophy is that he adds to this system the proposition that writing is a remedy. This addition of not p does not, however, constitute deconstruction as such, for deconstruction is both a first- and a second-order analysis; and it is an originary supplement to metaphysics. Derrida is an abnormal philosopher not by virtue of his *critical* points, which apply equally to normal and abnormal philosophy, but rather by dint of his generating abnormal philosophical readings for *tactical* reasons.

Floyd Merrell suggests that Gödel is 'perhaps the greatest

"deconstructor" the Western World has seen'.[35] This overshoots the mark somewhat, not least because Derrida's case is based upon undecidable *words* whereas Gödel's theorem turns on *propositions*. More particularly, it is in the distinction between criticism and tactics where the analogy between deconstruction and Gödel's theorem breaks down. Derrida cannot claim that truth is a more powerful notion than provability, since it is the value of 'truth' which comes under scrutiny. Also, Gödel's claim is considerably weaker than Derrida's: he need establish only that there is *at least one* proposition which is formally undecidable with respect to a system; but Derrida can go further and claim that there is *no* distinction within a text which is not susceptible to deconstruction. One distinction is chosen in preference to another for historical and tactical, not critical, reasons. As I have already suggested, these tactical reasons include a political agenda; they also fulfil a formal role, though: the generation of abnormal readings serves to defamiliarise a given text (in this case, Plato's *Phaedrus*) and a tradition of philosophy as metaphysics.

To follow normal or abnormal philosophy is not solely a matter of choice, because the choice arises only on account of structure. At first glance it would seem possible to thematise this distinction between the normal and the abnormal by way of the proper and the non-proper and, by extension, philosophy and literature. But this turns out to be a good deal more complicated than it seems. The obvious place to begin would be Aristotle's remarks on the proper and the non-proper, but – as Derrida is quick to report – Aristotle does not have 'a very simple, very clear, i.e. central, opposition of what will be called proper, literal meaning/figurative meaning. Nothing prevents a metaphorical lexis from being proper, that is appropriate *(prepon)*, suitable, decent, proportionate, becoming, in relation to the subject, situation, things'.[36] Individual writers aside, what philosophy demands is not that the text be proper but that the text's *meaning* be proper – a situation which applies as much to literary criticism as to philosophy.

In the last chapter I defined meaning as the allegory of a

35 Merrell, *Deconstruction reframed* (West Lafayette, IN: Purdue University Press, 1985), p. 66.
36 Derrida, *Margins of philosophy*, p. 246.

text. This is of assistance to us in several ways. To begin with, we can use it to place an important objection to one side. Paul Ricœur argues that deconstruction misses its critical object: deconstruction, the case runs, offers a critique of 'sign' but meaning is located at the level of the sentence, not the sign.[37] Both remarks in this objection are correct, yet this does not constitute a case against Derrida. For Derrida's analysis does not rely upon the sign as the irreducible unit of meaning but rather on the hierarchic distinction between presence and sign. No doubt one can argue that meaning abides with the sentence, but as soon as one does so one finds that the hierarchic distinction between presence and sign is repeated in the distinction between meaning and sentence or, if you like, between allegory and text. The structure of 'text and allegory' is exactly the same as the structure of 'sign and presence' or 'signifier and signified'. This returns us to binary oppositions. If we look for the figure which forms an oppositional pair with allegory, the strongest candidate is irony; and as the strongest theoretician of these tropes is Paul de Man, it is to him that we turn.

The first thing one notices is that de Man softens the distinction between allegory and allegoresis. 'Allegory' traditionally signifies a particular narrative mode in which a series of concrete events invite reconstruction as a second narrative. De Lorris's *Roman de la rose* and Bunyan's *Pilgrim's progress* stand as examples of this literary genre. 'Allegoresis', on the other hand, is a mode of interpretation – what I called, in the second chapter, 'the allegorical hermeneutic' – in which the meaning of a text is held to be constituted outside that text as another discourse. De Man's point is that all allegoresis takes the form of a narrative and, to that extent, is an allegory. Allegoresis, Philo tells us, is a 'wise Master-builder' concerned to establish a tower wherein the living truth may abide forever, outside the ravages of time and the slippages of textual meaning.[38] But if allegoresis is grounded in allegory, as de Man contends, the tower – like the tower of Babel – nonetheless remains subject to that which it seeks to transcend. De Man's point thus comes to be close to Walter Benjamin's famous contention against Hegel, that 'Alle-

---

37 This is the general thrust of Ricœur's analysis of Derrida's account of metaphor in *The rule of metaphor*, trans. Robert Czerny with Kathleen McLaughlin and John Costello, SJ (London: Routledge and Kegan Paul, 1978), esp. p. 294.
38 Philo, *On dreams*, II.ii. 8 (*Philo*, Vol. 5).

gories are, in the realm of thought, what ruins are in the realm of things'.[39] De Man's second major point also follows tradition, going back directly to Quintillian.[40] It is that both allegory and irony share an identical structure, since 'in both cases, the relationship between sign and meaning is discontinuous . . . the sign points to something that differs from its literal meaning and has for its function the thematization of this difference'.[41] Both points are of use to us, but we need the second immediately.

If allegory and irony share identical structural conditions for their realisation, irony is not wholly exterior to allegory. To distinguish between them we must go beyond necessary conditions and locate the differentia in the sufficient conditions which are, of course, supplied by the expectations of generic convention and tone. One further point: classically understood, allegory is a trope of closure – it seeks to fix the meaning of a text. Irony, however, is always a trope of non-closure, forever indicating the difference between text and meaning and therefore calling allegorical closure into question. With this in mind, we can listen to one of Derrida's most explicit formulations of the process of deconstruction:

> The movements of deconstruction do not destroy structures from the outside. They are not possible and effective, nor can they take accurate aim, except by inhabiting those structures. Inhabiting them *in a certain way*, because one always inhabits, and all the more when one does not suspect it. Operating necessarily from the inside, borrowing all the strategic and economic resources of subversion from the old structure, borrowing them structurally, that is to say without being able to isolate their elements and atoms, the enterprise of

39 Benjamin, *The origins of German tragic drama*, trans. John Osborne (London: NLB, 1977), p. 178. For an extended analysis of the relation between allegoresis and allegory, though stated in rather different terms, see J. Hillis Miller, 'The two allegories', in *Allegory, myth, and symbol*, ed. Morton W. Bloomfield. Harvard English Studies 9 (Cambridge, MA: Harvard University Press, 1981), pp. 255–70.
40 Quintillian, *Institutio oratoria*, trans. H. E. Butler. Loeb Classical Library. (Cambridge, MA: Harvard University Press, 1976), Vol. III. Book IX. ii. Norman Knox informs us that Quintillian is followed in this taxonomy by Cocondrius and Bede; and we may add Isidore of Seville to this list. See *The word IRONY and its context 1500–1755* (Durham, NC: Duke University Press, 1961), p. 6.
41 De Man, *Blindness and insight*, 2nd ed., revised (London: Methuen, 1983), p. 209.

deconstruction always in a certain way falls prey to its own work.[42]

To translate this into the language of rhetoric: allegory supplies the necessary structure for its ironic subversion, and of course the subversion brought about by irony is itself open to be overturned to the extent to which the ironic becomes canonised as 'literature' (as with Swift) or 'philosophy' (as with Socrates). In passing from allegory to irony there is a movement that is at once violent and miniscule, through the agency of an adopted tone or attitude. So while allegory in no way entails irony or *vice versa*, deconstruction can be seen to subvert allegory by realising the ironic possibilities inherent in its structure. Indeed, the rhetorical and critical operations invite parallel descriptions. 'As in jiujitsu, the expert presses gently and the victim ties himself in knots', writes Worcester concerning satire; and Marshall, describing deconstruction, remarks in the same terms that 'as with the jiu-jitsu wrestler, the opponent is made to trip himself up by having his own weight and force turned against him'.[43]

Needless to say, perhaps, not even deconstruction can claim immunity from irony in this state of affairs. A deconstructive reading of a text, despite what it does to previous readings, will always be an allegory of the text and, as such, be subject to a deconstruction to the second degree. At this level of sophistication, irony is exactly as described by Friedrich Schlegel, 'a permanent parabasis'.[44] So for de Man irony is always one step ahead of allegory: as a contingent temporal sequence, of course, but also because the possibility of being ironised is written into the structure of allegory. If this is true, de Man is perfectly correct to remark that 'Irony is no longer a trope but the undoing of the deconstructive allegory of all tropological cognitions, the systematic undoing, in other words, of understanding'.[45] Or in the vocabulary we have refined: irony is not simply a trope, it is also, when generalised, *both* the condition of possibility for all

42 Derrida, *Of grammatology*, p. 24.
43 David Worcester, *The art of satire* (New York: Russell and Russell, 1960), p. 94. Marshall's remark on deconstruction is from his unpublished paper, read in the Department of English at Yale, 'Sophism and deconstruction'. I am indebted to Professor Howard Felperin of Macquarie University for drawing this paper to my attention.
44 Quoted by de Man, *Allegories of reading*, p. 300.
45 De Man, *Allegories of reading*, p. 301.

tropes *and* the condition of impossibility for any cognition which is not conditioned by tropes.

Is Derrida an ironist, as this discussion would lead us to believe? There is a sense, to be sure, in which Derrida's project is not merely philosophy. Like Bataille, Derrida's concern is 'To laugh at philosophy (at Hegelianism)'.[46] Allan Megill suggests that Derrida is 'undoubtedly the most accomplished ironist of our age'.[47] Charles Altieri has remarked that Derrida remains trapped 'in an ironic or demonic version of the logic he wishes to deconstruct'; Harold Bloom advises us to 'oppose. . .the abysses of Deconstruction's ironies'; and Richard Bernstein invites us to picture Feyerabend and Derrida as satirists.[48] It is also tempting to consider irony in part responsible for what many take to be Derrida's obscure and affected style. And we may note, in passing, Wayne Booth's suggestive observation that 'irony is usually seen as something that undermines clarities, opens up vistas of chaos, and either liberates by destroying a dogma or destroys by revealing the inescapable canker of negation at the heart of every affirmation'.[49] There is a connection here between Derrida and Hume. Writing of Humean irony John Price draws a nice distinction, 'To treat philosophies ironically and yet remain a cogent philosopher is no small task. Irony, however, is not only a concept, it is a way of dealing with concepts'.[50] Sure enough, there are parallels between Hume and Derrida in the tactical way in which they deal with concepts. Here is Price on Hume's treatment of miracles:

> By temporarily assuming the alleged 'truth' of the reasoning which links testimony, miracles, and the Christian religion, Hume was later able to destroy the logic of that 'truth' by carrying the logical implications of the propositions concerned to their ultimate limit. Once the 'logic' of those propositions is pushed as far as it will go, the inherent contradictions, Hume believes, will be seen. The irony is apparent: what better way

46 Derrida, *Writing*, p. 252.
47 Megill, *Prophets of extremity* (Berkeley: University of California Press, 1985), p. 260.
48 Altieri, 'Wittgenstein on consciousness and language: a challenge to Derridean literary theory', *Modern Language Notes*, 91 (1976), p. 1398. Harold Bloom, *Deconstruction and criticism*, p. 37. R. J. Bernstein, *Beyond objectivism and relativism* (Oxford: Blackwell, 1983), p. 63.
49 Booth, *A rhetoric of irony* (Chicago: University of Chicago Press, 1974), p. ix.
50 Price, *The ironic Hume* (Austin: University of Texas Press, 1965), p. 25.

to undermine an opponent than to use his own argument against him?[51]

Hume's tacit acceptance of a text's prevailing logic in order to uncover its inherent contradictions is remarkably similar to Derrida's own strategy as stated in *Of grammatology*. This is not to agree with E. D. Hirsch, though, that Hume may be considered 'the deconstructionist *par excellence*' by virtue of his view in the *Treatise* that 'the understanding, when it acts alone, and according to its most general principles, entirely subverts itself and leaves us not the lowest degree of evidence in any proposition'.[52] Hume's is a formula for epistemological scepticism; Derrida, however, is not concerned with a thematics of certainty and doubt but with an analysis of the textual *effects* of such claims.

A comparison between Derrida and Hume goes some way towards clarifying Derrida's use of irony; but a consideration of Kierkegaard's reflections upon Socratic irony will take us a good deal further. The ironist, Kierkegaard tells us, 'conceals his jest in seriousness and his seriousness in jest';[53] and it is evident that what is being concealed in each case is a weapon. If Derrida is, as he signs himself on one occasion, 'the laughing rabbi', he nonetheless conceals his laughter successfully in a tome such as *Of grammatology*; and if a performance like *Glas* with all its puns, antonomasia and other legerdemains is at times very amusing indeed, this should not distract us from the number of serious points which we are there urged to accept. More pressing is Kierkegaard's remark upon the strategy of the ironist. 'As the ironist does not have the new within his power, it might be asked how he destroys the old, and to this it must be answered: he destroys the given actuality by the given actuality itself'.[54] We

51 Price, p. 56.
52 Hirsch, 'Derrida's axioms', *London Review of Books*, 21 July–3 August 1983, p. 17.
53 Søren Kierkegaard, *The concept of irony*, trans. Lee M. Capel (London: Collins, 1966), p. 273. Kierkegaard's formulation seems to be an unacknowledged quotation from Aristotle's *Rhetoric* in which we are told that Gorgias was right to say 'that you should kill your opponents' earnestness with jesting and their jesting with earnestness', *The works of Aristotle*, ed. W. D. Ross, Vol. XI, *Rhetoric*, 1419b.
54 Kierkegaard, p. 279. Cf. p. 234. It is also possible to construe irony as a *pharmakon*. Consider the following: 'irony is a healthiness insofar as it rescues the soul from the snares of relativity; it is a sickness insofar as it is unable to tolerate the absolute except in the form of nothingness', p. 113.

recall Derrida's formulation of deconstruction, how it must operate 'necessarily from the inside, borrowing all the strategic and economic resources of subversion from the old structure'.[55] So parallels can doubtless be drawn – and what is more, be seen to converge in the distance.

Such, at least, is Mark C. Taylor's view. For upon his reading Kierkegaard anticipates deconstruction, being 'the first thinker of writing'.[56] Without disagreeing with Taylor, we can nonetheless secure another viewpoint. We know how Derrida uses the familiar opposition between Greek and Jew in working towards the deconstruction of Greek metaphysics. Derrida's strategy is to take what seems to be a difference between Greek and Jew, namely between concept and *écriture*, then demonstrate that the Greek notion of conceptuality is already conditioned by a generalised version of *écriture*. Speaking of the father of all metaphysics, Parmenides, and of Plato's inability to escape the rule of his ideas, Derrida enquires, 'But will a non-Greek ever succeed in doing what a Greek in this case could not do, except by disguising himself as a Greek, by *speaking Greek*, by feigning to speak Greek in order to get near the king?'[57] Kierkegaard provides us with a suggestive answer to this question. It is not a non-Greek who brings about the end of Hellenism, he tells us, but a Greek, Socrates, who employs irony 'even in destroying Hellenism'.[58] Derrida is referring here to using language under erasure, it may be objected; but what is irony if not the trope of erasure? We can resolve this more sharply if we attend to Kierkegaard on the Greeks and the Jews:

> With respect to the chosen people, the Jews, it was necessary for the scepticism of the Law to prepare the way, by means of its negativity to consume and burn away the natural man, as it were, in order that grace should not be taken in vain. It is the same with the Greeks – who might well be called the chosen people of fortune whose native soil was harmony and beauty, a people in whose development the purely human traversed its determinations, a people of freedom – so also with the Greeks, I say, in their intellectual world void of sorrow it was necessary for the silence of irony to become the negativity preventing subjectivity from being taken in vain. Irony, like

55 Derrida, *Of grammatology*, p. 24.   56 Taylor, *Erring*, p. 91.
57 Derrida, *Writing* p. 89.
58 Kierkegaard, p. 281.

> the Law, is a demand; indeed, irony is an enormous demand, for it disdains reality and demands ideality.[59]

This passage is remarkable in various respects, not the least because of its strong Hegelian overtones in a book otherwise concerned to fight against the Hegelian system. The characterisation of the Greeks as a happy people, and the account of the Jewish Law as negativity are both Hegelian; yet Kierkegaard is resolutely unHegelian in linking Athens and Jerusalem through different principles of negativity, irony and the Law. And we can perhaps see the beginnings of a deconstructive move in Kierkegaard's conception of both Athens and Jerusalem as equally subtended by a principle of negativity, modified as irony and Law respectively.

Reasons why Kierkegaard should be seen as a precursor of Derrida could doubtless be multiplied, but our interest in him is otherwise. I have shown how deconstruction can be read as a mode of irony, and we need not question the efficacy of this in the hands of a conceptual rhetorician such as de Man. What Kierkegaard shows us, though, is that while we may accept deconstruction as a permanent parabasis, the thematic *direction* of this parabasis is neither natural nor inevitable. There is no doubt that, for de Man, the ironies of deconstruction enforce a militant atheism. But Kierkegaard shows us that irony – a proto-deconstructive use of irony, moreover – can be turned to apologetic ends. As Bloom reminds us, the ironies of deconstruction are linked to a despiritualisation of thought.[60] Kierkegaard meanwhile points us away from irony as a trope of disaffection to irony as a trope of elliptic affirmation. 'Irony', he tells us, 'is like the negative way, not the truth but the way'.[61] And if this identification of trope and religious practice seems odd, we have only to remember that 'apophasis' names both the negative way to God and the trope of denial. Once more, we seem to be able to accept Derrida's critical points in the service of other tactical points.

59 Kierkegaard, pp. 235–6.
60 Harold Bloom, *A map of misreading* (New York: Oxford University Press, 1975), p. 79 and p. 85.
61 Kierkegaard, p. 340.

3 Whose 'general text'?

Throughout this discussion I have stressed two distinctions – one between the phenomenal and the transcendental, and one between the critical and the tactical – and I have sought to draw out the relations between them. One problem has kept circling around our analysis, that the heuristic value of these distinctions is continually threatened by their critical and tactical functions. Just as the doctrines of erasure and palæonymy require that the distinction between the phenomenal and the transcendental be blurred, so too the very distinction between the critical and the tactical must be called into question. As soon as we accord a special privilege to the critical over the tactical, we open ourselves to a deconstruction which will affirm that the critical is a determined modification of the tactical. It little matters if we define deconstruction analytically (by way of recursion) or rhetorically (as the effect of parabasis), the point remains the same: deconstruction may be pressed into the service of certain first-order positions, but it will be the first to check the will to totalise at work within those positions.

We have observed how Rorty reads Derrida as a radically anti-Kantian philosopher, and there is some truth in this construction. For one thing, Derrida rejects the notion of *a priori* transcendental grounds in demonstrating that any text requires transcendental conditions of possibility which are not *a priori*. As far as Derrida is concerned, there is no such thing as 'necessary conditions for experience in general'; even the notion of 'experience' must be used under erasure, since it 'has always designated the relationship with a presence'.[62] Derrida's critique of Kant's necessary conditions for experience is an issue in its own right (which I shall discuss in chapter 7), but I would like to take up another, related issue: what seems to be a curiously Kantian move in defining a 'general text' in the first place. I say 'Kantian' not because Derrida adduces *a priori* reasons for what counts as a text but rather because he allows some particular oppositions the status of generality but does not heed others with as good a claim. For whom is the 'general text' general? Suppose we first fathom what Derrida means by 'general text', then develop our criticisms.

62 Derrida, *Of grammatology*, p. 60.

In the second chapter I considered the opposition between 'book' and 'text'. Since then, though, I have unravelled the phenomenal and the transcendental senses of 'text'. So when Derrida tells us 'There is nothing outside of the text'[63] we should take this to be a transcendental claim. There is, Derrida tells us, nothing which is not already conditioned by a generalised version of the difference which marks phenomenal script. A text is 'a differential network, a fabric of traces referring endlessly to something other than itself, to other differential traces'.[64] It is true that any piece of writing will have traces of other texts, whether we are talking of stylistics, semantics or syntactics. This is the basis of concepts as otherwise divergent as Harold Bloom's 'anxiety of influence' and Julia Kristeva's 'intertextuality'. But Derrida's claim goes further than this. We saw in the opening chapter that, given Derrida's definitions, we cannot rightly talk of a 'trace of a presence' but only of a 'trace of a trace'. All texts, accordingly, are composed of traces of moments of presence which can never be said to have presented themselves: Derrida's point thus concerns phenomenal texts, but also the transcendental underpinnings of textuality. Following the strategy of palæonymy, Derrida calls this transcendental realm 'the text'; and this transcendental text is, as we have said, a generalised version of the phenomenal text.

To say that there is nothing outside the text can lead to confusion – in particular to the view that things exist only because they are written about (thereby making Derrida into an idealist) or to the Borgesian conceit that the universe is one vast library. Yet Derrida's meaning is otherwise: 'it was never our wish', he says, 'to extend the reassuring notion of the text to a whole extra-textual realm and to transform the world into a library'.[65] However, if Derrida admits that there is an extra-textual realm, what can he mean by the formula that there is nothing outside the text? The quickest route to an answer, oddly enough, is via the philosophy of the thing itself rather than of the text itself. Deconstruction, we are told, 'can no more break with a transcendental phenomenology than be reduced to it'.[66]

63 Derrida, *Of grammatology*, p. 158. Italics deleted. Cf. 'If there is no extratext it is because the graphic-graphicity in general – has always already begun, is always implanted in "prior" writing', *Dissemination*, p. 328.
64 Derrida, 'Living on', p. 84.   65 Derrida, 'Living on', p. 84.
66 Derrida, *Of grammatology*, p. 62.

That is to say, deconstruction cannot be reduced to phenomenology because it thinks the ground of phenomenology. At the same time deconstruction is not entirely unphenomenological in its procedure; its intentional object, the text, is constituted by an endless series of noetic modifications: the noema is forever subject to noesis. Accordingly, when Derrida claims that there is nothing outside the text, he is making a remark concerning constitution, not concerning what *is*. In other words, he does not say that everything is *only* a text but that everything is *also* a text.

'Text', then, in both its phenomenal and transcendental senses has a very general extension; but this does not quite give us what Derrida means by the phrase 'general text'. In fact Derrida's account of the general text is explicitly given in one place only: in his interview with Jean-Louis Houdebine and Guy Scarpetta, when for the first time in print he openly addresses a range of political issues. In the midst of distinguishing *différance* from the totalising drive of the Hegelian *Aufhebung*, Derrida observes that *différance*, since it can never be totally resolved, 'marks its effects in what I call the text in general, in a text which is not reduced to a book or a library, and which can never be governed by a reference in the classical sense'.[67] Later in the interview Derrida underlines these remarks in a tangled and somewhat frenzied fashion:

> *There is* such a general text everywhere that (that is, every-
> where) this discourse and its order (essence, sense, truth,
> meaning, consciousness, ideality, etc.) are *overflowed*, that is,
> everywhere that their authority is put back into the position of
> a *mark* in a chain that this authority intrinsically and illusorily
> believes it wishes to, and does in fact, govern. This general
> text is not limited, of course, as will (or would) be quickly
> understood, to writings on the page. The writing of this text,
> moreover, has the exterior limit only of a certain *re-mark*.
> Writing on the page, and then 'literature', are determined
> types of this re-mark. They must be investigated in their speci-
> ficity, and in a new way, if you will, in the specificity of their
> 'history', and in their articulation with the other 'historical'
> fields of the text in general.[68]

67 Derrida, *Positions*, p. 44. Derrida's earliest invocation of the general text, though without overt political ramifications, is to be found in *Of grammatology*, p. 14.
68 Derrida, *Positions*, p. 60.

Let us first put this into manageable English. The general text comprises not just the written texts of western thought but also the material institutions which house them. This knowledge, along with the assurance that no presence can totalise a textual field, provides us with new ways of criticising literature and philosophy. In particular, it shows us that historicism and formalism are forever bound up with one another: formalist critique – the theory as well as the practice – is always framed by historical context, but historicised readings can never totalise a text.

I have already argued that deconstruction proceeds along two lines at the same time, as a theoretical and as a political critique. And this is because there are two sites which mark the 'other' of philosophy as metaphysics: the groundless ground of philosophy, *différance*, which provides us with a theoretical critique, and the realm of the political, from which one derives a political critique. Now while these critiques can be distinguished, they are not distinct. Because, first, deconstruction seems required to double itself in order to remain what it is: it must be both theoretical and political. Secondly, it follows from the extension granted to 'metaphysics' that the political is always already in league with the metaphysical. Consequently, while Derrida insists that the theoretical critique must precede the political in order to prevent a naïve reconfirmation of metaphysics under the guise of a political rhetoric, this does not commit him to a naïve valuing of theory over praxis.

This calls for a more detailed discussion. The instituting distinction of metaphysics, Derrida maintains, is that between the intelligible and the sensible. The Saussurean sign, for instance, is metaphysical because the distinction between the signified and the signifier converges with that between the intelligible and the sensible. And the same holds for the familiar philosophical distinctions between mind and body, identity and difference, truth and error, logic and rhetoric, as well as for the distinctions between Apollo and Dionysos, man and woman, management and labour, and so forth. Thus, when Derrida is engaged with the theoretical deconstruction of, say, the distinction between identity and difference in a text he is also, simultaneously, unsettling the distinction between management and labour. (Whereas Quine allows for a person's web of beliefs to be revised from its empirical edges *inwards*, Derrida holds that the deconstructive revision of the general text must necessarily proceed *outwards*, from the instituting distinctions of metaphysics.) Theoretical deconstruction implies a political deconstruction, then; but Derrida is adamant that we also need a specifically political deconstruction, one that is addressed to particular political situations. Theoretical deconstruction may be involved with the political *(le politique)*, but it needs a supplement to deal with politics *(la politique)*.

We know Derrida's characteristic move that supplements are structurally necessary, but a non-structural choice is introduced here. Nancy Fraser provides us with a rewarding commentary on this problem. Reporting on the rise and fall of the 'Centre for Philosophical Research on the Political', a group established largely to discuss questions relating to the overlap between deconstruction and politics, we are told that Derrida said that he had 'deliberately not produced a discourse against revolution or Marxism in order to avoid contributing to the "anti-Marxist concert" of the *circa* 1968 period. He did not and *does* not want to weaken "what Marxism and the proletariat can constitute as a force in France". Despite his distrust of the idea of revolution *qua metaphysical* concept, he does not "devalue what [this idea] could contribute . . . as a force of 'regroupment' *(rassemblement)*"'.[69] The words 'deliberately', 'in order to avoid', 'want' and so forth underline the role that choice plays in this matter. But what are we to make of Derrida's statements regarding choice and deconstruction? I have in mind familiar remarks such as 'I do not believe that today there is any question of *choosing* [between one of the two interpretations of interpretation]' and 'The *incision* of deconstruction . . . does not take place just anywhere . . . it can only be made according to lines of force and forces of rupture that are localizable in the discourse to be deconstructed'.[70]

One thing is certain: if Derrida deliberately elects to exempt Marxism from deconstruction at the present time for local reasons of French politics, he is engaging in a choice of some sort and is plainly not attending to the apparent necessity of the 'lines of force' which doubtless occur in the text of Marx and in the Leninist reading of Marx. What interests me here is not so

69 Fraser, 'The French Derrideans: politicizing deconstruction or deconstructing the political?', *New German Critique*, 33 (1984), p. 133.
70 Derrida, *Writing*, p. 293 and *Positions*, p. 82.

much the choice that Derrida makes, whether or not to support Marxism in France at the present moment, but at what level the issue of choice takes root in deconstruction. For it is obvious that Derrida chooses to accent the political aspect of the general text rather than, say, its theological aspect. Just as the realm of the political is within the general text yet indicates philosophy's 'other', so too with the realm of the theological. If we accept Derrida's account of metaphysics, we can readily assent to the view that oppositions such as those between management and labour, man and woman, are of a piece with metaphysics; but we can also trace another chain of oppositions within the general text, all of which are gathered around the distinction between the God of metaphysics and the God of faith. In his remarks upon Catholic French theology after Derrida, Claude Geffré supplies us with a useful list of these oppositions:

> It is a theology that takes note of the decline of metaphysics and that strives to let God be the God of revelation rather than reconstructing him conceptually. Rather than think God in the discourse of representation, it seeks to think God in terms of advent . . . It is concerned to contemplate the advent of a God who reveals himself in the events of history and of the world, who appears more in alterity than in identity; in the gap, gratuitousness and excess more than in the immediacy of his presence. In this regard, one must not neglect the growing influence of the work of E. Levinas on French theologians.[71]

And to underline this final point we may add the particular opposition which has oriented this study, that between God regarded as the highest being and God as otherwise than Being.

We can go further. Just as Derrida draws from the general text a wide variety of oppositions – between concept and concept, genre and genre, synecdoche and synecdoche – so, too, it is an easy matter to follow other threads within the general text. Rather than attend to the ways in which Joyce unsettles Husserl, Nietzsche disturbs Rousseau, Mallarmé undoes Plato, and so forth, we could examine the following couples: St Augustine and St Gregory Nazianzus; Aquinas and Eckhart; Descartes and Pascal; Kant and Hamann; Hegel and Kierkegaard; not to mention configurations of non-contemporaneous authors –

71 Geffré, 'Silence et promesses de la théologie catholique française', *Revue de théologie et de philosophie*, 114 (1982), p. 239.

Gilson and Tertullian, for example. Note the parallels between this set of oppositions and Derrida's. Each first-mentioned writer is, in one way or another, associated with a thematics of presence in a way which each second-mentioned writer is not. This is not to say, of course, that any of these new oppositions can be easily resolved into a distinction between the metaphysical and the non-metaphysical, only that they are congruent with Derrida's own oppositions.

St Augustine, to be sure, can hardly be considered a philosophical theologian in any straightforward sense of the phrase. His *De doctrina Christiana*, however, with its emphasis upon the one true interpretation of scripture (that which most contributes to the reign of charity) is palpably metaphysical in Derrida's sense of the word. It is equally plain, though, that St Gregory's *Poemata quæ spectant ad alios*, with its extraordinary thesis that all interpretations of the scriptures are equally true, is – whatever else it is – not simply metaphysical.[72] Another example might be useful. Even though Kant's entire project is directed against dogmatic metaphysics, its doctrines of the *a priori* categories and the transcendental subject render it metaphysical in Derrida's sense of the word. One consequence of these doctrines is that language, like reason, is held to operate properly only within the realm of the phenomenal. Hence scripture is not held to be a trustworthy passage to knowledge of God: that privilege is accorded solely to practical reason. Hamann, however, can be read as calling the metaphysics of Kant's project into question, specifically in his remarks concerning the relation of reason and revelation to language. Language, he contends, conditions both reason and revelation.[73]

We need not explore the views of St Gregory and Hamann in any further detail, for the truth or falsity of these views is not our immediate concern. Our object has been to demonstrate that the general text is far more heterogeneous than Derrida indicates. More particularly, we have seen that while deconstruction has a

---

72 The relevant section of St Gregory's poem is to be found in *Patrologiæ cursus completus: series Græca*, ed. J. P. Migne (1882; rpt. Westmead, Hants.: Gregg Press, 1965), Vol. 37, Col. 1561f.

73 'I am quite at one with Herder that all our reason and philosophy amount to tradition . . . For me it is not a matter of physics or theology, but language, the mother of reason and revelation, their alpha and omega. It is the two-edged sword for all the truths and lies'. Hamann to Jacobi, 28 Oct., 1785. Quoted by R. G. Smith in his *J. G. Hamann 1730–1788* (London: Collins, 1960), pp. 252–3.

critical function, what is chosen as a critical object is a matter of tactics, and that this choice depends largely upon how one understands philosophy. Derrida's deconstruction is in terms of the oppositions philosophy/literature and philosophy/politics; ours, however, is by way of philosophy/theology.

III | Dialogue

Here it is required to surrender *everything*; not only wife and child as one is accustomed to say, but whatever there is, even God, because even he, as far as this standpoint is concerned, is a being. Thus he who wants to attain the initial stage of a truly free philosophizing must give up even God. Here it is true: He who wants to keep it shall lose it, but he who surrenders it, he shall find it.

cf. GMHopkins

Friedrich Schelling

6 | The economy of mysticism

Introduction

Let us recollect the argument. It has two related stages, one negative and one positive. In the first place, I have argued against what I have called the 'common view' of deconstruction in which Derrida's programme is framed as a straightforward affirmation of groundlessness and hence as anti-theological. This 'common view' is in fact a family of views; but we may take a remark by Eugene Goodheart to be characteristic: 'Epistemologically, deconstructive skepticism is opposed to logocentric knowledge; theologically, to belief or faith.'[1] Upon my reading, this is mistaken on several counts. (1) Deconstruction is not a collection of first-order positions about knowledge or being but a second-order discourse on epistemology and ontology, one that traces the effects of their will to totalise. Since it deals with particular texts, deconstruction finds its starting-point in material situations – texts and institutions; but its vantage point is the gap between materiality and phenomenality. Unlike Pyrrho, Derrida does not hold the sceptical view that we cannot prefer one position to another because every argument for a position is balanced by an equally persuasive argument against it. Derrida's position is closer to (though not identical with) Gödel's: any metaphysical reading of a text will generate at least one element which cannot be decided within metaphysics. So Derrida does not advocate scepticism – it is not even a considered position for him. (2) Deconstruction is not opposed to logocentrism; indeed, it is the will to totalise in the Hegelian and structuralist notions of 'opposition' which Derrida seeks to convict. Far from opposing philosophy, deconstruction is an originary supplement to phil-

1 Goodheart, *The skeptic disposition in contemporary criticism*, p. 10.

osophy. (3) Deconstruction is not a critique of theology as such but a questioning of the limits of metaphysics. Consequently, it has a legitimate interest in the ways in which metaphysics is licensed by theology.

This leads us to the positive stage of the argument. Given (3) above, deconstruction would seem to be able to unravel the relationships between theology and metaphysics, especially with regards to the elusive notion of non-metaphysical theology. Deconstruction has already been linked to non-metaphysical theology under the rubrics of mysticism and negative theology. Instead of working to discredit these discourses, as Derrida sometimes seems inclined to do, deconstruction may in fact help us to understand how they work.[2] Deconstruction can illuminate how mysticism and negative theology work as discourses: certain concepts and textual manoeuvres developed by Derrida can be used to analyse the mystical theologian's use of language and his or her attitude to it. And most importantly, deconstruction can clarify how mysticism and negative theology work *within philosophy*. On various important occasions in the history of philosophy, mysticism has been regarded as the 'other' of philosophy, as that which must at all costs be excluded from philosophical discourse. Deconstruction supplies us with the means to trace the effects within a discourse of exactly this kind of exclusion; and to do so would lead to a greater understanding of the history of both 'philosophy' and 'mysticism'. But this situation also has consequences for deconstruction; for if, as Derrida tells us, deconstruction seeks to question philosophy from a site philosophy cannot name, and if the mystical is one such site, there is reason to probe possible connections between deconstruction and mysticism.

1 A restricted economy

'Mysticism' has proved to be one of the most elusive yet most recalcitrant words used in discussing religious experience and discourse. 'This expression is so extremely vague that it seems

---

2 Although Derrida often takes negative theology to be a phase of positive theology, he does not always seem content with this construction. Thus: 'I believe that what is called "negative theology" (a rich and very diverse corpus) does not let itself be easily assembled under the general category of "onto-

better to avoid it', writes Schleiermacher of the word 'mystical', and elsewhere he notes that 'mysticism' is often given an 'unfortunate nuance' when used in theological polemics.[3] Widely disseminated throughout history and across cultural boundaries, 'mysticism' and its grammatical forms can refer to an entire spectrum of particular experiences, ranging from the prayer of quiet to the soul's union with God. They can refer, with equal ease, to a diverse body of writings which straddles literature and philosophy or seems to slip between their dividing lines. Mystical texts differ in kind – from alleged autobiographical testimonies to speculative treatises – as well as in degree, and a general taxonomy of such texts would be a redoubtable project. To facilitate discussion, though, we may resolve 'mysticism' into five areas: mystical experience; mystical testimony; mystical theology; the *via negativa*; and the mystical (or allegorical) hermeneutic.

We are familiar with the allegorical hermeneutic, and I have already said something of mystical experience in earlier chapters; what we need now is a definite idea of mystical theology and the *via negativa*. And to see these in perspective we first need to draw a broader distinction. In discussing theology one is generally concerned with what is known in the west as 'positive theology' and in the east as 'kataphaticism', in which God is taken to manifest Himself by way of a katabasis, a descent: the Father is revealed by the Son in and through the Spirit, thereby positing a God that can be described, albeit imperfectly, in positive and negative predicates. In 'apophaticism', however, 'knowledge' of God is gained through successive denials of 'God', resulting in an anabasis, an ascent to God through the darkness of unknowing. Let us concentrate upon this negative movement, and refine matters by agreeing that 'theology' names a discourse which critically reflects upon the phenomenon *and* discourse of religion. If this is so, we may distinguish between the *via negativa*, a religious programme of practices by which the soul progressively denies all that is not God in order to become

theology to be deconstructed"'. 'Letter to John P. Leavey', *Derrida and biblical studies*, p. 61.
3 Friedrich Schleiermacher, *The Christian faith*, Vol. 2, ed. H. R. Macintosh and J. S. Stewart (New York: Harper and Row, 1963), p. 429; 'The aphorisms on hermeneutics from 1805, and 1809/10', trans. R. Hass and J. Wojcik, *Cultural Hermeneutics*, 4 (1976–77), p. 370.

one with God, and negative theology, the discourse which reflects upon positive theology by denying that its language and concepts are adequate to God. The religious practice and the theological reflection are often inextricably entwined, but the distinction is nonetheless useful. Whereas the aim of the *via negativa* is union with God, the critical object of negative theology is the concept of God. In order to embark upon the *via negativa* one must be motivated by love; yet while the love of God may prompt one to engage with negative theology, this is also elicited by epistemological concerns.

What, then, is *negative* about 'negative theology'? I have said that negative theology denies the adequacy of the language and concepts of positive theology, and 'denial' requires some comment. *Apophasis*, in its strict Aristotelian sense, signifies 'negation'; yet when we talk of apophatic theology we must take into account the influence of two other Greek words which became linked with it. *Aphairesis*, meaning 'abstraction', was used interchangeably with *apophasis* in the early development of negative theology; and negative theology was itself called *analysis*, meaning 'the way of successive abstractions'. We can see how *aphairesis* and *analysis* illumine the kind of negation at work in negative theology by attending to what will be our guiding text, *The mystical theology*. Speaking of the ineffable God of faith, Pseudo-Dionysius provides us with a catalogue of what God is not:

> nor is It personal essence, or eternity, or time; nor can It be grasped by the understanding, since It is not knowledge or truth; nor is It kingship or wisdom; nor is It one, nor is It unity, nor is It Godhead or Goodness; nor is It a Spirit, as we understand the term, since It is not Sonship or Fatherhood; nor is It any other thing such as we or any other being can have knowledge of; nor does It belong to the category of non-existence or to that of existence; nor do existent beings know It as It actually is, nor does It know them as they actually are; nor can the reason attain to It to name It or to know It; nor is it [sic] darkness, nor is It light, or error, or truth; nor can any affirmation or negation apply to it [sic] . . .[4]

4 Pseudo-Dionysius Areopagite, *The divine names and the mystical theology*, trans. C. E. Rolt (London: S.P.C.K., 1940), pp. 200–1. I shall have recourse to two other translations: *The works of Dionysius the Areopagite*, trans. Rev. John Parker (1897–1899; rpt. NY: Richwood Pub. Co.,1976); and Pseudo-Dionysius Areo-

We shall return to this rich passage, but for the present it emphasises that simple negation has no special privilege with respect to discourse on God. What *is* denied within negative theology is the claim that God can be described adequately by positive or negative predicates, and in this way negative theology seeks to abstract our attention from concepts of God to the true God who cannot be conceptualised. The negative theologian continually points to the status of human discourse on God. In this passage Pseudo-Dionysius focuses upon the inadequacy of *both* Aristotelian ('essence', 'unity', 'existence') *and* theological vocabulary ('kingship', 'wisdom', 'Sonship', 'Fatherhood') before the mystery of the unnameable God.

Now what of the relations between these terms? One of the first things one notices in reading commentaries on mysticism is their tendency to link the element under consideration with one or more other elements. Thus Hans-Georg Gadamer has noted, in a passing reference to Pseudo-Dionysius, that 'The allegorical procedure of interpretation and the symbolical procedure of knowledge have the same justification'; and Joel Fineman has remarked, without further explanation, that 'it is significant that Philo, who was the first to employ an extensively allegorical mode of scriptural criticism, was also the first to introduce the terms of negative theology into theological discourse'.[5] It is this relationship between the allegorical hermeneutic and negative theology which chiefly concerns us, as one connection in what appears to be a far more comprehensive economy. When reading a work of negative theology, commentators will often attempt to find evidence of the author's mystical experience, as though to validate a theological position. Similarly, testimonies of mystical experience will be studied for signs of the author's theological commitment. It is as though where any one element of mysticism occurs, several others must also be present. This may be a useful heuristic or a misleading fiction. At any rate, we shall call it 'the economy of mysticism' and examine it further.

pagite, *The divine names and mystical theology*, trans. and introd. John D. Jones (Milwaukee, WI: Marquette University Press, 1980).
5 Hans-Georg Gadamer, *Truth and method*, ed. G. Barden and J. Cumming (London: Sheed and Ward, 1975), p. 66; J. Fineman, 'The structure of allegorical desire' in *Allegory and representation*, ed. S. J. Greenblatt. Selected Papers from the English Institute, 1979–80. New Series, No. 5 (Baltimore: Johns Hopkins University Press, 1981), p. 29.

Think of Origen, perhaps the first Christian theologian in whose writings this economy is seen to be at work. To begin with, de Lange tells us that 'Origen was the founder of the science of hermeneutics in the Church', and Etienne Gilson observes that it is in Origen's theology that one finds the origins of negative theology within Christian thought.[6] Andrew Louth tells us that Origen's 'interpretation of Scripture lies at the very heart of his mystical theology'; and Rowan Greer agrees when he suggests that 'Origen's approach to Scripture or his hermeneutical principle is really nothing more than his theological view'.[7] So we have *prima facie* connections between negative theology and the allegorical hermeneutic, and there is evidence in Origen's *Commentary on the Song of Songs* that he advocates the *via negativa*.[8] More difficult to establish, though, is if Origen enjoyed mystical experience of any kind. Most commentators take Origen's mysticism to be a matter of intellectual contemplation rather than of personal experience. It is all the more worthy of note, therefore, to find C. W. MacLeod stressing the relation between allegorical interpretation and mystical experience. Following Philo, Origen maintains that the exegete must be inspired before he can properly interpret scripture. In Origen's Christian vocabulary, understanding scripture presupposes purity of heart and the gift of God's grace: the Word is held to be incarnate in scripture as well as in Jesus of Nazareth. 'If, then, we consider the belief and doctrines which animate Origen's allegory', MacLeod infers, 'we have surely the right to talk of a mystical experience in some sense, one which is implicit in the nature of his faith; for allegory is the expression *par excellence* of the spiritual life'.[9] This move certainly grants a

6 N. R. M. de Lange, *Origen and the Jews* (Cambridge: Cambridge University Press, 1976), p. 134; E. Gilson, *History of Christian philosophy in the middle ages* (London: Sheed and Ward, 1955), p. 37.

7 A. Louth, *The origins of the Christian mystical tradition*, p. 54; and R.A. Greer, trans. and introd. *An exhortation to martyrdom, prayer and selected works*. The Classics of Western Spirituality: Origen. Pref. Hans Urs von Balthasar (London: S.P.C.K., 1979), p. 32.

8 Consider, for example, 'For with these preliminaries accomplished by which the soul is purified through its acts and habits and conducted to the discernment of natural things, the soul comes suitably to doctrines and mysteries, and is led up to the contemplation of the Godhead by a genuine and spiritual love', Origen, *Commentary on the Song of Songs*, in R. A. Greer, p. 234. Cf. p. 231 and p. 252.

9 C. W. MacLeod, 'Allegory and mysticism in Origen and Gregory of Nyssa', *Journal of Theological Studies*, NS 22 (1971), p. 371.

remarkable extension to 'mystical experience'. If we grant this extension, we have a positive idea of how the economy of mysticism works; but if we do not accept it we have something perhaps even more revealing, an instance of the working of the *desire* to establish a relationship between the allegorical hermeneutic and mystical experience. And this invites us to ask if there are other, hidden forces which motivate this desire for a restricted economy.

One such motivation is the desire to win mysticism for orthodoxy. Thus Newman's remark, when discussing the various merits and demerits of the Alexandrian and Antiochene schools of theology, that 'it may be almost laid down as an historic fact, that the mystical [i.e. allegorical] interpretation and orthodoxy will stand or fall together'.[10] As Newman rightly insists, 'the school of Antioch, which adopted the literal interpretation, was the very metropolis of heresy';[11] but this is not to conclude that there is a necessary connection between the allegorical hermeneutic and orthodoxy. Indeed, textual evidence constrains us to say that many of the orthodox Fathers drew a fine, though not always straight, line between doctrine and the allegorical method. Thus the three.great Cappadocians critically built on Origen's hermeneutics yet rejected certain doctrinal conclusions reached by Origen, in particular his subordinationalism. Similarly, St Athanasius repudiated Origen's account of the Trinity while approving features of his hermeneutic. The allegorical hermeneutic may have helped to shape a number of orthodox doctrines, but it also served to mould various heterodox doctrines. The same is substantially true of the literalist hermeneutic of the Antiochenes.

What is significant, however, is that while positive theology was developed by both the Alexandrians and the Antiochenes, it was only those who followed the allegorical hermeneutic who developed negative theologies. The Alexandrians Philo, Clement and Origen – and those who were greatly influenced by Alexandrian hermeneutics, such as St Gregory Nyssa – are precisely the early writers with whom we associate negative theology. Vladimir Lossky suggests that orthodoxy and apophaticism

10 J. H. Newman, *An essay on the development of Christian doctrine*, ed. and introd. J. M. Cameron (1845; rpt. Harmondsworth: Penguin, 1974), p. 340.
11 Newman, p. 340.

are correlative in the fourth century and beyond.[12] A detailed assessment of this claim is quite outside the scope of this study. Suffice it to say, by way of passing, that a late literalist such as Theodoret rejected the notion of immediate communion with God, and in this he was following a theme, deeply opposed to experiential mysticism, which began with Theophilus of Antioch and which characterised Antiochene theology in its entirety. Also, far from Antioch, Eunomius held that the divine essence could be expressed conceptually, a view that was exhaustively combated by each of the Cappodocians who argued against it on the basis of apophaticism. In short, Lossky's relating of orthodoxy and negative theology is far more plausible than Newman's close identification of orthodoxy and allegorising.

We must leave the question of orthodoxy to the theologian and return to philosophical concerns, specifically to a point of methodology. Our access to mystical experience is through texts and, unless we become mystics ourselves, we know of mysticism – at least in its highest reaches – vicariously, at the level of concepts. The fact that mystics frequently draw attention to their inability to represent their experiences in a satisfactory manner serves only to compound the problem: language is a medium that reveals mystical experience while simultaneously hiding it from inspection. Disturbing as it is, this is merely the surface of the problem. Whilst many are happy to agree that there have been genuine Christian mystics there is far less agreement as to who they are and how they can be distinguished from those who merely seem to have been mystics. MacLeod does not hesitate to call Origen a mystic, yet Dodds classes him as a 'mystic manqué'.[13] Augustine and Aquinas agree that St Paul enjoyed a mystical experience on the road to Damascus, yet Walter Stace concludes that there is insufficient evidence to call Paul a mystic.[14] Lack of agreement over what one means by 'mystic' is one explanation for these divergent views, and different criteria for evidence is another; yet even if agreement on these issues could be reached a problem would remain.

For not only is mystical experience refracted rather than

12 See V. Lossky, *The mystical theology of the eastern Church* (London: James Clarke and Co. Ltd., 1957), Ch. 2.
13 C. W. MacLeod, 'Allegory and mysticism', p. 368.
14 Aquinas, *Summa theologiæ*, 2a2æ Q.175 art. 3; W. Stace, *The teachings of the mystics* (New York: Mentor, 1960), p. 132.

reflected in texts but the texts themselves are endlessly refracted by other texts, by entire traditions of textual practices. Although what we may take to be a presence may *institute* a text it cannot function as the *origin* of the text's significations; nor can it be recovered by a reading of the text, since we cannot even talk of a trace of a presence in a text, only of a trace of a trace. This situation is not a matter of much concern with literary texts: whether Wordsworth really did see a field of golden daffodils before composing the famous lyric should not arise in any important sense when we evaluate Wordsworth's talent as a poet. However, whether Angela of Foligno actually did hear Christ say to her 'Thou art I and I am Thou' must arise when deciding if her writings are mystical texts. Questions touching upon the subject's psychology, not to mention phenomenological questions concerning her foreconception of the experience, can be placed to one side here. My point is merely that questions of experience and intention must be posed when dealing with mystical texts, but that textuality ensures that neither experience nor intention can ever be confidently recovered from texts.

Here is an example. 'Broadly speaking mystical theology can be divided into two categories – descriptive and theological', writes William Johnston.[15] He later wields this distinction with great confidence. It can 'scarcely be doubted', he tells us, that *The cloud of unknowing* testifies to the author's personal mystical experience; other texts by the same writer – *A treatyse of the stodye of wysdome* and his modified translation of Pseudo-Dionysius's *The mystical theology* – merely 'give the theoretical or theological basis' for such experience.[16] Whether or not the *Cloud* - author was a mystic worries me less than Johnston's reason for concluding that one text is testimonial while the others are theoretical. Only one reason is offered:

> the sureness of touch with which he writes indicates clearly enough that he himself experienced the sapiential repose in silence which he describes with a serene authority arising, one feels, not only from deep theological study but also from silent communion with God at the sovereign point of his own spirit.[17]

15 W. Johnston, *The mysticism of The cloud of unknowing.* Foreword by Thomas Merton (1978; rpt. Wheathampstead, Herts.: Anthony Clarke, 1980), p. xiv.
16 Johnston, pp. 3, 4.   17 Johnston, p. 4.

The argument is that personal experience is necessary for persuasive writing. Many objections could be raised. One could point to any number of poems or novels which effectively describe events of which the author has had no direct experience. Conversely, rhetorical skill is requisite for persuasive writing, even if one is writing from direct experience. *The cloud of unknowing* may seem realistic, but the very concision of the text suggests that material has been selected and framed, which implies that the text does not so much report raw experience as deploy a realist code. There may be traces of direct experience in the text, but the argument from literary persuasiveness to personal experience will not help us isolate them.

Questions of genre, style and tradition – not to mention the humility of the writers themselves, their desire not to appear as beneficiaries of special graces – qualify all inferences from text to experience. Our knowledge of mystical experience is textual, and on the basis of textual experience alone one cannot judge if a text refers to a lived experience or to another text about such experience, if the writer is a practising mystic, a theorist, or both. It may well be that we can never know for sure if *The cloud of unknowing* or Origen's *Homilies on Numbers* refract actual experience; however, we can talk with far more certainty about mystical theology. That is, while we can never be absolutely certain that a specific text answers to a particular experience, we can be sure that any 'mystical' text is underpinned by or underwrites a theology. It may be that Origen and the *Cloud* - author were mystics; but it is certain that they used and developed negative theologies.

On the basis of these distinctions it may be polemic to cast philosophers such as Kant, Hegel and Derrida as mystics, but it would be an entirely different matter to ascribe to them the status of negative theologians. In this way one does not attribute to them any experience of God or any personal belief in God, but one claims that their texts underwrite a certain attitude towards discourse on God. Kant's inveighing against mysticism as 'monstrosities on reason' and his hope that Herder will 'attain to that serenity which is peaceful yet full of feeling and is the contemplative life of the philosopher, just the opposite of that dreamed of by the mystic' are well known.[18] However, this is not to say

18 Kant, *Critique of practical reason*, trans. L. W. Beck (Indianapolis: Bobbs-Merrill Educational Publishing, 1956), p. 125; Letter to Herder in Riga, 1768.

that Rosenzweig is necessarily wrong to talk, in the one breath, of 'the negative theology of Nicholas of Cusa or of the sage of Koenigsburg'.[19] One can tell a similar story of Hegel. Benedetto Croce is in part correct to maintain that 'Hegel became ferociously satirical against mysticism, with its frenzies, its sighings, its raising the eyes to heaven, its bowing the neck and clasping the hands, its faintings, its prophetic accents, its mysterious phrases of the initiates'.[20] It is true that Hegel did object to religious enthusiasm and to undialectical claims to know God, though this hardly amounts to a complete rejection of 'mysticism', as Hegel's admiration for Meister Eckhart and Jacob Böhme makes clear. However, even if Hegel does reject the possibility of immediate experience of God, this does not commit one to disagree with Quentin Lauer's characterisation of Hegel's philosophy as 'negative theology'.[21] And finally, although Derrida distinguishes deconstruction from 'the violences of mysticism' and Spivak emphasises that grammatology 'is not "mystical"', Crossan's suggestion that 'what Derrida is saying leads straight into a contemporary retrieval of negative theology' is not thereby contradicted.[22]

2 Derrida and mysticism

Just as there are a number of casual remarks which associate allegory and negative theology, so too with deconstruction and negative theology. At first glance it would seem that at least one of these associations is mistaken, for deconstruction is always the unravelling of allegoresis. Yet deconstruction does not work by opposing itself to another discourse: so it may be possible that both associations are of use to us. Mikel Dufrenne, Geoffrey Hartman and Susan Handelman have sketched parallels between deconstruction and negative theology, while Paul Ricœur and Henri Meschonnic have suggested that all such

Quoted by E. Cassirer, *Kant's life and thought*, trans. J. Haden and introd. S. Körner (New Haven: Yale University Press, 1981), p. 85.

19 F. Rosenzweig, *The star of redemption*, trans. W. W. Hallo (New York: Holt, Rinehart and Winston, 1971), p. 23.

20 B. Croce, *What is living and what is dead of the philosophy of Hegel*, trans. D. Ainslie (London: Macmillan, 1915), p. 6.

21 Q. Lauer, S.J. 'Hegel's negative theology', *Journal of Dharma: An International Quarterly of World Religions*, 6 (1981), p. 47.

22 Derrida, *Writing*, p. 87; G. Spivak, 'Translator's preface' to *Of grammatology*, p. lxxviii; J. D. Crossan, *Cliffs of fall*, p. 11.

parallels are illusory.[23] Whilst there has been no sustained discussion of the problem, the most persistent and provocative contribution to the debate has come from John Dominic Crossan.

We noted Crossan's first formulation that 'what Derrida is saying leads straight into a contemporary retrieval of negative theology', and of particular importance is his gloss upon this remark: a negative theology, it turns out, is 'a theology articulating itself by a philosophy of absence'.[24] The main obstacle Crossan has to face here is Derrida himself, especially a familiar passage from 'Différance' which I quote *in extenso*:

> the detours, locutions, and syntax in which I will often have to take recourse will resemble those of negative theology, occasionally even to the point of being indistinguishable from negative theology. Already we have had to delineate that *différance is not*, does not exist, is not a present-being *(on)* in any form; and we will be led to delineate also everything *that* it *is not*, that is, *everything*; and consequently that it has neither existence nor essence. It derives from no category of being, whether present or absent. And yet those aspects of *différance* which are thereby delineated are not theological, not even in the order of the most negative of negative theologies, which are always concerned with disengaging a superessentiality beyond the finite categories of essence and existence, that is, of presence, and always hastening to recall that God is refused the predicate of existence, only in order to acknowledge his superior, inconceivable, and ineffable mode of being. Such a development is not in question here, and this will be confirmed progressively. *Différance* is not only irreducible to any ontological or theological – onto-theological – reappropriation, but as the very opening of the space in which ontotheology – philosophy – produces its system and its history, it includes onto-theology, inscribing it and exceeding it without return.[25]

So deconstruction is neither a negative theology nor a philosophy of absence: a point which Derrida has been at pains to stress in a

23 Mikel Dufrenne, *Le poétique*, p. 21f. G. Hartman, *Saving the text*, p. 7. S. Handelman, 'Jacques Derrida and the heretic hemeneutic', in *Displacement*, ed. M. Krupnick, *passim*. P. Ricœur, 'A response', *Biblical Research*, 24/25, p. 74. H. Meschonnic, *Le signe et le poème*, p. 403.
24 J. D. Crossan, *Cliffs of fall*, p. 11. This chapter of Crossan's book first appeared as 'Paradox gives rise to metaphor: Paul Ricœur's hermeneutics and the parables of Jesus', *Biblical Research*, 24/25 (1979–80).
25 Derrida, *Margins of philosophy*, p. 6. Cf. Derrida's other remarks on negative theology in *Derrida and difference*, pp. 4, 130, 132.

recent essay, 'Comment ne pas parler'.[26] This point allows us to see the root of Crossan's difficulty in associating negative theology with deconstruction. It is this: Crossan assumes that the distinction between positive theology and negative theology converges with that between a philosophy of presence and a philosophy of absence. And upon this model, negative theology – far from having a rapport with deconstruction, as Crossan would wish – will always be open to deconstruction.

In a subsequent essay Crossan refines his position, observing that 'there can certainly be little communication between Derrida and negative theology if that is conceived as a simple alternative strategy within onto-theology'.[27] This is a decisive move; unfortunately, though, Crossan does not indicate *how* we are to re-think negative theology. Finally, in a further essay, he comes to the brink of a solution: 'Derrida's thematics of absence could be extremely important for negative theology. But even more important would be the thought of difference for that theology which is neither positive nor negative but paradoxical'.[28] What prevents Crossan from actually finding a solution is, once more, his insistence upon construing positive theology and negative theology along the lines of presence and absence. The distinction at issue is, rather, between presence and representation. Derrida does not maintain that presence is a modification of absence but that presence is always already a representation. Similarly, the negative theologian is not so much concerned with the existential problem of God's absence as with the double bind that God imposes upon man: Represent me, but on no account represent me.

It may be worth spelling this out. Representation is usually thought as derived from presence, but when the distinction between presence and representation is deconstructed we must think representation otherwise, as that from which presence is derived. We see here the workings of the familiar distinction between a marginal element's phenomenal and transcendental senses: as phenomenon, representation is *within* the realm of

26 See Derrida, 'Comment ne pas parler: dénégations', in *Psyché*, pp. 537–45. Unfortunately this essay appeared only just as this book was in press and I am therefore unable to discuss it in the detail it deserves.
27 Crossan, 'Difference and divinity', in *Derrida and biblical studies*, p. 38.
28 Crossan, 'Stages in imagination', in *The archeology of the imagination. Journal of the American Academy of Religion Studies*, 48 (1981), ed. C. Winquist, p. 59

presence, but as transcendental it is *outside* that realm because it is the condition of possibility for that realm. In other words, we do not need a third theology, one neither positive nor negative – a theology of paradox – for negative theology, properly understood, *is* that theology: a discourse which works at once inside and outside onto-theology, submitting its images of God to deconstruction. My position is not that deconstruction is a form of negative theology but that negative theology is a form of deconstruction.

One point which is liable to introduce unnecessary difficulties into the discussion is the view that Derrida speaks of *différance* in a language which recalls how negative theologians write of God. Responding to Derrida's description of *différance* as 'the structured and differing origin of differences', Mark C. Taylor observes, 'This is a remarkable formulation, for it suggests a striking similarity between Derridean *différance* and what theologians have traditionally called "God"'.[29] Derrida warns us that 'the detours, locutions, and syntax' he must adopt in talking of *différance* 'will resemble those of negative theology, occasionally even to the point of being indistinguishable from negative theology'.[30] And this prompts Crossan to ask, 'Why, then, are the syntactics so similar if the semantics are so different?'[31] The similarity between the discourses answers to the fact that in each case its subject is ineffable; and we may answer Crossan's question by distinguishing between ineffability as a consequence of the subject being *transcendent* and because of the subject being *transcendental*. If God is understood as transcending the phenomenal world, one cannot hope to describe Him because language is restricted in its scope to the realm of the phenomenal. Similarly, if *différance* enables concepts to emerge it cannot be described adequately by concepts.

It may be objected that while the God of onto-theology is transcendent He also fulfils a transcendental role. And this is surely correct. God is absolutely in and for Himself, and thus transcendent, and is also an absolute ground, and in that sense transcendental. But we must recall the distinction between 'transcendental ground' and 'transcendental': God is understood to

29 Taylor, *Deconstructing theology*, p. 99.
30 Derrida, *Margins of philosophy*, p. 6.
31 Crossan, 'Difference and divinity', p. 39.

constitute a transcendental ground because He is pure self-presence; but *différance* is transcendental yet cannot constitute a ground because it must always differ from itself. The apparent similarity of the theological and grammatological vocabularies betrays a fundamental difference. The God of onto-theology reveals *that* He is yet conceals *what* He is; the play of *différance* is revealed in the phenomenal differing and deferring of meaning yet is concealed at the level of the transcendental, not because it is inaccessible but because there is no independent transcendental realm.

This last point needs to be teased out a little. We can say that *différance* originates at the level of the phenomenal text because prior to writing there is no *différance*: it is not a transcendental principle which could theoretically be articulated in a world without phenomena. However, Derrida argues that metaphysics presupposes a generalised version of the difference it systematically devalues. This is *différance* in its transcendental sense; and because it is a condition of possibility it is also an origin. Strictly speaking, *différance* is constituted by a doubled origin, at once phenomenal and transcendental. The transcendental is implied by the phenomenal, and the phenomenal turns out to be conditioned by the transcendental. This is what Derrida means by describing *différance* as 'the structured and differing origin of differences'.

The ineffability that concerns the theologian differs, then, from the ineffability that perplexes the deconstructionist. Having reached this point, we can weigh Derrida's views on mysticism and negative theology. Whilst it has become an *idée reçue* of much contemporary discussion of mysticism to remove mysticism from the operations of reason – to argue, as Rudolph Otto does, that the experience of the holy is fundamentally non-rational[32] – Derrida locates a complicity between 'rationalism and mysticism'.[33] This puzzling association is not to be confused with Harnack's definition of mysticism as 'nothing else than rationalism applied to a sphere above reason' nor with Inge's polemic revision of this definition in which mysticism is characterised as 'reason applied to a sphere above rationali-

---

32 Rudolf Otto, *The idea of the holy*, trans. J. W. Harvey (London: Oxford University Press, 1971), Ch. 1.
33 Derrida, *Of grammatology*, p. 80.

sm'.[34] Whereas Harnack and Inge at least agree that there is a marked difference between philosophy and mysticism, Derrida suggests that both may serve the same obscure end. This immediately places Derrida at odds with the common view whereby mysticism is the *other* of philosophy. There are, to be sure, traces of this view throughout the history of philosophy; but its point of maximum force is first felt in Kant and variously drawn out by neo-Kantianism. This relation between philosophy and mysticism will pass under review in the following chapters, and we can best prepare ourselves for this inquiry by probing Derrida's reasons for assimilating mysticism to philosophy.

Although he names Meister Eckhart, and while he often has Pseudo-Dionysius in mind when evoking negative theology (he characterises the God of negative theology as a 'superessentiality'), Derrida is not especially interested in mystical texts. The recent essay 'Comment ne pas parler' is something of an exception, yet even here he is more concerned to justify and clarify his earlier, occasional remarks on negative theology than to explore the texts of Pseudo-Dionysius and Meister Eckhart in any detail. Apart from his heuristic assumptions, such as that all metaphysics addresses presence, Derrida's general statements are usually rooted in readings of particular texts; and he is concerned to find texts which have been systematically relegated to the margins of philosophy – as mystical texts certainly have. What attracts Derrida, however, is the *distinction* between philosophy and mysticism, especially when it is drawn along the lines of metaphysics and non-metaphysics. Derrida's move, here as elsewhere, is to show that what seems free of metaphysics is in fact already indebted to it. Thus the mystic's characteristic claims to enjoy immediate experience of God, to hear God's voice, and to pass beyond the confines of human concepts, are metaphysical in that they value immediacy over mediation, speech over writing. In fine, Derrida's moves against mysticism are all programmatic and – perhaps because of this – often phrased too briefly to be of much moment.

Derrida's remarks upon negative theology, however, are far more pressing. For while they are often dogmatic, they also show signs of a certain unease. The dogmatism is explained by Derrida's perfectly legitimate desire to establish that his dis-

34 W.R. Inge, *Christian mysticism* (1899; rpt. London: Methuen and Co., 1948), p. 21.

course is not a negative theology, while the unease perhaps answers to his anxiety that negative theology be seen, as in my view it should be, as a deconstructive discourse. What, then, does Derrida say about negative theology? Writing of Pseudo-Dionysius, Meister Eckhart or even Georges Bataille, Derrida has the one theme: 'The negative movement of the discourse on God is only a phase of positive ontotheology.'[35] Negative theology, he holds, may be recuperated by positive theology, since both ultimately posit 'a "superessentiality"; beyond the categories of meaning, a supreme being and an indestructible meaning'.[36]

How persuasive are these assessments of mysticism and negative theology? It is possible to adduce a wealth of evidence in favour of the view that many mystics remain complicit with Platonism and hence with metaphysics. Consider St Teresa of Avila. Writing of an experience in which Christ changes the cross of a rosary into four large stones, St Teresa comments that they were 'much more precious than diamonds – incomparably more so, for it is impossible, of course, to make comparisons with what is supernatural, and diamonds seem imperfect counterfeits beside the precious stones which I saw in that vision'.[37] Similarly, in her vision of hell St Teresa tells us that the pictorial and verbal representation of the suffering of the damned 'is like a picture set against reality'.[38] Whatever else is happening in these passages, it is evident that St Teresa is positing a hierarchy of presence over representation and is doing so in an overt Platonic manner. Given that St Teresa feels herself unable to communicate her experience of Christ's presence, her comparisons cause her some anxiety. According to the theology to which St Teresa subscribes, there is only one way in which her comparisons can be validated, and that is if they are confirmed by Christ. It must be Christ because only He is both the full presence of God and the representation of God in human form. And this is exactly what happens in St Teresa's narrative of her mystical experiences: after pondering the validity of one of her images of God, Christ answers her by saying 'The comparison thou hast made is a good one'.[39] St Teresa's *experiences* may or

35 Derrida, *Writing*, p.337, n.37.
36 Derrida, *Writing*, p. 271. Derrida continues to argue the same line in 'Comment ne pas parler'.
37 St Teresa of Avila, *The life of the Holy Mother Teresa of Jesus*, in *The complete works of St Teresa of Jesus*, trans. E. Allison Peers (London: Sheed and Ward, 1978), Ch. XXIX, p. 190.
38 St Teresa, *Life*, Ch. XXXII, p. 217.   39 St Teresa, *Life*, Ch. XXXIX, p. 289.

may not be of a metaphysical state of affairs, but her *account* of them is surely metaphysical.

One could find similar evidence to argue that the various treatises of St John of the Cross are metaphysical, at least in part. But we need not labour the point: it may well be that a mystic's testimony is metaphysical, but this is not to say that it is *simply* metaphysical. There may be elements in his or her discourse which call metaphysical claims into question. With this in mind, let us describe the model of negative theology which Derrida assumes. The Thomist and Hegelian models present themselves as starting points, so I shall take them, very briefly, one at a time.

I have already distinguished between the main ways in which one can know God. In positive theology God is known in His effects, while in negative theology one gains 'knowledge' of God by successively abstracting God from images of Him. The one assumes a movement from presence to representation, the other a movement from representations to presence (or, perhaps more accurately, to that which is otherwise than presence). There is, however, a third position – the way of eminence, or analogical theology; it was developed by Celsus and Albinus, but our interest is in St Thomas's adaptation and refinement of it. St Thomas develops this position when answering the question, Can we say anything literally about God? On the one hand, he says, it seems as though no word can be used literally of God, for every predicate we apply to God is drawn from our discourse on creatures, and so can only be used metaphorically of God. On the other hand, St Thomas is committed to the view that there are propositions which are literally true of God, such as, for example, that God is both trinity and unity. His solution is as follows:

> We have to consider two things, therefore, in the words we use to attribute perfections to God, firstly the perfections themselves that are signified – goodness, life and the like – and secondly the way in which they are signified. So far as the perfections signified are concerned the words are used literally of God, and in fact more appropriately than they are used of creatures, for these perfections belong primarily to God and only secondarily to others. But so far as the way of signifying these perfections is concerned the words are used inappropriately, for they have a way of signifying that is appropriate to creatures.[40]

40 Aquinas, *Summa theologiæ* Ia Q.13 art. 3.

St Thomas is referring here to *proper* predicates, those which signify the transcendental properties of being such as unity, truth, goodness and beauty. Excluded from consideration are all those *improper* predicates which specify the various perfections of each created species; these can only ever be applied to God in a metaphorical manner. With the scope of St Thomas's remark in mind, we may isolate his central point: negations correspond only to the mode of signification, not to what is signified. But how does this square with Pseudo-Dionysius's remarks on negation? St Thomas tells us that this is in fact what Pseudo-Dionysius meant: 'The reason why Dionysius says that such words are better denied of God is that what they signify does not belong to God in the way that they signify it, but *in a higher way*'.[41] For St Thomas, therefore, the transcendental properties of being belong eminently to God. If this is so, negative theology and positive theology work together in a dialectic; moreover, this dialectic has a positive accent, for it affirms that God is the highest value. For the moment we can bracket whether St Thomas's distinction between positive theology and negative theology does indeed correspond to Pseudo-Dionysius's and turn, instead, to a second model of negative theology – that of Hegel.

Why Hegel? I have said that both models of negative theology are dialectical. This is true, but negative theology for St Thomas is part of a closed dialectic – it *corrects* the anthropomorphisms inherent in positive theology and plays no further role – while negativity for Hegel plays a *constitutive* role. But does Hegel offer us a negative theology? Quentin Lauer thinks so, and he quotes in support of this view one of Hegel's most puzzling yet most often cited passages:

> The life of God and divine intelligence, then, can, if we like, be spoken of as love disporting with itself; but this idea falls into edification, and even sinks into insipidity, if it lacks the seriousness, the suffering, the patience, and the labour of the negative. *Per se* the divine life is no doubt undisturbed identity and oneness with itself, which finds no serious obstacle in otherness and estrangement, and none in the surmounting of this estrangement. But this 'per se' is abstract generality, where we abstract from its real nature, which consists in its being objective to itself, conscious of itself on its own account

41 Aquinas, *Summa theologiæ* Ia Q.13 art. 3. My emphasis.

(für sich zu sein); and where consequently we neglect altogether the self-movement which is the formal character of its activity.[42]

To place this passage in its historical context, Hegel is arguing here against Schelling's notion of God as an undifferentiated Absolute. Considered as a pure abstraction, without regard for its inner workings, the Absolute appears to be a natural self-identity. But far from being an abstraction, the Absolute, for Hegel, is what *is*; and actual reality is differentiated, so the Absolute must contain difference and negativity within itself. As Hegel says elsewhere, the nature of the Absolute 'is to differentiate itself within itself, and thus to preserve within itself the element of difference, but yet to do this in such a way as not to disturb the universality which is also there. Here universality [or the Absolute] is something which has this element of difference within itself, and is in harmony with itself.'[43]

It is crucial to recognise that in Hegel's understanding God is driven by His nature to posit that which is other than Himself. And as we saw in our discussion of Hegel's account of the Fall, this self-estrangement is repeated in man: 'the step into opposition, the awakening of consciousness, follows from the very nature of man'.[44] We know that for Hegel philosophy is the tracing of the dialectic, and that as the dialectic is nothing other than an *itinerarium mentis in deum*, philosophy *is* theology. We know too that the forward movement of the dialectic is given by the negativity in God and consequently in man: the dialectic proceeds by successively negating what is inadequate in a form of knowing. So there is a sense in which we may rightly call Hegel's philosophy a negative theology; and this, in short, is Lauer's thesis.

Quite clearly, Lauer's sense of 'negative theology' does not correspond to my own use of the term. Moreover, Hegel would reject the sense I have given to 'negative theology'.[45] For in my view negative theology seeks to guarantee that human speech about God is in fact about *God* and not a *concept* of God. This

42 Lauer's translation, 'Hegel's negative theology', p. 47.
43 Hegel, *Lectures on the philosophy of religion*, trans. R.B. Spiers, Vol. III, p. 9.
44 Hegel, *Logic*, p. 43.
45 The same case is argued, at length, by R. Williamson, 'The mystery of god [*sic*] in Hegel's philosophy', in *The via negativa* (*Prudentia*, Supplementary Number 1981), eds. D. W. Dockrill and R. Mortley, pp. 107, 114.

implies that there is, in principle, something which man cannot know about God, and it is this position against which Hegel's entire project is directed: a perfectly adequate account of what God is in and for Himself, Hegel would argue, is already given in his *Encyclopædia*. I develop the Hegelian model of negative theology, however, not in order to promote it as true but because it is needed to clarify Derrida's idea of negative theology. To this end, we may observe that, different though they are, the Thomist and Hegelian models of negative theology share a fundamental similarity: in each case, the negative moment of theology is subdued to the positive moment. We have already seen that Derrida's main objection to linking deconstruction and negative theology is that 'The negative movement of the discourse on God is only a phase of positive ontotheology'.[46] I would suggest that Derrida's conception of negative theology is circumscribed by either or both the Thomist and Hegelian models; and that these models supervene even when his remarks are based upon Pseudo-Dionysius or Meister Eckhart. Derrida assumes the *Thomist* reading of Pseudo-Dionysius and the *Hegelian* reading of Meister Eckhart. That is, Derrida always regards negative theology as part of a *dialectic* with positive theology.

One place where Derrida argues that negative theology remains in fee to positive theology is in his reading of Bataille's reading of Hegel. Derrida distinguishes Bataille's atheology from negative theology: 'Even in its discourse, which already must be distinguished from sovereign affirmation, this atheology does not, however, proceed along the lines of negative theology; lines that could not fail to fascinate Bataille, but which, perhaps, still reserved, beyond all the rejected predicates, and even "beyond being", a "superessentiality"; beyond the categories of beings, a supreme being and an indestructible meaning'.[47] Bataille develops this position (or, better, non-position) by locating the blind spot in Hegel's discourse, the point of radical negativity or non-reserve which cannot be designated as positivity or negativity within the Hegelian system. Thus Hegel's theology is held to be conditioned by an atheology. Derrida, in turn, isolates the

---

46 Derrida, *Writing*, p. 337, n. 37.
47 Derrida, *Writing*, p. 271. Bataille titles volumes five and six of his *Oeuvres complètes* (Paris: Gallimard, 1973) 'La somme athéologique'.

blind spot of Bataille's reading of Hegel, the place where Bataille's transgression of the Hegelian system presupposes that system. In my turn I wish to draw attention to the blind spot in Derrida's account of negative theology, and I shall do this by reference to his reading of Bataille on Hegel.

3 From a restricted to a general economy

'He did not know to what extent he was right', he had no idea 'with what exactitude he described the movement of Negativity'.[48] Bataille refers here to two passages, one of which I have already discussed, namely Hegel's remarks in the preface to the *Phenomenology* upon 'the labour of the negative'. Hegel is right, Bataille argues, to take negativity as fundamental to the dialectic; but in the preface Hegel restricts negativity to the narrow compass of seriousness, suffering, patience and labour, to the secure realm of history and meaning, and thus negativity is always recuperated in advance by positivity. Here Hegel is blind to what he has already written in the body of the *Phenomenology*, the sovereignty of the negative in the form of death. Hegel's insight occurs in the parable of the Lord and Bondsman. We enter the story half-way through with Hegel talking of the lord and master's independent – and therefore limited – consciousness:

> Still, it does in fact contain within itself this truth of pure negativity and self-existence, because it has experienced this reality within it. For this consciousness was not in peril and fear for this element or that, nor for this or that moment of time, it was afraid for its entire being; it felt the fear of death, the sovereign master. It has been in that experience melted to its inmost soul, has trembled throughout its every fibre, and all that was fixed and steadfast has quaked within it. This complete perturbation of its entire substance, this absolute dissolution of all its stability into fluent continuity, is, however, the simple, ultimate nature of self-consciousness, absolute negativity, pure self-referent existence, which consequently is involved in this type of consciousness.[49]

In this description of consciousness risking its life in order to gain freedom, we see Hegel almost coming to an understanding

48 Quoted by Derrida, *Writing*, p. 260 from Georges Bataille, *Hegel, la mort et le sacrifice*, p. 36.
49 Hegel, *The phenomenology of mind*, p. 237.

of the true scope of negativity. Yet even here negativity is perceived as constructive work. Bataille again: 'Hegel, elaborating the philosophy of work (it is the *Knecht*, the freed bondsman, the worker, who in the *Phenomenology* becomes God) suppressed chance – and laughter'.[50] What Hegel overlooks, Bataille contends, is a kind of radical negativity which resists conversion into positivity; and Bataille takes *potlatch* as a representative instance of this radical negativity.

Marcel Mauss's discussion of *potlatch* amongst the Tlingit, the Haida, the Tsimshian, and other people of the northwestern coast of North America, is well known.[51] A community may make a large gift of various goods to a rival community with the intention of humiliating the recipients; in order to overcome this shame, the recipients must respond with a larger gift. Humiliation can also be aroused, however, by a community or its representative being seen to destroy accumulated wealth; and the only acceptable way of saving face is to raze more of one's own property and possessions. Quite clearly, Bataille is not drawing attention to Hegel's ignorance of this particular social practice; it is the principle which is pertinent. 'As a game, *potlatch* is the opposite of a principle of conservation', Bataille observes; 'At no time does a fortune serve to *shelter its owner from need*. On the contrary, it functionally remains – as does its possessor – *at the mercy of a need for limitless loss*'.[52] The Hegelian dialectic works with a restricted economy – Hegel speculates only with the hope of making a return on his conceptual layout: the *Aufhebung* advances us towards absolute knowledge – and remains blind to all that is excessive and transgressive in negativity: chance, eroticism, laughter, sacrifice, play.

Bataille proposes a displacement of the Hegelian system. Negativity will no longer be recuperated by positivity: there will be a transgressive overflow which will remain negative. This view seems entirely coherent from a distance, but upon closer inspection it resolves into distinct positions. Bataille wishes to push the Hegelian dialectic as far as it will go: whereas a limited

50 Bataille, *Le coupable*, in *Oeuvres complètes*, Vol. V (Paris: Gallimard, 1973), p. 341.
51 See Marcel Mauss, *The gift*, trans. I. Cunnison (New York: Norton, 1967).
52 Bataille, *Visions of excess*, ed. and introd. A. Stoekl, trans. A. Stoekl, C.R. Lovitt and D.M. Leslie, Jr. Theory and History of Literature, Vol. 14 (Minneapolis: University of Minnesota Press, 1985), pp. 122–23.

negativity of work is *sublated* with Hegel, a radical negativity of eroticism, laughter and sacrifice is *embraced* by Bataille. Yet Bataille recognises that the unlimited loss which characterises radical negativity does serve a need; in providing an outlet for excess energy it paradoxically helps to preserve norms.[53] In this sense, excess and transgression turn out to be yet one more ruse of the dialectic. Bataille remains Hegelian even as he transgresses the Hegelian system. Derrida nicely captures this double movement of subversion and reversion in the subtitle to his essay on Bataille, 'an Hegelianism without reserve', meaning both 'an Hegelianism without reserve funds' and 'an unqualified commitment to Hegelianism'.

Upon Bataille's account, Hegel's insight into negativity is directly related to his blindness with regards to the scope of negativity; but on Derrida's reading, Bataille's insight into Hegel is itself related to a similar blindness. Derrida sees Bataille as working towards deconstruction in recognising that the Hegelian dialectic excludes play and chance; and, following from this, in drawing a distinction between a restricted and a general economy. Bataille's reading of Hegel is exemplary, then, in that it displaces the dialectic and situates it in a new configuration of concepts governed by a re-interpretation of Hegel's own notion of absolute negativity in terms of chance, eroticism, laughter, sacrifice and play. Through his analyses of these various instances of transgression and excess, Bataille maintains that unlimited loss is prior to conservation, or – in his vocabulary – that general economy is structurally prior to restricted economy. However it is instantiated, the principle of unlimited loss confirms the structural stability of a society; but for Bataille it does so only as a phenomenal supplement, as a social particular which is simultaneously excluded and required. And upon Derrida's reading, this is where Bataille remains blind to the scope of negativity.

What Bataille fails to think through is the relation between that which is excluded by the Hegelian dialectic and the enabling

53 Thus Bataille remarks, 'But a transgression is not the same as a back-to-nature movement; it suspends a taboo without suppressing it' then notes, 'There is no need to stress the Hegelian nature of this operation which corresponds with the dialectic phrase described by the untranslatable German 'aufheben': transcending without suppressing.' Bataille, *Death and sensuality* (New York: Walker and Co., 1962), p. 36.

condition of that dialectic. Bataille overturns Hegel's valuing of conservation over loss, work over play, by attending to the structural role played by the supplements of play; but in not questioning the structurality of that structure, he allows his critique to be gathered back into the dialectic. For although a supplement adds itself as a surplus, appearing to work for completeness, it is always unequal to the task. That which requires supplementation already has within it a trace of what the supplement brings: just as speech already harbours the difference which marks the supplement of script, so too labour is always already marked from within by play. Here is Derrida explicating Bataille on Hegel but already moving into position to question Bataille's idea of play:

> In interpreting negativity as labor, in betting for discourse, meaning, history, etc., Hegel has bet against play, against chance. He has blinded himself to the possibility of his own bet, to the fact that the conscientious suspension of play (for example, the passage through the certitude of oneself and through lordship as the independence of self-consciousness) was itself a phase of play; and to the fact that play *includes* the work of meaning or the meaning of work, and includes them not in terms of *knowledge*, but in terms of *inscription*: meaning is a *function* of play, is inscribed in a certain place in the con-figuration of a meaningless play.[54]

Implicit here, and later drawn out by way of *archi-écriture*, is that play is always already doubled: it is both the supplement of phenomenal play and the transcendental play of *différance*. Bataille may observe that 'In the world of play philosophy dis-integrates',[55] but Derrida accuses Bataille of not thinking 'play' radically and thus allowing philosophy to be reintegrated by the dialectic. Whereas Bataille embraces the negativity of trans-gression and excess, at the level of the phenomenal eroticism, play and so forth, Derrida affirms these at both a phenomenal and a transcendental level. *Différance* at once accounts for the excess of textual meaning at the level of discourse and names the condition of possibility for meaning as such. Or in terms of supplementation, Bataille proposes the structural importance of excess while Derrida shows that the supplement of phenomenal excess leads us to recognise that the entire self-grounding dialec-

54 Derrida, *Writing*, p. 260.   55 Bataille, *Death and sensuality*, p. 275.

tic is inescapably bound up with groundless play. The supplement's excess goes beyond what Bataille imagines: it underwrites meaning and the dialectic which accounts for meaning.

Let us step back for a moment and see Derrida's reading of Bataille in perspective. Derrida's analysis consists of two stages: after he *retraces* Bataille's distinction between restricted and general economies, he then *supplies* it with what it lacks, an account of the structurality of structure. This supplement is more than adequate to fill the gap in Bataille's reasoning, however, for the account of structurality Derrida provides exceeds what is required: it points to the implicit transcendental commitment of Bataille's phenomenal distinction. Bataille has already espoused play as negativity, but Derrida points out the extent of this commitment. 'The supplement', Derrida tells us elsewhere, 'can only respond to the nonlogical logic of a game. That game is the play of the world'.[56] We can therefore distinguish between two sorts of supplement and, accordingly, two sorts of negativity: the phenomenal, which works within a restricted economy and thus within metaphysics; and the transcendental, which defines a general economy and which questions metaphysics. And as explained in part II, the phenomenal and the transcendental are mutually dependent, so restricted negativity will always involve general negativity, and *vice versa*.

To return to the argument. Just as Bataille convicts Hegel of a blindness with regards to the scope of negativity, so too with Derrida on Bataille. Yet there is a sense in which Derrida also remains blind to the scope of negativity: not because there is anything more negative than the play of *le supplément*, but because Derrida fails to recognise that negative theology has deconstructive power. We are used to Derrida's insistence that negative theology always answers to positive onto-theology. Here, though, his remarks are guarded:

> Bataille's atheology is also an a-teleology and an aneschatology. Even in its discourse, which already must be distinguished from sovereign affirmation, this atheology does not, however, proceed along the lines of negative theology; lines that could not fail to fascinate Bataille, but which, perhaps, still reserved, beyond all the rejected predicates, and even 'beyond being', a 'super-essentiality'; beyond the categories of being, a

56 Derrida, *Of grammatology*, p. 259.

supreme being and an indestructible meaning. Perhaps: for here we are touching upon the limits and the greatest audacities of discourse in Western thought.[57]

As the words 'superessentiality' and 'beyond being' suggest, Derrida has Pseudo-Dionysius in mind. However, it is equally clear that Derrida's reading of Pseudo-Dionysius is largely determined by *Aquinas's* reading of that author.

There is no reason to assimilate St Thomas's version of negative theology to deconstruction, but does *The mystical theology* accord with St Thomas's interpretation? Textual evidence constrains us to say no. Even *The divine names*, which is usually taken as the source of Pseudo-Dionysius's positive theology, begins and ends by stating that negative theology is to be preferred to positive theology. The text starts by telling us that positive theology is necessary but necessary only as a route to negative theology. The point of theology is to pass from knowing to unknowing, to attain 'that Union which exceeds our faculty, and exercise of discursive, and of intuitive reason'.[58] In the middle of the text Pseudo-Dionysius reminds us of the superiority of negative theology, informing us that 'the Divinest Knowledge of God, the [*sic*] which is received through Unknowing, is obtained in that communion which transcends the mind'.[59] And the text concludes with Pseudo-Dionysius underlining the point: 'we have given our preference to the Negative method'.[60] Rather than serving to correct positive theology, as St Thomas would have it, negative theology is argued to be correct in itself.

But if negative theology is the correct way to talk of God it must be correct in a peculiar sense of the word. For negative theology is engendered only with respect to positive theology, and this would seem to grant priority to positive theology. The theologies are bound up with one another, as Pseudo-Dionysius remarks in his ninth letter:

> The theological tradition is double, being on the one hand, a tradition which is not expressed in words and which is mystical and, on the other hand, a tradition which makes manifest

57 Derrida, *Writing*, p. 271.
58 Dionysius, *The divine names* I.i. 585B–588A (Rolt, p. 51).
59 Dionysius, *The divine names* VII. iii. 872B (Rolt, p. 152).
60 Dionysius, *The divine names* XIII. iii. 981B (Rolt, p. 198).

199

and is better known. One is symbolic and aims at initiation; the other is philosophical and demonstrative. What is not said is woven together with what is said. One persuades and makes known the truth of what is said, the other fulfills and situates souls in God through a mystical guidance which is not learned by teaching.[61]

So, the theologies are not separately developed. Despite Pseudo-Dionysius's appeal to silence, negative theology is prized in *The divine names*, and positive theology is assumed in *The mystical theology*. The difference between the texts is a matter of emphasis. But while negative theology may be superior to positive theology, we still have no definite idea as to their relationship. We cannot just deny St Thomas's point that negative theology confirms positive theology. There are passages throughout the *Areopagitica* which suggest that the progressive negations of negative theology serve to reveal and affirm God's preeminence – and these cannot be easily dismissed.[62]

John Jones is of assistance here. In his acute and timely commentary on *The divine names* and *Mystical theology*, he draws attention to a doubling within theology and negative theology:

> There is a double sense to negative theology. On the one hand, negative theology functions within affirmative theology or, more specifically, metaphysics to express the preeminence of the divine cause. Here, if you will, the negations are 'super affirmations'. On the other hand, negative theology provides the foundation for mystical unity with the divinity. Here negative (mystical) theology denies all that is and all reference to beings and, by my interpretation, ultimately denies all affirmative theology and, hence, metaphysics. Negative (mystical) theology involves the ultimate denial of divine causality and preeminence.[63]

First of all, we can use this distinction to clarify what happens in St Thomas's account of negative theology. St Thomas contends

---

61 Dionyius, Letter IX. 1106C-D. Quoted by J. D. Jones in his introduction to *The divine names and mystical theology*, p. 102.
62 Consider, for example, '. . .that we may offer Him that transcends all things the praises of a transcendent hymnody, which we shall do by denying or removing all things that are like as men who, carving a statue out of marble, remove all the impediments that hinder the clear perceptive of the latent image and by this mere removal displace the hidden statue itself in its hidden beauty', *Mystical theology* II. 1025B (Rolt, p. 195).
63 John D. Jones, trans. *The divine names and mystical theology*, p. 20, n.20.

that theology is characterised by its *positive* statements about God; negative theology is required only to draw attention to the imperfections in the predicates we attach to God. In the vocabulary we have developed, negative theology supplements positive theology; it comes to fill a lack in positive theology, a lack which results from the use of improper predicates.

There is no difficulty in agreeing with Jones that negative theology, thus understood, is metaphysical. But we cannot agree that what he calls negative (mystical) theology provides us with an exit from metaphysics, as the *denial* of metaphysics is itself a metaphysical gesture. The relation between the two negative theologies is one of supplementarity. Negative theology is invoked to supply what is lacking within positive theology; however, in supplying what is needed the supplement supplants what calls for supplementation. Negative theology supplies positive theology with what it lacks: a guarantee that improper predicates can speak of *God*, not solely a human image of God. As soon as this occurs, though, attention is drawn to the distinction between the proper and the improper. Even the proper predicates which one ascribes to God in positive theology – that He is good, He is one and that He is truth, and so on – are seen to be improper and so require negation if they are to refer to God. Pseudo-Dionysius acknowledges this at the end of *The mystical theology* when the proper names of God are denied just as the improper names have been:

> nor does It belong to the category of non-existence or to that of existence; nor do existent beings know It as It actually is, nor does It know them as they actually are; nor can the reason attain to It to name It or to know It; nor is it [*sic*] darkness, nor is It light, or error, or truth; nor can any affirmation or negation apply to it [*sic*]; for while applying affirmations or negations to those orders of being that come next to It, we apply not unto It either affirmation or negation, inasmuch as It transcends all affirmation by being the perfect and unique Cause of all things, and transcends all negation by the pre-eminence of Its simple and absolute nature – free from every limitation and beyond them all.[64]

So for Pseudo-Dionysius, negative theology is both within metaphysics, as a restricted economy, and outside it as a general economy. That is, negative theology plays a role within the

64 Dionysius, *The divine names and the mystical theology* (trans. Rolt), p. 201.

201

phenomenon of positive theology but it also shows that positive theology is situated with regards to a radical negative theology which precedes it. In short, negative theology performs the deconstruction of positive theology. This description is important to us, for several reasons: it allows us to describe negative theology and its complex relations with positive theology with far more precision than has yet been available; it clarifies 'non-metaphysical theology', explains in what sense negative theology can be a non-metaphysical theology, and establishes the limits within which this description is accurate; and it demystifies certain descriptions of deconstruction as an atheological discourse: on the contrary, in some contexts it is theological discourse *par excellence*.

It may be objected that even at the end of *The mystical theology* Pseudo-Dionysius makes positive statements about God; in chapter 5, God is still the transcendent 'superessentiality' addressed in chapter 2. And if this is so, we cannot rightly say that negative theology is a mode of deconstruction, since deconstruction is always directed against presence. While this objection is pressing when addressed to Rolt's translation, it is beside the point when one returns to the actual text of Pseudo-Dionysius. The word Rolt translates by 'superessential' is *hyperousios*. The English word, when used to describe God, suggests that God is the highest being, that He exists yet in a way which transcends finite beings. The Greek word, however, makes no such claim; indeed, the prefix *'hyper'* has a negative rather than a positive force. To say that God is *hyperousios* is to deny that God is a being of any kind, even the highest or original being. As Jones remarks, Pseudo-Dionysius denies that God is a being and denies that God is be-ing *(on)*. The divinity, he says, is 'beyond be-ing beyond-beingly before all' or – to borrow Levinas' concise formulation – *otherwise than being*.[65] Given this, Derrida is wrong to say that negative theology reserves a supreme being beyond the categories of being. Just as 'sign' must be crossed out in the deconstruction of metaphysics, so too must 'God' in the deconstruction of positive theology.[66] The God of negative theology is transcendent in that He transcends being, all conceptions of being as presence, as well as the categories of gender.

65 Jones, p. 32, n. 64. Jones is referring to *The divine names* V. 8. 824B.
66 J.-L. Marion, for example, crosses out 'Dieu' throughout *Dieu sans être*.

The negative theologian uses language under erasure; and this, I think, gives us a better account of what happens in mystical discourse than has been done under the familiar rubric of 'paradox'.

This brings us to the end of our discussion of negative theology as supplement; but before we can conclude we must return, very briefly, to what I have called the economy of mysticism. We saw at the beginning of the chapter that allegory, negative theology and mystical experience are often taken to be mutually implicative. Since then, however, our discussion of supplementarity has put us in a position where we can explain more fully the working of this economy. The logic of the supplement begins to operate whenever we have an hierarchic distinction between an inside and an outside – just the situation we have with the economy of mysticism. Allegory, mystical experience and negative theology has each been held, often at the one time, to be essential to Christianity; however, they have also been recognised as threatening the original purity of the faith.

The main argument against the orthodoxy of allegory rests on the claim that it is radically unhistorical whereas Christianity finds its meaning within history. Jean Daniélou draws a line between the 'general tradition of the Church and the private interpretations of the Fathers' in terms of typology and allegory.[67] The distinction is nicely made by Woollcombe. 'Typological exegesis is the search for linkages between events, persons or things *within the historical framework of revelation*', he writes, 'whereas allegorism is the search for a secondary and hidden meaning underlying the primary and obvious meaning of a narrative'.[68] There is, as he notes, no necessary connection between allegory and history; and, for Daniélou, 'it is necessary to set up a rigorous distinction' between them, between what is authentically Christian and what is inherited from Philo and the pagans.[69] Allegory, claims Daniélou, is capable of 'corrupting . . .

67 Jean Daniélou, *From shadows to reality* (London: Burns and Oates, 1960), p. 149.
68 K. J. Woollcombe, 'The Biblical origins and patristic development of typology', in *Essays on typology* by G. W. H. Lampe and K. J. Woollcombe. Studies in Biblical Theology No. 22 (London: SCM Press, 1957), p. 40.
69 Daniélou, 'The problem of symbolism', *Thought* (New York), 25 (1950), p. 435.

the whole nature of true typology'; it is 'a perpetual danger that menaces the symbolic interpretation of Scripture'; it is a 'distortion' and 'entirely foreign to genuine tradition'.[70]

These oppositions between normality and abnormality, interiority and exteriority, purity and corruption, are also to be found in accounts of mystical experience. For Margaret Smith, mysticism is the 'most vital element in all true religion, rising up in revolt against cold formality and religious torpor'; Evelyn Underhill agrees, remarking that mysticism represents 'in its intensive form the essential religious experience of man'; and Otto Pfleiderer also recognises mysticism as 'the religious life at its very heart and centre'.[71] Yet, as David Knowles remarks, mysticism is also frequently 'regarded as something abnormal and occasionally, if not wholly, "extraordinary"'; and Lossky comments how 'mysticism is frequently opposed to theology'.[72] In his influential *Agape and eros*, Anders Nygren argues that whereas the Agape motif defines true Christianity, mysticism derives from the Greek motif of Eros and is consequently outside the original purity of the faith, entering it only as a corrupting element. Interestingly enough, Nygren finds a link between the domestication of the Eros motif and the allegorical hermeneutic. 'Thus the conflict between Hellenistic piety and Christianity is settled for the Alexandrian theologians; Eros and Agape have come to terms', he writes, '*But the Eros motif retains the ascendency, for it is allowed to represent the deeper, spiritual meaning of Christianity*'.[73] For Nygren, allegory and mysticism are inextricably linked, and alien to the spirit of Christianity.

If both mysticism and the allegorical hermeneutic are thus associated and condemned as parasitical, the same is true of negative theology. 'Argument about the roots of negative theology is part of the old question: What is there common between

70 The first two quotations are from Daniélou's 'The problem of symbolism', p. 438; the second two are from his 'The Fathers and the scriptures', *Theology: A Monthly Review*, 57 (1954), pp. 86, 88.
71 Margaret Smith, *An introduction to the history of mysticism* (1930; rpt. Amsterdam: Philo Press, 1973), p. 3; E. Underhill, *Mysticism* (1911; rpt. New York: E.P. Dutton, 1961), p. vii of 1930 Preface; Otto Pfleiderer, *Primitive Christianity*, quoted by Smith, p. 3.
72 David Knowles, *What is mysticism?* (London: Burns and Oates Ltd., 1967), p. 43; V. Lossky, *The mystical theology of the eastern Church*, p. 7.
73 Anders Nygren, *Agape and eros*, trans. P.S. Watson (London: S.P.C.K., 1953), p. 353.

Athens and Jerusalem?' remarks Ardley.[74] Without the 'proper stance' of St Thomas's harmonising of negative and positive theology, he suggests, negative theology is 'in peril of drifting to disaster' and 'prey to aberrations'.[75] And here Ardley seems to have in mind the sort of accusations which have been levelled at Pseudo-Dionysius, that negative theology leads him to confuse Christ's person and nature. Allegory, mystical experience and negative theology are associated not because they are absolutely exterior to the faith but because they supplement it. Daniélou does not dismiss allegory out of hand; he devalues it in comparison with typology and suggests that it may serve to supplement the true interpretation of scripture. Similarly, Nygren does not seek to deny that certain persons have enjoyed mystical union with God; his point is that the Eros motif should remain marginal with respect to the Agape motif. And finally Ardley wishes to conserve negative theology but only as a supplement to positive theology. In each case the supplement is held to be limited, adequate to what it supplements.

At stake in construing each of allegory, mysticism and negative theology as a process of corruption, is the notion of an original purity, unique to Christianity and manifested in history. Each argument is directed at historical encroachments upon Christianity, and each assumes that there is an original, pure form of the faith that precedes the process of corruption. The situation is exactly parallel to that recorded in the *Corpus hermeticum*, the fear expressed by Hermes that 'there will be many who make philosophy [i.e. the Hermetic doctrine] hard to understand, and corrupt it with manifold speculations'.[76] And as the corruption of the Hermetic doctrine does not come entirely from outside but through the hermeneutic which preserved the doctrine for the initiated whilst simultaneously concealing it from the uninitiated, so too the 'process of corruption' claimed to infect Christianity in its historical development can be seen to be grounded within the faith itself. To distinguish typology from allegory, true interpretation from false, and thereby to maintain the purity of the faith, it is necessary to draw a line between

74 G. Ardley, 'From Greek philosophy to apophatic theology', in *The via negativa*, p. 135.
75 Ardley, p. 142.
76 W. Scott, ed. and trans., *Hermetica* (Oxford: Oxford University Press, 1936), Vol. 1, p. 311.

them, to divide the inside from the outside. For Daniélou, this line runs between the public and the private; typology, unlike allegory, 'expresses the inherent intelligibility of history' and is thus open to public inspection.[77] What makes history intelligible as a sequence of types, however, is revelation which, for Daniélou, must be public and must originate outside history. That is, the inside – typology – depends for its constitution upon what comes from outside history; and since it is the allegorical hermeneutic which removes the meaning of scripture from history, typology depends upon that which also constitutes allegory. This does not mean that we cannot distinguish between typology and allegory; but it does mean that, if allegory is a process of corruption, it is not wholly external to typology. Once more, a restricted economy is underwritten by a general economy.

77 Daniélou, 'The conception of history in the Christian tradition', *Journal of Religion*, 30 (1950), p. 173.

7 | Kant: mysticism and parerga

Introduction

The previous chapter identified and analysed a phenomenon which I called 'the economy of mysticism'. I was concerned there to see in what ways deconstruction could illuminate the workings of mystical discourse. Rather than being a restricted economy framed by positive theology, negative theology is, I argued, also a general economy which underwrites positive theology. At the beginning of my discussion, however, I sug-- gested that deconstruction could clarify how negative theology works within philosophy; and this suggestion answers to a more commonly acknowledged framing of mysticism as philosophy's 'other'. We could doubtless trace this framing of mysticism back past Russell and Wittgenstein to Leibniz and indeed back to a certain layer of Plato's text; but I wish instead to examine the point at which the full force of this distinction is felt, and that requires us to dwell upon the thought of Immanuel Kant.

Our examination will proceed along two lines, for we cannot discuss the distinction between philosophy and mysticism in any detail without also considering the economy of mysticism. So far I have considered this economy at work in theological discourse; now, though, I shall trace its more covert operations in Kant's philosophy. Whatever else it does, the Kantian transcendental consciousness performs a hermeneutic function of great force and consequence: it interprets representations according to its own rules, leaving the realm of presence outside hermeneutic inquiry. With respect to both philosophy and religion this hermeneutic systematically relegates mystical experience, as Kant conceives it, to a marginal position. Yet this exclusion, I shall argue, has a peculiar effect upon Kant's system. In denying mystical *experience* Kant's hermeneutic simultane-

207

ously leads him to affirm a mystical *theology*, in philosophy as well as religion. Derrida may tell us that negative theology travels 'through philosophical discourse as through a foreign medium',[1] but upon my reading Kant's philosophical discourse *is* a negative theology. If this is so, we may rightly say that the deconstruction of the Kantian philosophy is performed by that which Kant sets beyond philosophy, namely mysticism.

Derrida has written several essays upon Kant, and in developing my case I shall have recourse to his reading of Kant's remarks on frames and parerga. One of the issues which will direct our discussion, albeit from a distance, is a certain framing of Kant and Derrida, one I have already mentioned and one which will refine our view of the relation between philosophy and deconstruction. Rorty has argued that Derrida is suggesting 'how things might look if we did not have Kantian philosophy built into the fabric of our intellectual life'.[2] On the contrary, Derrida contends that one cannot unravel the Kantian philosophy from this fabric. Our intellectual life is composed of a philosophical warp and a non-philosophical woof. What Derrida does, and does very effectively, is show how any given text is a fabrication, how its tension varies, how one can detect loose ends in even the smoothest production. Indeed, as we shall see, Derrida cannot entirely unravel the Kantianism in his own discourse.

1 Mysticism and the 'death of philosophy'

From his early attack on Swedenborg, *Dreams of a spirit-seer*, to the late *Conflict of faculties*, Kant remains constant in his strong condemnation of what he calls 'mysticism' *(die Mystik)*. At no time, however, does he discuss or even allude to specific texts by Pseudo-Dionysius, the *Cloud*-author, Meister Eckhart, St Teresa of Avila, Jacob Böhme or, for that matter, any person who is taken to be a mystic; and it is possible that he had no first-hand knowledge of any of these writers. It is also unlikely that Kant had any direct acquaintance with the writings of the eastern mystics, although he sometimes has these in mind when addressing the subject. Our first task, therefore, is to work out what Kant understands mysticism to be.

1 Derrida, *Writing*, p. 116.   2 Rorty, *Consequences of pragmatism*, p. 98.

Kant's most sharply focused description of mysticism is found in his *Lectures on philosophical theology*. 'We men know very little a priori, and have our senses to thank for nearly all our knowledge', he begins.[3] He goes on to distinguish between man's knowledge and God's. God has no *conceptus*, only *intuitus*: so whereas God knows things as they are in themselves, *modum noumenon*, man can know things only as they appear to us, *modum phænomenon*. After this brief rehearsal of the critical epistemology, Kant turns his attention to mysticism:

> If we were to flatter ourselves so much as to claim that we know the *modum noumenon*, then we would have to be in community with God so as to participate immediately in the divine ideas, which are the authors of all things in themselves. To expect this in the present life is the business of mystics and theosophists. Thus arises the mystical self-annihilation of China, Tibet, and India, in which one is under the delusion that he will finally be dissolved in the Godhead.[4]

Upon Kant's understanding, the *sine qua non* of mysticism is immediate contact with God. Mysticism is therefore prone to two kinds of objections. First, the claim that one can enjoy an unmediated experience of God is epistemologically untenable. Experience, for Kant, involves a synthesis of sensible intuitions with the concepts of the understanding. And as the concepts necessarily mediate objects of experience, for human beings there can be no experience of immediate intellectual intuition. A 'transcendental [*übersinnliche*] experience', Kant insists, 'is impossible' because it is contradictory.[5] Second, Kant distrusts mysticism on moral grounds, fearing that the mystic may claim an individual privilege to act in a manner which would defy the moral law: this is the basis for his association of mysticism and fanaticism (*Schwärmerei*). In short, he fears that mystical experience could be cognitively or morally significant.

Kant's understanding of mysticism is both more narrow and more broad than is usual today. It is true that he distinguishes between gradations of mysticism: that which claims to know God, and that which claims to feel God's presence. All the same, Kant defines mystical experience in terms of immediacy, and

---

3 Kant, *Lectures on philosophical theology*, p. 86.   4 Kant, *Lectures*, p. 86.
5 Kant, *Der Streit der philosophischen Fakultät mit der theologischen*, in Kant's *Werke*, ed. E. Cassirer *et al*. (Berlin: Bruno Cassirer, 1912–22), p. 358.

this is a long way from the finely discriminating taxonomy of mystical experience one finds in the writings of individual mystics. St Teresa, for instance, is positive that some mystical experiences occur when one is *not* enjoying immediate union with God. 'It should be noted', she writes, 'that we never, I think, see visions or hear these words when the soul is in union during an actual state of rapture, for then . . . all the faculties are wholly lost, and at that time I do not believe there is any seeing, hearing or understanding at all'.[6] At the same time, Kant's notion of mysticism is wide enough to accommodate alchemy and occultism. If, as Kant proposes, we are to subsume theosophy under 'mysticism' it can only be on account of its adherence to something like the Neoplatonic theory of emanation. And while Swedenborg and others do seem to have believed that all reality is, in some sense, spiritual, this is far too lax a criterion by which to label them 'mystics'. We need a way of distinguishing between a claim that God has revealed Himself to someone and the claims which follow from adopting a philosophical system; and Kant does not offer this.

So it may be that Kant's particular remarks upon mysticism are chiefly of historical curiosity. Yet the ways in which Kant *frames* mysticism have been decisive, in the post-Kantian reception of mysticism and in the determination of 'philosophy'. From the institution of philosophy as an autonomous academic subject in the Enlightenment to the latter half of the twentieth century, philosophers have shown little interest in the problems generated by the claims of mystics. It was common enough before Kant for philosophy to define itself against poetry or theology; but it is Kant who, more vividly than any before him, introduces mysticism to this role: 'supernatural communication' and 'mystical illumination' become, for Kant, 'the death of all philosophy'.[7] What gives life to the mystic brings death to philosophy: such is the burden of Kantian philosophy. The fundamental distinctions which establish the critical philosophy – between knowing and thinking, cognition and intuition, work and Grace, the moral law and vision – also serve to distinguish philosophy from mysticism. The immediate clarity of the mystic's vision is thus to

6 St Teresa, *The life of the Holy Mother Teresa of Jesus* in *The complete works of St Teresa of Jesus*, trans. E. Allison Peers Vol. 1, p. 158. All further references will be to this edition.
7 Kant, *Von einem neuerdings erhobenen vornehmen Ton*, in Kant's *Werke*, Vol. VI, pp. 487, 495.

be opposed by a clarity of another kind which is revealed in and through a rigorous analysis of concepts, a logical enquiry into the scope and status of human knowledge, and, now more than was ever envisioned in the Enlightenment, an inspection of the connections between the structures of language and knowledge. By these means philosophers since Kant have established a discipline that can look outside its borders with an achieved confidence, folding what is outside into its own territory, expanding itself by means of the familiar formula 'the philosophy of x' where the unknown element can be replaced by almost any other area of enquiry. History, science, theology, psychology, law, and the many other areas that philosophy interrogates as a matter of course, share assumptions with philosophy, particularly a faith in the eminence of reason, which enables philosophy to bring them under its surveillance.

Yet if the borders of philosophy are continually expanding, it is nonetheless true that mysticism represents philosophy's 'other', a discourse (or, at any rate, a family of discourses) concerned with truth and reality but which repudiates philosophical method and which prizes certain experiences over reason and language. Whereas philosophy licenses itself as prosecutor and judge, mysticism appears closed to dialectical inspection. The mystic's vision finds expression in metaphors, hyperboles, oxymorons, prosopopoeia – in tropes of every kind – which are anathema to philosophical lucidity, and all the more alien to philosophy since the thought which gives rise to them seems anything but confused. Resisting attempts to be exclusively classified as 'literature', mystical texts often claim a special authority which stands at odds with that of philosophy and, at times, that of theology. Thus while the philosophy of religion has become a standard branch of philosophy, the description 'philosophy of mysticism' is seldom used when discussing mystical experiences or mystical texts. Problems arising from mysticism are conventionally treated under the rubric of the philosophy of religion, as a species of problem rather than as a different kind. Indeed, for Kant 'the philosophy of mysticism' would be a contradiction. It would be nothing less than the philosophy of the death of philosophy.

If philosophy and mysticism are to be distinguished in such a manner, how then is it possible for Kant to philosophise about mysticism? He draws another distinction, this time between religion and mysticism. It surely comes as no surprise to find that Kant relegates anything which could be associated with mysticism – works of Grace, miracles, mysteries, and the means of Grace – to the status of parerga to religion properly regarded. In order to make sense of this move, we must become clear as to what Kant understands by 'parergon'. In *The critique of judgement* we are informed that a parergon is 'only an adjunct, and not an intrinsic constituent in the complete representation of the object', and that 'in augmenting the delight of taste [it] does so only by means of its form'.[8] Examples are then offered: 'Thus it is with the frames of pictures or the drapery on statues, or the colonnades of palaces'; and Kant is quick to point out that parerga – unlike what he calls *finery* – play some role, albeit limited, in the composition of the art work.[9]

It is Kant's later remarks upon parerga in *Religion within the limits of reason alone*, however, which most concern us. His introductory observations on the matter are worth attention:

> This General Observation is the first of four which are appended, one to each Book of this work, and which might bear the titles, (1) Works of Grace, (2) Miracles, (3) Mysteries, and (4) Means of Grace. These matters are, as it were, *parerga* to religion within the limits of pure reason; they do not belong within it but border upon it. Reason, conscious of her inability to satisfy her moral need, extends herself to high-flown [*überschwenglich*] ideas capable of supplying this lack, without, however, appropriating these ideas as an extension of her domain. Reason does not dispute the possibility or the reality of the objects of these ideas; she simply cannot adopt them into her maxims of thought and action.[10]

So not everything which is beyond the scope of reasonable religion is a parergon to it: the four parerga answer to acknowledged *moral* needs. As is well known, the essence of religion for Kant is morality: 'Religion', he tells us elsewhere, 'is the recognition of all duties as divine commands'.[11] Also, while a parergon

---

8 Kant, *The critique of judgement*, trans. J. C. Meredith (Oxford: Clarendon Press, 1952), Part I, p. 68.

9 Kant, *The critique of judgement*, Part I, p. 68.

10 Kant, *Religion within the limits of reason alone*, trans. T. M. Greene and H. H. Hudson with a new essay by J. R. Silber (New York: Harper and Row, 1960), pp. 47–48.

11 Kant, *Critique of practical reason and other writings in moral philosophy*, trans. and ed. Lewis White Beck (Chicago: University of Chicago Press, 1949), p. 232. Also see *Religion*, p. 142.

is, as the word itself suggests, beside the work *(ergon)* it nonetheless maintains a rapport with the work. The relation between work and parergon does not admit a rigorous distinction between the essential and the accidental, or the inside and the outside.

What we have, in sum, are four notions which are required for religion and morality yet which are, at the same time, beyond rational discussion. *Dogmatic* faith, Kant tells us, claims to know what is beyond the realm of pure reason, and consequently places its authority in jeopardy. On the other hand, the theory of parerga at once answers to the richness and complexity of religious experience while removing from temptation all questions regarding the realm of the transcendent: it allows a space for faith, but for *reflective* faith. Just as the critical philosophy seeks to replace dogmatic metaphysics, so too reflective faith offers itself as a more circumspect and more honest replacement for dogmatic faith. Transcendental illusions arise from the nature of reason yet are exposed and limited by critique; similarly, the experiential illusions of faith which comprise mysticism arise from the nature of religious feeling and are kept at bay only by the critical theory of parerga. Not only will reflective faith protect us from unreasonable dogma, it will also enable us to avoid the manifold dangers of mysticism:

> As regards the damage resulting from these *morally-transcendent* ideas, when we seek to introduce them into religion, the consequences, listed in the order of the four classes named above, are: (1) [corresponding] to imagined inward experience (works of grace), [the consequence is] *fanaticism*; (2) to alleged external experience (miracles), *superstition*; (3) to a supposed enlightening of the understanding with regard to the supernatural (mysteries), *illumination*, the illusion of the 'adepts'; (4) to hazardous attempts to operate upon the supernatural (means of grace), *thaumaturgy* – sheer aberrations of a reason going beyond its proper limits and that too for a purpose fancied to be moral (pleasing to God).[12]

To protect ourselves from all this we need to have reflective faith; but what is it? 'Faith', Kant writes, 'is the moral attitude of reason in its assurance of the truth of what is beyond the reach of theoretical knowledge'.[13] Thus there is an essential connection

---

12 Kant, *Religion*, p. 48.   13 Kant, *The critique of judgement*, Part II, p. 145.

between faith and morality; moreover, faith is grounded in its moral specificity. In order to characterise this connection, though, we need to draw out a distinction occluded in the word 'assurance'. For Kant elsewhere distinguishes between necessary belief, which is guaranteed by transcendental argument, and pragmatic belief. The latter works in the context of other possible conditions yet is sufficient to form the ground for 'the actual employment of means to certain actions'.[14]

Both kinds of faith fall under the aegis of practical reason, since the only way in which faith can become assertoric is to yield to the guidance of the moral law. Our belief in God as the moral author of the world is necessary, Kant contends, because only the existence of God could possibly underwrite our judgements and because there can be no exemption from judging. Quite plainly this sort of critical faith is not claimed by the mystic. Nor can he or she lay claim to pragmatic faith, Kant thinks, as this requires the weighing up of alternatives which is just what the mystic does not do. A doctor prescribing medicine for a patient in a critical condition relies upon pragmatic belief, but in this instance there is always the possibility that another doctor, called in for a second opinion, might propose a sounder diagnosis. When a mystic claims to have experienced the immediate presence of God, however, Kant thinks that the issue of alternatives cannot arise. And if this is so, the mystic has no moral grounds for belief or action and thus lapses into fanaticism. The problem here, of course, is that there are cases when even someone familiar with a range of mystical experiences, such as St Teresa, considers the possibility that one may be misled in hearing supernatural locutions. One should not act upon a supernatural voice, she recommends, 'without taking the advice of a learned confessor. . . even though one may understand the locutions better and better and it may become evident that they are of God'.[15]

Kant's general case against mysticism may show a contempt for (or even ignorance of) the particular case, but let us put this to one side and concentrate upon his framing of the situation which is, as we have seen, a discourse upon the *frame*. The parerga, recall, cannot be wholly eliminated from the system of

---

14 Kant, *Critique of pure reason*, A 824/B 852.
15 St Teresa, *The interior castle*, Vol. II, p. 283.

religion considered within the limits of reason alone: they supply a lack within that system. One of the things which recommends reflective faith is the honesty of admitting that 'if in the inscrutable realm of the supernatural there is something more than she [Reason] can explain to herself, which may yet be necessary as a complement to her moral insufficiency, this will be, even though unknown, available to her good will'.[16] Kant expands upon this modesty of reason in *The conflict of faculties*:

> One can add to this, that faith in this complementation [*Ergaen-zung*: also 'supplementation'] is beatific, because it is only through this that he can summon up courage and a firm attitude toward a God-well-pleasing conduct (as the only pre-condition for the hope of blessedness), that he does not despair in the successful outcome of his end-goal (to be well pleasing to God). – But that he must know and must certainly be able to state, wherein the means of this compensation [*Ersatzes*: also 'replacement', 'restitution'] which in the end is still excessive (and, despite all that God Himself wants to have told us about it, is for us incomprehensible) consists.[17]

Thus the parergon shares the same structure as the supplement: it supplies what is recognised as a lack within religion considered within the limits of reason alone. It would be useful to explore this in more detail, focusing upon mystery, grace and revelation.

One notices, first of all, that in each case there is a quantity of connection between what is within religion, as Kant understands it, and what is rendered marginal. Although Kant plainly regards works of Grace as incomprehensible, an aberration from the point of view of rational religion, he concedes that there is a morally legitimate form of Grace: 'if by nature . . . is understood

---

16 Kant, *Religion*, p. 48.
17 Kant, *Der Streit*, p. 355. Cf. 'The thesis of the moral destiny of our nature, viz. that it is able only in an infinite progress to attain complete fitness to the moral law, is of great use, not merely for the present purpose of supplementing the impotence of speculative reason, but also with respect to religion', *Critique of practical reason*, p. 226; also 'It may even be conceded that one is privileged to supplement this unavoidable lack by a permissible and wholly reasonable hypothesis to the effect that since wisdom, beneficence, etc., are displayed in all the parts offered to our more exact knowledge, it will be the same with the rest', p. 241. Kant also discusses the supplement in these terms in letters to J.C. Lavater, April 26, 1775 and some time after this date. See A. Zweig, ed. and trans., *Kant: philosophical correspondence 1759–99* (Chicago: University of Chicago Press, 1967), pp. 81–83.

the general capacity for accomplishing with one's own power a certain purpose, so is grace nothing more than the essence (*Wesen*) of man'.[18] The same holds true for mysteries. Kant associates special mysteries with superstition and devalues them accordingly, yet allows place within rational religion for the mysteries of the divine call, atonement and election. And finally, while specific revelations are pushed to the borders, general revelation is contained within rational religion: 'God has indeed revealed His will through the moral law in us, but the *causes* due to which a free action on earth occurs or does not occur He has left in . . . obscurity'.[19] Kant is perfectly happy to consider these various parerga as supplements, but if his system is to work these must remain within a restricted economy, supplying a lack yet never supplanting the whole.

But does his system work? We shall see if it does with regards to just one parergon – revelation. Kant allows that God reveals Himself in the moral law, and if this is so he cannot subscribe to a firm distinction between natural and revealed religion. It may be that God reveals Himself in ways other than through the moral law, but the only way in which we can be certain of not being deceived is by trusting the revelation that comes to us mediated by nature, that is, in the moral law. To use his own words, Kant is a 'pure rationalist', one who 'recognizes revelation, but asserts that to know and accept it as real is not a necessary requisite to religion'.[20] The immediate problem that arises here is how Kant can reconcile this with the institution of a revealed religion such as the one he professes to be true, Christianity. At first glance it would seem as though he must admit a special revelation and thereby place the moral law in jeopardy. In order to avoid this, Kant draws another distinction, between natural and learned religion. 'This distinction is very important', he assures us, 'for no inference regarding a religion's qualification or disqualification to be the universal religion of mankind can be drawn merely from its origin, whereas such an inference is possible

18 Kant's negative remarks upon grace as parergon may be found in *Religion*, pp. 48-49 and p. 162. The partial assimilation of 'grace' and 'nature' is found in *Der Streit*, p. 43. I have used Carl A. Raschke's translation as found in his *Moral action, God and history in the thought of Immanuel Kant*, American Academy of Religion Dissertation Series, No. 5 (Missoula, Mont.: Scholars Press in conjunction with A.A.R., 1975), p. 168.
19 Kant, *Religion*, p. 135.   20 Kant, *Religion*, p. 143.

from its capacity or incapacity for general dissemination, and it is this capacity which constitutes the essential character of that religion which ought to be binding upon every man'.[21]

The true religion, Kant thinks, must be able to be accepted universally. And in order for a religion to be universal it must be capable of being disseminated. If this is so, however, the religion cannot be instituted purely and simply by a special revelation; since upon Kant's understanding a special revelation is *ipso facto* ineffable and cannot be communicated. The possibility of universal communication depends upon that which is naturally common to all people and that is, of course, the moral law. This is Kant's solution:

> Such a religion, accordingly, can be *natural*, and at the same time *revealed*, when it is so constituted that men *could and ought to have discovered it* of themselves merely through the use of their reason, although they *would* not have come upon it so early, or over so wide an area, as is required. Hence a revelation thereof at a given time and in a given place might well be wise and very advantageous to the human race, in that, when once the religion thus introduced is here, and has been made known publicly, everyone can henceforth by himself and with his own reason convince himself of its truth. In this event the religion is *objectively* a natural religion, though *subjectively* one that has been revealed; hence it is really entitled to the former name.[22]

We know that Kant's epistemology is, at least in part, an answer to and displacement of Leibniz's strict distinction between truths of reason and truths of fact. Of moment here, though, is the theological consequence of this displacement, what happens when Leibniz's distinction is made in theology. This was Lessing's move when he insisted on a radical separation of events and truth: 'accidental truths of history can never become the proof of necessary truths of reason'.[23] Sympathetic as he is to Lessing's distinction, Kant nonetheless manages to reconcile natural practical reason and supernatural revelation. The supplement of revelation takes place, it seems, at the origin of the Christian religion; it remains, however, secondary to the moral law. Speaking disparagingly of the Jewish faith, Kant argues as follows:

21 Kant, *Religion*, p. 143.   22 Kant, *Religion*, pp. 143-44.
23 H. Chadwick, ed. and trans., *Lessing's theological writings* (Stanford: Stanford University Press, 1957), p. 53. Italics deleted.

when a religion of mere rites and observances has run its course, and when one based on the spirit and the truth (on the moral disposition) is to be established in its stead, it is wholly conformable to man's ordinary ways of thought, though not strictly necessary, for the historical introduction of the latter to be accompanied and, as it were, adorned by miracles, in order to announce the termination of the earlier religion, which without miracles would never have had any authority. Indeed, in order to win over the adherents of the older religion to the new, the new order is interpreted as the fulfilment, at last, of what was only prefigured in the older religion and has all along been the design of Providence. If this be so it is quite useless to debate those narratives or interpretations; the true religion, which in its time needed to be introduced through such expedients, is now here, and from now on is able to maintain itself on rational grounds.[24]

Whereas before we had just two categories to adjust – the natural and the supernatural – Kant now draws our attention to a third. Miracles may be admitted in the institution of true religion; the moral law, being universal, is necessary; and interpretation falls between the two. Just as judgement is found between understanding and reason, in a realm which is neither simply practical nor simply theoretical, so here interpretation is a middle ground between the natural and the supernatural, the necessary and the contingent. Furthermore, interpretation is viewed with a certain ambivalence by Kant. From one point of view, it is necessary if the Jews are to be convinced of Christianity's truth; from another, its necessity is merely historical and is to be replaced by the moral law.

Essential yet dispensable, exterior yet in communication with an interior, interpretation has the structure of a parergon. Doubtless Kant needs this description, as his system requires that adherence to the moral law replace interpretation. A problem arises, though, for what is the moral reading of scripture if not an interpretation? Kant can of course reply that it is the *correct* interpretation, and therefore not an interpretation in the sense which would make it a parergon. But a difficulty nonetheless remains. For when interpreting scripture we need to know what is within the text and what frames it from outside; however, if Kant tells us that the frame is a parergon, an exterior

24 Kant, *Religion*, p. 79.

which helps to constitute an interior, the act of interpretation immediately becomes problematic. Rather than solving the problem of the institution of the true religion, interpretation seems to introduce complications which cannot be easily smoothed over. The problem seems to reside in Kant's hermeneutics, so let us examine this more closely.

2 Kant's hermeneutics and negative theology

The critical philosophy works with two interpretative constraints, both of which appeal, in different ways, to the imposition of structure. In the first place, we have the interpretative role of the transcendental consciousness; and we can best get into a position to discuss this by reconstituting Kant's account of the relation between consciousness, knowledge and interpretation. Knowledge can begin only with the appearing of a phenomenon in the pure forms of sensible intuition. Once presented, this manifold of sensible intuition is synthesised and schematised in an act of the imagination. Before we have knowledge of a phenomenon, however, there must be both an individual consciousness and a guarantee that there *is* a relation between the represented manifold and an object. Both conditions can be met. The understanding supplies us with a concept of an object in general – that which is conceived as substance, perceived in relations of cause and effect, and so forth. We cannot pass from represented manifold to particular object without reference to consciousness, though, since there must be a constant unity of consciousness to accompany each represented manifold. Without this 'pure apperception', as Kant calls it, representations would be impossible or void of import. Yet in becoming conscious of objects, I also become conscious of myself as conscious of objects. Self-consciousness and intentional consciousness are therefore correlative for Kant. Indeed, unless there is a unity of pure apperception and representation there can be no knowledge. In other words, the unity of apperception is transcendental.

The understanding, Kant tells us, is 'nothing but the faculty of combining *a priori*, and of bringing the manifold of given representations under the unity of apperception'.[25] Phenomena,

25 Kant, *Critique of pure reason*, B 134.

therefore, are ultimately subject to the *a priori* concepts of the understanding. Unlike the forms of intuition, which – although *a priori* – are passive and immediate, the concepts of the understanding are actively engaged in mediation. Understanding judges; but as 'judgement' means no more here than mediate knowledge of an object, we may say, with at least as much accuracy, that the categories *interpret* phenomena, though only formally.[26] The first interpretative constraint, then, is the structure of the human consciousness. And the second constraint has already entered our discussion: it is the restriction of context, without which no interpretation could begin. We need not go into the various relations between the active faculties of imagination, understanding and reason to see that the activity of interpretation is framed by understanding. And we will not dwell upon this framing with regards to consciousness, since the same points can be made, with greater pertinence, if we turn to Kant's framing of mysticism.

Rational religion is bordered by four elements which we may associate with mysticism. This entire picture, however, is itself framed – not just once but twice. First of all, religion is framed by the moral law. Kant is plain that morality does not depend upon religion but, on the contrary, that the moral law provides the only reliable path to God. 'The moral law commands us to make the highest possible good in a world the final object of all our conduct'; yet this highest good can be attained only with God's help, and so religion must be 'added' to morality.[27] This addition recalls something we have already discussed, Kant's assurance of reason's entitlement to believe in God's supplementation of our inadequate justness. We have a complicated situation, then. Without morality, religion would not know that mysticism was merely supplementary and, consequently, would remain threatened by the various dangers of mysticism. So morality protects religion from the supplement. At the same time, morality recognises a lack within itself which only religion can supply and thus fashions religion as a supplement to itself. Furthermore, once supplemented, morality allows the possibility, on its own terms, of divine supplementation. The difference between religion before and after its moral basis has been provided is that the

26 Despite appearances, this characterisation of the categories is not simply and directly traceable to post-structuralist interest in interpretation. Writing in 1929, F. E. England describes the categories as 'principles of interpretation', *Kant's conception of God* (1929; rpt. New York: Humanities Press, 1968), p. 99.
27 Kant, *Critique of practical reason*, p. 232.

supplement has been limited to a restricted economy; it is no longer morally dangerous.

The second framing of religion comes from Kantian epistemology. Before the critical philosophy, religion was not aware of the impossibility of mystical experience: only God can possibly have an intuition which is purely intelligible, and so only God can have experience and knowledge of Himself. The framing of religion by concepts, by the privileged realm of epistemology, responds not to a lack of concepts in religion but to what Kant considers an illegitimate use of concepts. There must be, he says, a strict distinction between knowing and thinking. Theoretical reason assures us that there is nothing logically impossible in the concept of God; practical reason tells us that there is a God; so it is entirely reasonable, indeed it is our duty, to think God, though not to claim knowledge of Him. All this is familiar, so familiar perhaps that it prevents us from seeing something very odd: a way in which Kant, despite himself, manages to supply the basis for a mystical theology.

We will get further more quickly, I think, if we put to one side one possible way of construing the critical philosophy as a displaced mysticism. One finds with Fichte, Schelling, and the young Hegel a particular reading of Kant which centres upon re-interpreting the doctrine of pure apperception. Walter Cerf puts it well when, in his imaginative reconstruction of a discussion between Kant, Schelling and Hegel, the latter two philosophers demonstrate what they take to be a fundamental flaw in Kant's system. The flaw they point out is that Kant unknowingly makes 'intellectual intuition the ultimate basis of all knowledge claims'; and the argument they propose consists in showing that the unity of nature depends ultimately upon the unity of the Kantian 'I think' in its act of thought; and that in this very move Kant unwittingly gives transcendental apperception the characteristic which marks intellectual intuition. 'To think oneself as thinking – pure self-consciousness – is to give oneself existence as a pure I', they argue, doubtless thinking of Kant's remark in the first *Critique* that 'The "I think" expresses the act of determining my existence'.[28]

28 Walter Cerf, 'Speculative philosophy and intellectual intuition: an introduction to Hegel's *Essays'*, in Hegel's *The difference between Fichte's and Schelling's system of philosophy*, p. xxviii; and I. Kant, *Critique of pure reason*, B 159 a. Consider, in this regard, the following remark by Schelling: 'This intellectual intuition takes place whenever I cease to be an object for myself, when –

Cerf makes no mention of Fichte in this regard, but there is an obvious connection. Introducing the second edition of his *Science of knowledge*, Fichte retraces the connection of ideas in the Kantian system and supplies it with what it seems to lack:

> Intellectual intuition in the Kantian sense is a wraith which fades in our grasp when we try to think it, and deserves not even a name. The intellectual intuition alluded to in the Science of Knowledge refers, not to existence at all, but rather to action, and simply finds no mention in Kant (unless, perhaps, under the title of *pure apperception*). Yet it is nonetheless possible to point out also in the Kantian system the precise point at which it should have been mentioned. Since Kant, we have all heard, surely, of the categorical imperative? Now what sort of consciousness is that? . . . – This consciousness is undoubtedly immediate, but not sensory; hence it is precisely what I call 'intellectual intuition'.[29]

Fichte does not argue on the basis of this that Kant's argument from epistemology against mysticism is radically mistaken. If we were to accept the reading of Kant circulating amongst Schelling, Fichte and the young Hegel, this option would be open to us. But the question is whether this reading of intellectual intuition is persuasive, and a glance at its use in the first *Critique* is sufficient to see that it is not.[30]

While we cannot convict Kant's case against mystical experience on the charge of internal inconsistency, it is nevertheless open to other objections. We could contest what Kant means by 'mystical', arguing – as we have already begun to do – that not all mystical experience is unmediated. And we could also, like Hamann and Hegel, draw attention to the narrow sense Kant attributes to 'possible experience' in setting his 'necessary conditions of possible experience'.[31] Either line of attack would put

withdrawn into itself – the intuiting subject is identical with the intuited. In this moment of intuition, time and duration vanish for us; it is not we who are in time, but time is in us; in fact it is not time but rather pure absolute eternity that is in ourselves. It is not we who are lost in the intuition of the objective world; it is the world that is lost in our intuition'. F. W .J. Schelling, 'Philosophical letters on dogmatism and criticism', in *The unconditional in human knowledge*, trans. and commentary Fritz Marti (Lewisburg: Bucknell University Press, 1980), p. 181.

29 J. G. Fichte, *Science of knowledge*, ed. and trans. Peter Heath and John Lachs (Cambridge: Cambridge University, Press, 1982), p. 46.

30 Kant, *Critique of pure reason*, B. xl n.

31 Hamann insists, *contra* Kant, that 'Experience and revelation are one and the same' in his letter to Jacobi, 14 November, 1784. This is quoted by R. G. Smith, *J. G. Hamann 1730–1788*, p. 77. Also see Hegel's *Lectures on the history of philosophy*, Vol. III, p. 425.

pressure on Kant's case; but I wish to try another approach. A moment ago I suggested that we are perhaps overfamiliar with Kant's epistemological framing of religion and mysticism. And now I want to follow this up by arguing that this framing is something of a frame-up. For what reason is there to suppose, as Kant does, that the mystic wants to make epistemological claims? What if it were epistemology which he or she wished to render problematic in discourse with and on God? To be sure, it cannot be denied that the mystic's discourse makes an epistemological claim. That is not at issue; what is in question, though, is the status of that epistemological claim. These considerations point us in a different direction from that which Fichte seems to offer, a direction which is anticipated by several descriptions of Kant as a negative theologian.[32]

Our most suitable point of entry is Kant's treatment of interpretation. To avoid confusion, we shall distinguish between the interpretative function of the transcendental consciousness and the textual practice of exegesis. And to start with we shall take stock of Kant's view of the relation between textual interpretation and mysticism. This topic receives its most focussed discussion in *The conflict of faculties* where we find a dispute between the biblical theologian and the philosopher over biblical exegesis. The biblical theologian, Kant says, is apt to take 'the cloak of religion for religion itself' and this occurs, 'when he must explain, e.g. the whole Old Testament as a continuing allegory of prototypes and symbolic images [*Vorstellungen*] of the state of religion that is yet to come, when he does not want to assume that what happened in those days was already true religion, whereby the new (that surely cannot be truer than true) would be made dispensable'.[33] What Kant objects to here is not allegory as such but typology; and it is typology, he tells us, which allows the mystics to find evidence in support of their own claims. Against this mystical interpretation, with all its dangers, Kant proposes a philosophical mode of exegesis. 'As regards the

32 See F. Rosenzweig, *The star of redemption*, p. 23; Pearson's remark is quoted by Rufus M. Jones, *Studies in mystical religion* (London: Macmillan and Co., 1923), p. 229 n. 1; D. M. MacKinnon, *The problem of metaphysics* (Cambridge: Cambridge University Press, 1974), p. 9 and 'Kant's philosophy of religion', *Philosophy*, 50 (1975), p. 141; Don Cupitt, 'Kant and the negative theology', in *The philosophical frontiers of Christian theology*, ed. Brian Hebblethwaite and Stewart Sutherland (Cambridge: Cambridge University Press, 1982), pp. 55–67.
33 Kant, *Der Streit*, p. 356.

so-called mysticism of exegesis by reason [*Vernunftauslegung*], when philosophy has espied a moral meaning in written passages, nay when it [philosophy] presses it upon the text, then this is exactly *the only means* with which to keep mysticism (e.g. that of Swedenborg) at bay.'[34]

There are a couple of odd things here. In the first place, the philosophical mode of exegesis is allegorical: it claims that text and meaning are discontinuous and that this meaning is ahistorical. If we were to follow Derrida in claiming that the mystical is invariably complicit with the intelligible, we would have to say that Kant is consistently caught up in what he rejects. Yet we need not invoke Derrida to find a difficulty for Kant. In fact we need not look past Kant's account of typology. To be sure, this account sets Kant apart from the mainstream of post-Reformation biblical hermeneutics, but it also sets Kant apart from himself. For we recall that, in *Religion*, we are told that 'in order to win over the adherents of the older religion to the new, the new order is interpreted as the fulfilment, at last, of what was only prefigured in the older religion and has all along been the design of Providence'.[35] If this is so, the condition of possibility for the institution of the true religion is also, and at the same time, the condition of possibility for mysticism. Kant's hermeneutics, it seems, involves him in substantial difficulties.

We can go further, however, if we change direction a little and consider the interpretative function of the transcendental consciousness. To recapitulate: the interpretative function of the categories excludes *a priori* the possibility of mystical experience as Kant defines it; yet in doing so it generates a particular sort of negative theology. Kant believes in God on the basis of practical rather than theoretical reason. The Idea of God is commended to us as regulative, not constitutive. We cannot represent God adequately because the interpretative role of the pure concepts of the understanding does not legitimately extend to the realm of the transcendent. So if we are to talk of God we cannot say anything which positively describes Him. Moreover, the theology which issues from this position must contest the statements of any theology which does make dogmatic positive assertions about God. In short, Kant's theology is a negative theology.

What does this mean? If we go back to Philo Judæus, perhaps

---

34 Kant, *Der Streit*, p. 357. My emphasis.   35 Kant, *Religion*, p. 79.

the first negative theologian, it is evident that the tradition Philo founds is oriented around God's nature or essence. 'In a word', says Philo summing up his position, 'who can make any positive assertion concerning His essence or quality or state of movement?'[36] Furthermore, Philo makes it clear that no positive assertions of God's essence can be made because this essence is a simple unity.[37] If Kant develops a negative theology, it is one which answers not to the ineffability of God's *essence* but to our inability to know that God *exists*. As Don Cupitt observes, what distinguishes Kant from the scholastic theological tradition is his insistence that we have an idea of God and sufficient practical reason to act upon that idea. And indeed it is this insistence which also maps out a distinctive negative theology. Cupitt also draws our attention to a second difference between these ways of developing a negative theology. 'The Greek Fathers', he reminds us, 'invoke a sense of the mystery of the divine transcendence in order to awaken heavenly longings. Their language is designed to *attract*, whereas Kant's language is designed to *repel*.'[38]

In short, Kant presents us with a negative theology spun from philosophical considerations – from the structure of the transcendental consciousness – and not from experience. Despite their marked differences, both Philo and Kant agree that God cannot be expressed conceptually, which entails that the transcendent Christian God cannot be positively expressed in language. In denying the mediation of concepts with regards to God, however, both negative theologies allow for God to be 'known' through unknowing, though Kant of course would never admit the paradox as it implies an analogy between knowing and thinking. Yet if one keeps their differences in mind, it is possible to point to several parallels between the writings of Kant and particular mystics. For example, Kant would doubtless agree with St Teresa's emphasis that 'the important thing is not to think much, but to love much'; and that 'The highest perfection consists . . . in the bringing of our wills so closely into conformity with the will of God'.[39] And if we allow a little room to manoeuvre with regards to vocabulary,

36 Philo, *Allegorical interpretation*, III. lxxiii. 206.
37 Philo, *On the giants*, 11.52.
38 Cupitt, 'Kant and the negative theology', p. 63.
39 St Teresa, *Interior castle*, p. 233; *Book of the foundations*, p. 23.

Kant would agree, too, with St John of the Cross that 'though faith brings certitude to the intellect, it does not produce clarity, but only darkness'; that 'intellectual comprehension of God . . . is impossible'; that the soul 'should desire to journey to God by unknowing'; and that 'the supernatural does not fit into the natural, nor does it have anything to do with it'.[40]

Further parallels could be drawn. Crucial, however, is the recognition that it is the interpretative function of the transcendental consciousness which at once denies the possibility of mystical experience yet simultaneously establishes the means for a negative theology. Kant's framing of mysticism in epistemological terms, as the immediate *knowledge* of God, unwittingly leads him to provide the basis for a negative theology. Moreover, Kant does not merely elaborate a negative theology as part of his philosophy of religion; it constitutes, rather, the entire project of the critical philosophy. He comes to the threshold of our problem when he establishes that all talk of God must be conceptual but that theology must be non-cognitive. Faced with this aporia, Kant steps back and ponders the religious person's moral duty, and this is where his conclusions are worked out. At no time, though, does Kant work towards the deconstructive move, found in the text of Pseudo-Dionysius, that the language of negative theology must undo the conceptual commitment of individual propositions. The Kantian construction of philosophy as negative theology accordingly remains metaphysical, a restricted negative theology, and therefore open to deconstruction. And yet just as the texts of Kant and of certain mystics are near counterparts, so also with Kant and Derrida. Despite his deconstruction of Kant, Derrida remains, as we shall see, within the shadow of the critical philosophy.

3 Kant and Derrida

One of the most common framings of Derrida is that he stands in a distinct tradition from that instituted by Kant. I have already explored several aspects of this framing and found various problems with it. In particular, I have taken issue with Rorty's picture of Derrida. According to Rorty, 'philosophy –

40 St John of the Cross, *The ascent of Mount Carmel*, pp. 119, 126, 99 and *The living flame of love*, p. 623.

Kantian philosophy, philosophy as more than a kind of writing – is an illusion' and it is Derrida, he thinks, who, along with other edifying writers, is responsible for drawing our attention to this illusion.[41] 'The twentieth-century attempt to purify Kant's general theory about the relation between representations and their objects by turning it into philosophy of language is, for Derrida, to be countered by making philosophy even more impure – more unprofessional, funnier, more allusive, sexier, and above all, more "written"'.[42] And thus western philosophy becomes a family romance of 'Father Parmenides, honest old Uncle Kant, and bad brother Derrida'.[43] The relations between Kant and Derrida are not entirely straightforward, however, as Rorty admits. There is the Derrida Rorty admires, the writer who is suggesting 'how things might look if we did not have Kantian philosophy built into the fabric of our intellectual life'. Yet Derrida at times seems to succumb to the lure of transcendental philosophy in the great Kantian tradition: 'The worst bits of Derrida are the ones where he begins to imitate the thing he hates and starts claiming to offer "rigorous analyses"'.[44]

Rorty's claim, then, is that there are two traditions, the Kantian and the non-Kantian, the one a matter of argument and the other a matter of vocabulary. What is more, he contends that it is possible to distinguish between the Kantian and non-Kantian parts of Derrida along the lines of specific texts: thus, in *Of grammatology* one finds Derrida fashioning a counter-philosophy based upon the trace, while in *Glas* Derrida 'does not want to comprehend Hegel's books; he wants to play with Hegel'.[45] On the contrary, I have argued, 'Kantianism' and 'non-Kantianism' are not historical traditions but structural elements of any discourse, whether philosophical or literary. It follows from my reading of Derrida that the deconstruction of Kant will be bound up with certain structural elements of Kantianism. Here, for example, are two placing shots. Rorty characterises Derrida's distance from Kant by specifying that Kantian philosophy is an illusion. True, Derrida sees metaphysics as leading to illusions; but what could be a more orthodox Kantian move? It is also true that Derrida seeks to displace

---

41 Rorty, *Consequences*, p. 93.   42 Rorty, *Consequences*, p. 93.
43 Rorty, *Consequences*, p. 92.
44 Rorty, *Consequences*, p. 98 and 'Deconstruction and circumvention', p. 9.
45 Rorty, *Consequences*, p. 96.

Kant; but when he does so it is by way of developing a 'new transcendental aesthetic'.[46] This recognition of Derrida's residual Kantianism helps us understand Derrida's views of theology and mysticism but it is also, and more importantly, of help in recognising problems which arise in trying to articulate deconstruction and theology.

First of all, it is important to realise that Kant's epistemology has generated completely opposing judgements of both mysticism and interpretation. Thus we have Rudolf Otto who reconciles mystical experience with Kantianism by arguing that the holy is an *a priori* category; while Albrecht Ritschl's neo-Kantianism is firmly opposed to any mystical element in Christianity. Both writers agree, though, with Kant's fundamental assumption, that mystical experience is primarily a matter of *knowing* that something is or is not the case. Similarly, contemporary theories of interpretation draw opposing inspirations from the critical philosophy. As Ricœur has amply demonstrated, although 'Husserl *did* phenomenology . . . Kant *limited* and *founded* it'.[47] All in all, it is the Kantian emphasis upon the primacy of the constituting subject which animates that extended family of interpretation theories, ranging from Schleiermacher and Dilthey to Jauss and Gadamer, which passes under the general title of 'hermeneutics'. Broadly opposed to these hermeneuticists are the structuralists and semiologists, from Lévi-Strauss to Todorov; yet structuralism is also deeply rooted in Kantian epistemology, in the very idea of *a priori* structures of human consciousness.

This is perhaps most clearly seen in the Ur-text of structuralism, *The course in general linguistics*. It is not that the signifier is arbitrary with respect to a given signified, Saussure argues, but that the *relation* between signifier and signified is arbitrary: neither the signified nor the signifier is able to form a ground. The familiar empiricist doctrine of the arbitrariness of the signifier is here combined with a far more radical thesis, that of the reciprocity of signifier and signified. If we are to talk of 'ground' in Saussurean linguistics we must turn to the linguistic system itself, since signifiers and signifieds achieve definition only by

46 Derrida, *Of grammatology*, p. 290.
47 Ricœur, *Husserl: an analysis of his phenomenology*, trans. Edward G. Ballard and Lester E. Embree (Evanston: Northwestern University Press, 1967), p. 201.

virtue of their place in the system. If we combine the three notions of arbitrariness, reciprocity and system, we have a powerful case against the idea that language names a set of concepts which precede language. And if this is so, Saussure is Kantian to the extent that he argues for the impossibility of our having direct experience of reality as it is in itself. The difference between Kant and Saussure is that the one finds the determining structures in the transcendental consciousness while the other locates them in language. To expand Ricœur's observation on Lévi-Strauss, if structuralism is a Kantianism without the transcendental consciousness, hermeneutics is a Kantianism without the *a priori* structures.[48]

Derrida's response to these sets of opposed judgements may be readily anticipated. Both the prizing and rejection of mystical experience remain ensnared by metaphysics. For as we have seen, Otto's mysticism is complicit with Ritschl's rationalism and both assume the instituting distinction of metaphysics, that between the intelligible and the sensible. Similarly, phenomenological hermeneutics and structuralism are equally comprehended by metaphysics. Both are haunted by the lack of a perfect fit between linguistic and logical categories, a space which allows the play of difference. This gap can be closed in either of two ways: by the development of a pure logical grammar, such as Husserl attempted in the *Logical investigations*, or by the elaboration of a more formal grammar such as semiology announces. And it is these attempts to erase the differences between grammar and logic which are submitted to Derrida's most persistent critiques. Both early phenomenology and structuralism attempt to cover the entire textual field with a calculus, be it a grammar raised to a logic or a logic condensed to a grammar.

So deconstruction seems to call into question everything which issues from Kant. But while Derrida manages to dislodge the critical philosophy he does not succeed in entirely escaping it, nor would he claim to do so. In one respect at least Kant and Derrida are similar: both set out to limit metaphysics yet remain within its closure. Kant's argument that 'we can know *a priori* of things only what we ourselves put into them' necessarily eliminates the metaphysical as a possible area of positive know-

48 Ricœur, *The conflict of interpretations: essays in hermeneutics*, ed. Don Ihde (Evanston: Northwestern University Press, 1974), p. 33.

ledge.[49] Like Condillac before him, Kant distinguishes between good and bad metaphysics. Good metaphysics is to be found in the method of transcendental deduction which supplies a firm ground to speculation; what is beyond dogmatic metaphysics turns out to be critical metaphysics. Derrida's situation is at once similar and different. Derrida demonstrates that metaphysics depends transcendentally upon *différance*, but metaphysics is not thereby eliminated. Indeed, it is *différance* which produces metaphysics: 'Differance produces what it forbids, makes possible the very thing that it makes impossible'.[50] Or in other words, *différance* enables metaphysics yet disables the totalisation of a text by metaphysics.

Whereas the critical philosophy establishes a transcendental ground, deconstruction locates a transcendental realm which cannot constitute a ground. It is a short step from here to a closer parallel. Just as Kant formulates 'necessary conditions of possible experience' so too Derrida establishes the 'general text' as the condition of possibility for the act of interpretation. And just as Kant's necessary conditions work with a narrow sense of 'experience', so too Derrida's general text is more closely specified than it at first seems. It is the third parallel, however, which is of particular interest. The critical philosophy seeks to dispose of dogmatic metaphysics and in the process decides the role and scope of any future metaphysics. Now Rorty would argue here that Derrida attempts to dispose of metaphysics as such yet, in arguing against metaphysics, constructs one more 'final' metaphysics – grammatology, the *logos* of the *grammè*. I disagree: Derrida satisfactorily shows that metaphysics is situated with respect to a site it cannot properly name without losing its specificity as metaphysics; but he also admits, as he must, that in naming this site – albeit provisionally, with all the strategic displacements of erasure and palæonymy – he is unable fully to escape metaphysics: *différance* is itself a metaphysical name.[51] Whereas Kant proclaims the *end* of dogmatic metaphysics, Derrida outlines its *closure*.

We should pause and look at this more closely. For Kant the speculative illusions of dogmatic metaphysics arise from the transcendent employment of the understanding and, more dis-

49 Kant, *Critique of pure reason*, B xviii. 50 Derrida, *Of grammatology*, p. 143.
51 Derrida, *Margins*, p. 26.

turbingly, from the transcendent employment of reason. It is in the nature of reason to generate ideas which go beyond possible experience; however, these ideas can be used legitimately or illegitimately. Reason misuses its ideas if it exceeds the bounds of the understanding, where what counts as knowledge is resolved, and attempts by itself to constitute positive knowledge of things. This is not to say that the ideas of reason have no constructive role to play. Far from it; practical reason gives us sufficient assurance that the ideas of reason are indispensable in regulating our thought. This distinction between the constitutive and the regulative roles of reason is therefore extremely important for Kant. But it also, I want to suggest, orients Derrida's diagnosis of the illusions of metaphysics.

Derrida's enterprise revolves around the possibility of finding a site which is unconditioned by metaphysics. This is a project he shares with modern thinkers as different as A. J. Ayer and Martin Heidegger. But what distinguishes Derrida from these people is the persistence of his recognition that, as he puts it, 'the limit or end of metaphysics is not linear or circular in any indivisible sense'.[52] While Derrida can demonstrate that metaphysics is conditioned by the transcendental play of *différance* he must also admit the structural impossibility of designating what is beyond metaphysics. The very question 'What is beyond metaphysics?' repeats the instituting question of philosophy, 'What is . . .?', and so the question turns out to manifest the problem. While the grammatologist can and should put 'the outside of metaphysics' to use as a regulative principle, only illusions will result from its constitutive use. Note the words 'can' and 'should'. The analytic point is one which Derrida accents repeatedly: the most that deconstruction can do is glimpse 'the yet unnameable glimmer beyond the closure'.[53] The moral point, however, while just as frequently made, is one which Derrida is less prepared to elaborate.

These aspects, the analytic and the moral, are at times difficult to separate. There are times when Derrida appears to anticipate the end of metaphysics as a particular event, almost, it seems, as part of salvation-history. In *Of grammatology*, for instance, we find talk of 'the future which proclaims itself at present, beyond

52 Derrida, 'Deconstruction and the other', p. 111.
53 Derrida, *Of grammatology*, p. 14.

the closure of knowledge'; we hear that this future 'can only be proclaimed, *presented*, as a sort of monstrosity'.[54] And this apocalyptic tone is intensified in 'Structure, sign and play'. Speaking of the problem of conceiving *différance*, Derrida remarks,

> Here there is a kind of question, let us still call it historical, whose *conception, formation, gestation*, and *labor* we are only catching a glimpse of today. I employ these words, I admit, with a glance towards the operations of childbearing – but also with a glance toward those who, in a society from which I do not exclude myself, turn their eyes away when faced by the yet unnameable which is proclaiming itself and which can do so, as is necessary whenever a birth is in the offing, only under the species of the nonspecies, in the formless, mute, infant, and terrifying form of monstrosity.[55]

These and other passages are sometimes cited as evidence that deconstruction does point the way beyond the closure of metaphysics to a realm of pure freedom; and it is not difficult to detect the moral significance with which this is imbued.

Gayatri Spivak, for one, argues that deconstruction unequivocally urges us to correct social injustices, such as the subjugation of women, and that Derrida is here urging us to open our discourse to an outside 'constituted by ethical-political contingencies'.[56] Michael Ryan seems to take this a step further, considering deconstruction within a moral frame. 'There is a difference', he tells us, 'between the angelic disinterestedness accompanying the hypothesis that no truth is determinable, no text readable, and the provisional limitation of a potentially unlimited and indeterminate textuality in the name of the political interest of countering the structures of power whose interests are served implicitly by the angelic disinterestedness of liberal detachment'.[57] And, finally, Jacob Rogozinski argues the more subtle thesis that there are two political views irreducibly

54 Derrida, *Of grammatology*, pp. 4, 5.
55 Derrida, *Writing*, p. 293. In 'A dialogue on language', Heidegger talks of two sites: metaphysics and a transformation to another site which must be left without a name. See *On the way to language*, trans. Peter D. Hertz (New York: Harper and Row, 1971), p. 42.
56 Gayatri Spivak, 'Il faut s'y prendre en s'en prenant à elles', in *Les fins de l'homme*, ed. P. Lacoue-Labarthe and J.-L. Nancy (Paris: Editions Galilée, 1981), p. 514.
57 Michael Ryan, *Marxism and deconstruction*, (Baltimore: Johns Hopkins University Press, 1982), p. 41.

at work in Derrida's discourse: the first resists political upheaval in an indefinite deferral of rupture and revolution while the second, found in the above passages, enjoins us to a radical revolution.[58] On this model there is no possibility of choice but, Rogozinski contends, it is morally and politically necessary to choose between them. And so, once more, deconstruction is questioned from within a moral – and political – frame.

All three readings agree that Derrida is addressing an epoch which will be constituted within history yet beyond metaphysics; and each assumes that what is beyond metaphysics is, at least in part, constituted by a moral imperative. Now I think this is a misconstruction of Derrida's intention and text. To begin with, it is *différance* which is glimpsed beyond the closure of metaphysics, and *différance* cannot be a value in itself. In the second place, the uncritical placing of deconstruction within an ethico-political frame ignores the arguments Derrida adduces against Levinas's insistence that 'the Good beyond essence' provides us with a point of entry into a non-metaphysical ethics. Far from freeing us from the metaphysical, Derrida argues, the realm of the ethical aids and abets metaphysics. This is the thrust of Derrida's case that the 'step beyond' (*le pas au-delà*) metaphysics leads us 'not beyond' metaphysics. There is no need to appeal even to these arguments, however, for Derrida's text makes it clear that in these debated passages he is not addressing a state to come, a post-lapsarian grammatological paradise.

The future world he characterises is one which 'will have put into question the values of sign, word and writing', one which is currently proclaiming itself.[59] It is proclaiming itself *today* because the values of sign, word and writing have been called into question, in one way or another, from Hegel to Heidegger, and more particularly because the very text which these words introduce, *Of grammatology*, is an explicit interrogation of those values. We have passed the initial stage of grammatology as a positive science and, in 1967, when this passage was written, we stand upon the threshold of the second stage, of grammatology as part of the project of deconstruction of metaphysics, including 'positivity' and 'science'. The images of monstrosity and abnormality do not refer to a time beyond metaphysics but rather to

58 J. Rogozinski, 'Déconstruire la revolution', in *Les fins de l'homme*, pp. 523–24.
59 Derrida, *Of grammatology*, p. 5.

the enterprise in which Derrida is engaged, the deconstruction of metaphysics, which – as I have argued – is an *abnormal* philosophy. (Whereas Kant uses the antinomies of pure reason to establish a discourse upon the limits of pure reason, Derrida uses what we could perhaps call the antinomies of impure genre to establish a discourse upon formal undecidability.) Exactly how this second stage of grammatology will be elaborated, Derrida cannot say; it is regulated, however, by the thought of *différance*. Derrida uses the future anterior, 'will have put into question', because *différance*, as a transcendental, always already precedes phenomenal texts. At the same time, though, *différance* can only be thought in reading specific phenomenal texts. This is partly done in the text Derrida is introducing here and will be part of a much larger project.

We must reject *both* the general view that 'beyond metaphysics' can be employed constitutively *and* the particular view that this realm is itself constituted by the ethical. Just as Kant maintains that 'freedom' has only a regulative role, so too Derrida contends with unlimited 'free play'. Yet there is a difference between Kant and Derrida here. For while Kant allows the unavoidable problems of God, freedom and immortality to play positive regulative roles, Derrida in effect distinguishes between positive and negative regulative roles. 'Free play' performs a positive role, but we need to recall that grammatology is itself regulated, albeit negatively, by the concepts of metaphysics. Metaphysics and the deconstruction of metaphysics are equally produced by *différance*, and while the question of symmetry does not arise here by virtue of the totalising claim of metaphysics, it is nonetheless true that deconstruction needs the resistance which metaphysics naturally supplies. To graft Kant's aphorism onto the Derridean problematic, 'The light dove, cleaving the air in her free flight, and feeling its resistance, might imagine that its flight would be still easier in empty space'.[60]

None of this is to deny, however, that what is glimpsed beyond the closure has moral significance; and this demands some attention. *Différance* may well be the 'nonethical opening of ethics' but it is also 'the origin of morality as of immorality': so while grammatology does not constitute a moral position of absolute freedom, it can be pressed into the service of such moral

60 Kant, *Critique of pure reason*, A 5.

positions as certain forms of feminism and socialism. As Jean-Luc Nancy shows, Derrida's text contains an axiomatics and suggestions of an axiology. When Derrida tells us *il faut déconstruire la philosophie, il faut penser l'écriture, il faut entendre doublement*, and so forth, we seem to be placed under an obligation of some sort.[61] Nancy follows Heidegger's 'Letter on humanism' in affirming that all that is currently addressed under the title of 'ethics' is part and parcel of western metaphysics.[62] Interestingly enough, Nancy's response here is that deconstruction 'does its duty' *(fait son devoir)* in resisting the call to develop an ethics; but what can the 'duty' of deconstruction be if not a *moral* duty? Regardless of how theoretical a discourse deconstruction sets itself up to be, it would seem that it generates practical demands upon the reader. In deconstructing the critical philosophy, and the distinction between theoretical and practical reason in particular, Derrida's discourse does not escape the *effects* of this distinction. The Kantian philosophy cannot be entirely unstitched from the fabric of our intellectual life, as Rorty suggests.

We have uncovered several places where Derrida repeats a familiar Kantian move, sometimes with the intention of displacing the critical philosophy yet sometimes with the effect of confirming it. It is possible to see that Derrida repeats Kant's move with respect to mysticism and finds himself in almost the same position. Kant frames mystical experience in epistemological terms, then relegates it to the status of a parergon only for it to exert a powerful force upon Kant's entire system, making the critical philosophy a negative theology. Derrida follows Kant exactly in framing mystical experience epistemologically and, in construing it as complicit with metaphysics, he relegates it to the status of a parergon within his own discourse. For as is surely apparent by now, metaphysics, once deconstructed, is a parergon to grammatology – it is pushed to the margins of Derrida's discourse where, like the idea of 'free play' but conversely, it has a regulative role. Unlike Kant, though, Derrida's discourse does not become a negative theology; it turns out, as chapter 6 showed, that negative theology is itself a mode of deconstruc-

61 J.-L. Nancy, 'La voix libre de l'homme', in *Les fins de l'homme*, p. 166.
62 Heidegger, 'Letter on humanism', in *Basic writings*, p. 195. See Derrida, *Writing*, p. 81 and p. 312 n. 5.

tion. The difference between the two philosophers on this score, then, is that Kant's philosophy is a restricted negative theology whereas Derrida's grammatology is a belated version of the deconstructive power of a general negative theology.

8 | Heidegger: the revealing and concealing of mysticism

Introduction

Neither the questioning of metaphysics nor the quest for a non-metaphysical theology is peculiar to this century. We have seen the two problematics intersect, first in Pseudo-Dionysius, then in the critical philosophy. Now, though, we must turn to a philosopher whose intervention in twentieth-century ideas has been decisive, a man whose thought has already exerted a considerable force throughout this study: Martin Heidegger. We can resolve this force in two directions. It is the Heideggerian project of the *Destruktion* of western metaphysics which is the immediate precursor of Derridean deconstruction. And it is Heidegger who, more than any single philosopher this century, has influenced the development of contemporary speculative theology. So if deconstruction is, as we have suggested, a rigorous revision of *Destruktion*, then surely we should expect it to clarify and extend the theological projects already begun under the aegis of Heidegger.

Yet we do not turn to Heidegger purely for historical reasons, and in passing from the eighteenth to the twentieth century we do not thereby step outside the shadow cast by the critical philosophy. After all, it is Heidegger who submits the critical philosophy to a rigorous and ground-breaking analysis; for unlike most commentators, Heidegger attends partly to Kant's doctrines and arguments and partly to what remains *unsaid* in Kant's text. Such is the burden of *Kant and the problem of metaphysics* and *What is a thing?*[1] In this way Heidegger begins his radical questioning of the relation between metaphysics and

---

1 Heidegger, *Kant and the problem of metaphysics*, trans. James S. Churchill (Bloomington: Indiana University Press, 1962); *What is a thing?* trans. W. B. Barton, Jr. and Vera Deutsch (Chicago: Henry Regnery Co., 1967).

interpretation, the problem for which he is perhaps best known. One of the things which remains unthought by Kant yet which specifies the character of his philosophical speculation, Heidegger tells us, is the principle of sufficient reason (or, as he often prefers, the principle of ground).[2] What interests me here is that it is just this principle which enables us to see the relation between metaphysics and interpretation as part of the wider configuration of metaphysics, interpretation and mysticism. We have seen how this configuration works in Kant's text, and now we shall examine the ways in which it is reworked by Heidegger.

1   Philosophy, mysticism and tone

In the last chapter we distinguished between the Kantian doctrine of the interpretative function of the transcendental consciousness and Kant's view of scriptural exegesis. These two are related, and this will enable us to get our bearings. As we have seen, mystical experience is foreclosed in the act of limiting pure reason while mystical interpretation is dismissed by the demands of practical reason. The speculative and the practical are jointly entertained in a late essay on the dangers of mysticism, 'About a recently raised superior tone in philosophy'. We enter Kant's discussion towards its conclusion, distinguishing between the adherents of *Gefühlsphilosoph*, such as Jacobi, who affirm the possibility of immediate intuition and thus opens the gate to mysticism, and Kant who stresses the primacy of mediation and the moral law:

> But, why now all this disputation between two parties, that at bottom have one and the same good intention, namely to make people wise and upright? – It is an uproar about nothing, disagreement out of misunderstandings, which does not require making it up with each other but rather only a reciprocal explanation ... The veiled goddess, before whom we on both sides bend our knees, is the moral law in us, in its invulnerable majesty. Although we hear her voice, and also understand her commandment well indeed; but are in doubt when listening, whether it comes from the person out of the might-fulness of his own reason, or whether it comes from

---

2 Heidegger, *The essence of reasons* (Evanston: Northwestern University Press, 1969), p. 9.

another whose being is unknown to him, and which speaks to
the person through this his own reason.[3]

The disagreement between the parties is not, therefore, over
interpretation, what something means, but over the grounds for
interpretation, its theoretical justification. There are two interpretations of interpretation: one which posits divine action *ab
extra* as its guarantee and one which is grounded in the knowing
subject. These modes of interpretation are not of equal value,
however, for the second – mystical – mode of interpretation is at
best a supplement to the first.

It might be useful to tease this out further. Kant distinguishes
between reason's voice and a voice beyond reason. Mystagogues
such as Jacobi fail to distinguish between speculative and practical reason; they confuse what can be *known* with what can only
be *thought*. The mystagogues cannot hear the difference between
the voices. (One might say that they do not have an 'ear for
philosophy'.) The mystical mode of interpretation has its use,
though, as long as it does not trespass from the realm of thought
to that of knowledge:

> Maybe at bottom we would do better just to pass over this
> inquiry; since it is only speculative, and what is obliged to be
> done by us (objectively) always remains the same, whether
> one may found it on the one or the other principle: only that
> the didactic proceeding is actually alone philosophical, to bring
> the moral law in us on to clear concepts according to logical kind
> of teaching, but that one [proceeding], to personify that law
> and to make a veiled ISIS out of the morally commanding
> reason, (if we straight away adjoin to this one no other quali-
> ties than the ones found according to that method), is an
> aesthetic kind of conceptualization of just the same item; of
> which one can well make use after, when through the former
> the principles have already been cleared up, in order to enliven
> those ideas through sensory even although only analogical
> representation, but always with some danger of happening
> into fanciful vision that is the death of all philosophy.[4]

It is clear, then, that the modes of interpretation are to be
characterised as the philosophical and the mystical. Moreover, it
is a special attitude towards interpretation which specifies the
difference between philosophy and mysticism. Kant is plain that

3 Kant, *Von einen neuerdings erhobenen vornehmen Ton in der Philosophie*, p. 494.
4 Kant, *Von einen neuerdings erhobenen vornehmen Ton*, pp. 494–95.

whereas the voice of reason 'speaks to each without equivo-cation', thus making univocality the medium of philosophical discourse, the voice of the oracle is equivocal, open to conflicting interpretations.[5] In other words, Kant distinguishes between moral and mystical interpretations by way of mutually exclusive processes of unveiling and reveiling. '

More than anything else, it is this equivocality which disturbs Kant. There can be hermeneuts only where there are equivocal texts. The hermeneut is therefore in a position of power which does not answer directly or indirectly to reason: a power which resides precisely in the ability to make out the oracle's secret whispers, that is, to employ a hermeneutic. As soon as this happens, Kant says, the mystagogue's tone leaps; he adopts a 'superior tone', bypassing the labour of philosophy in order to claim direct access to the truth. Thus we have a sharp division. There is the philosopher who listens to the unequivocal voice of reason, writes in prose and adopts a neutral tone befitting the patient investigation of the truth. And there is the mystagogue (and the mystic) who listens to the equivocal voice of a private oracle, lapses into poetry, adopts a high tone and, in short, threatens to bring about the death of philosophy.

So upon Kant's account the mystic must make some sort of leap, but exactly what this consists in is far from self-evident. Several questions arise: from what ground does the mystic leap? Where does the mystic come to rest? Or if he or she does not come to rest, what sort of fall is experienced? More generally, what relationship is presupposed between philosophy and mys-ticism in this account? To answer these questions we need to make something of a leap ourselves, from Kant to Heidegger. A leap forward, to be sure, yet also a leap slightly backwards. For the help we need from Heidegger is not to be found in his readings of Kant but in his analysis of Leibniz's principle of sufficient reason. Heidegger's contention is that there is a 'rapport between Leibniz and Kant'; indeed, the principle of sufficient reason is the hidden support of the entire archi-

5 Cf. Gershom Scholem's remark about revelation and mysticism: 'Here revela-tion, which has yet no specific meaning, is that in the word which gives an infinite wealth of meaning. Itself without meaning, it is the very essence of interpretability. For mystical theology, this is a decisive criterion of revelation', *The messianic idea in Judaism and other essays on Jewish spirituality* (New York: Schocken Books, 1971), p. 295.

tectonics of the critical philosophy.[6] 'Behind the formula "*a priori* conditions of possibility"', Heidegger insists, 'is hidden the sign of the sufficient reason which, as *ratio*, is pure reason'.[7]

To begin with, we need to reconstitute Heidegger's reading of the principle of sufficient reason. There is no doubt of the importance which Leibniz attributed to this principle. While he held the principle of contradiction to be 'the great foundation of mathematics', it must be combined with the principle of sufficient reason to ground metaphysics and natural theology.[8] Heidegger agrees with Leibniz's estimation of the principle's importance. Although the principle was explicitly stated by Leibniz as late as the seventeenth century it was always implicit in philosophy, Heidegger tells us, as far back as Plato. Not that Leibniz's discovery of the principle was accidental: the unveiling of the principle is part of the inscrutable *Seinsgeschick*. The important point is that, for Heidegger, the principle of sufficient reason is not peculiar to Leibniz's metaphysics but constitutes metaphysics as such. In offering a reading of this one principle, Heidegger is therefore claiming to present a reading of the text of philosophy, in both senses of *the* text of philosophy and the text of *philosophy*.

It is therefore important to establish the text of this principle; and this is not quite as easy as it seems. Heidegger distinguishes three versions: (a) the short, *principium rationis*; (b) the strict, *principium reddendæ rationis*; and (c) the complete, *principium reddendæ rationis sufficientis*:

(a) Nothing is without ground;
(b) Nothing is unless a ground can be rendered for it; and

---

6 Heidegger, *Le principe de raison*, trans. André Préau with preface by Jean Beaufret (Paris: Gallimard, 1962), p. 165. Apart from its concluding lecture, Heidegger's *Der Satz vom Grund* has not yet been translated into English. I shall use the French translation, cited above. The concluding lecture, 'The principle of ground' has been translated in *Man and World*, 7 (1974), pp. 207–22. All translations from the body of the text are my own, made in consultation with the German text and certain passages translated by John D. Caputo in *The mystical element in Heidegger's thought*, a book whose influence upon my account I gratefully acknowledge here.
7 Heidegger, *Le principe de raison*, p. 169.
8 H. G. Alexander, ed., *The Leibniz-Clarke correspondence* (Manchester: Manchester University Press, 1956), p. 16.

(c) Nothing is unless a sufficient ground can be rendered for it.[9]

Although Heidegger takes pains to establish the importance of the expression that a ground 'can be rendered', (b) and (c) chiefly serve to elucidate (a) which he takes as his text.

On the face of it, the difference between (a) and (b) is not so much between degrees of strictness in formulation as it is between a statement of ontology and epistemology; and if this is so, (c) is merely a refinement of an epistemological statement. Indeed, if one examines the correspondence between Leibniz and Clarke there appear to be three quite distinct principles advanced under the title 'principle of sufficient reason': that every event has a cause; that God requires a motive for acting; and that God acts for the best.[10] For Heidegger, these criticisms are largely beside the point. What is important, he would claim, is not whether he has recovered Leibniz's intention or reached a correct scholarly account of Leibniz's text but whether he has grasped the determining principle of philosophy as metaphysics. The fact that Heidegger holds this principle to come to light only with Leibniz in no way commits him also to maintain that Leibniz's *statement* of this principle is faultless. Despite all that one hears about Heidegger's break with phenomenology, what we have here, in fact, is a phenomenological reduction, performed with respect to a series of texts rather than the world. Heidegger wishes to hear what Being has to say, not what Leibniz says; so he must bracket the natural attitude which accords an explanatory role to Leibniz's intention. Heidegger's 'hermeneutical violence' is no more than phenomenology working with texts.

At any rate, it is the short version of the principle, 'Nothing is without ground', which Heidegger analyses. Heidegger nowhere makes any reference to Kant's essay 'About a recently raised tone in philosophy', so it is all the more curious that his analysis is based upon hearing a tonal difference between possible readings of the principle. Throughout the long tradition of onto-theology, we have heard the principle only in the one way, with the following accent: (1) *Nothing* is *without* ground. Heard in

---

9 Heidegger, *Le principe de raison*, pp. 79, 137.
10 Alexander, ed., *The Leibniz-Clarke correspondence*, p. xxii.

this key, we have the familiar statement of the principle. Most commentators on *Der Satz vom Grund* follow Heidegger in stressing the principle's ontological character to the virtual exclusion of its epistemological character. This is understandable, given Heidegger's suspicion of the distinction between ontology and epistemology; yet the distinction is required if we are to explain what is at stake here.

The epistemological character of (1) may be traced from Aristotle's insistence in the *Posterior analytics* that all statements have *archai* (except, of course, the *archai* themselves) to Husserl's remark in the *Logical investigations* that 'Scientific knowledge is, as such, *grounded knowledge*. To know the ground of anything means to see the necessity of its being so and so . . . To see *a state of affairs as a matter of law* is to see *its truth as necessarily obtaining*, and to have knowledge of the *ground of the state of affairs* or of its truth: all these are equivalent expressions'.[11] To say that every statement must have its reason is to remain within calculative thinking which is, in Heidegger's sense of the term, leagued with metaphysics. And this brings us to the ontological interpretation of the principle. Within metaphysics, Heidegger tells us, a being is understood as that which is grounded; and from Aristotle to the present day a being's ground is called Being. Given this, if we ask 'What is Being?' the only reply we have open to us is that it is the being of beings. The grounding principle of metaphysics – the principle of *ground* – is thus a statement about beings, not about Being. According to this reasoning, all that can be said of Being is that it is the ground of beings.

Is it possible to turn the logic which sustains this system against its starting-point? For within this world, in which everything must be grounded, it seems perfectly reasonable to inquire into the ground of Being. Within metaphysics, however, the question is inadmissible; it appears cogent in much the same way as in mathematics it seems reasonable to divide a number by zero. Yet just as there is a point of discontinuity between zero and the smallest real number, so too there is a radical difference between Being and a being: the one is construed as *essentia*, the other as *existentia*. The only answer that can be advanced here is that Being formally functions as an *archè*, as that which can be known though not demonstrated,

11 Husserl, *Logical investigations*, Vol. I, pp. 227–28.

and as such it serves to prevent an infinite regress. If this is so, we must accept that metaphysics is that discourse which *not only* elaborates itself within the difference between Being and beings *but also* assumes that there is nothing prior to Being.

Is this assumption entirely defensible? Heidegger does not think so; and, with striking critical insight, claims that the assumption is questioned from within the principle of sufficient reason itself. If one is attentive to the voice of Being, he tells us, it is possible to hear the principle in another key, thus: (2) 'Nothing *is* without *ground*'. Barely heard in the text of philosophy, the copula is a harmonic of ground. Epistemologically, Being and reason belong together: the thought of Being stands in its *own* reason, not *before* reason, as Kant's judiciary metaphor would have it. And ontologically, Being and ground belong together: Being is not a ground *for* beings; rather, Being *is* ground in and for itself. Being is not grounded in anything else because, in itself, Being is groundless.

It is tempting to object that Heidegger is simply confusing the 'is' of distribution with the 'is' of identity. But as a hermeneut of suspicion, Heidegger has a standard reply to this knock-down argument, that he is not concerned to hear what is *said* in the principle of sufficient reason but what remains *unsaid*: hermeneutical violence is the precondition of finding an exit from metaphysics. Heidegger may be right to claim that this reading of Being is not normally heard in the principle of sufficient reason; but the reading is common enough in transcendental idealism. Here is Schelling, for example: 'we cannot say of the true I that it *exists*: for it is the *Ground* of Existence – it *gives existence* in all Things, but *is* not itself. The eternal "I AM", or the *timeless* Act of Self-affirmation, needs no Being to support it, has no Substance or Substratum . . .'[12] Heidegger's originality depends upon finding this doctrine hidden in the principle of sufficient reason and in showing that, far from being part of transcendental idealism, it questions idealism.

We agreed earlier that metaphysics is that discourse which elaborates itself within the ontico-ontological distinction and

12 The translation is by Coleridge and is from an unpublished translation of part of Schelling's *System of transcendental idealism*. The passage is quoted by G. N. G. Orsini, *Coleridge and German idealism* (Carbondale: Southern Illinois University Press, 1969), p. 211.

assumes that nothing precedes this distinction. Upon this understanding, it is patent that (1) is the pre-eminent statement of metaphysics, in both the subjective and objective senses of the genitive. The assurance with which (1) is asserted within metaphysics is called into question, though, by (2); for here it is claimed that there is indeed something which precedes the ontico-ontological distinction and thus philosophy – the thought of Being. But in what sense is (2) non-philosophical? Heidegger moves from the grammatical function of the verb 'to be' to a statement about Being; yet, as he realises, the substantive verb can properly refer only to beings, not to Being. 'The goal of all ontology is a doctrine of categories', he says, while flatly denying that the essential characteristics of Being are categories.[13] Within metaphysics, beings are rendered intelligible to the extent that they accord with the system of predication; so Being remains essentially concealed within the epoch of ontotheology. More particularly, thought is in no way reducible to a univocal proposition:

> all true thought remains open to more than one interpretation – and this by reason of its nature. Nor is this multiplicity of possible interpretations merely the residue of a still unachieved formal-logical univocity which we properly ought to strive for but did not attain. Rather, multiplicity of meanings is the element in which all thought must move in order to be strict thought.[14]

Strictly speaking, (2) cannot be formally stated as a proposition. If (1) is thetic, (2) must be athetic: whereas the one is *Setzung*, concerned with position, the other is *Übersetzung*, translating us beyond position, back into the ground of metaphysics. Or as Heidegger elsewhere hints, (2) is a *thesis*, but in the original Greek sense of the word 'which means a setting up in the unconcealed ... bringing forth into what is present, that is, letting or causing to lie forth'.[15] So whereas (1) accords with the metaphysical notion of truth as correspondence between a proposition and reality, (2) works with the supposedly more

---

13 Heidegger, *An introduction to metaphysics*, trans. Ralph Manheim (New Haven: Yale University Press, 1968), p. 156.
14 Heidegger, *What is called thinking?*, trans. J. Glenn Gray (New York: Harper and Row, 1968), p. 71.
15 Heidegger, 'Addendum' to 'The origin of the work of art', in *Poetry, language, thought*, p. 82.

245

originary notion of truth as *aletheia*. Heidegger respects the protocol of this difference, expressing the import of (2) as 'Being and reason: the Same'.[16] Thus (2) is non-philosophical in the sense that it names the condition of possibility for philosophy and in that it resists reduction to a thesis.

Even so, we have still to puzzle out the relation between (1) and (2). There is a sense in which, if Heidegger is right, this cannot be satisfactorily done. For to explain the relation between the philosophical and the non-philosophical is to declare in favour of philosophy at the outset. And yet *not* to offer some sort of account of how one can at least pass from (1) to (2) would be to resign oneself to becoming a mystagogue, like those Kant condemned. In trying to accede to this latter demand, Heidegger also manages, I think, to show how the former problem can be evaded. The distance from (1) to (2) can be negotiated only by a leap. Heidegger neatly makes the point by means of an untranslatable pun: 'The principle [*Satz*] of reason is not only a *Satz* as supreme principle. It is a *Satz* in the special sense that it is a leap'.[17] There can be no continuous train of reasoning from (1) to (2) and therefore (2) cannot be governed by (1). At first this sounds like a Kierkegaardian 'leap of faith', not from non-belief to belief but from philosophy to non-philosophy.

It is worth noting, first of all, that in developing the non-relation between (1) and (2) Heidegger has recourse to a familiar metaphor. 'The change of tone is sudden', he tells us. 'It represents a leap of thought. Without the help of a bridge, that is to say without the continuity of a progression, the leap brings thought into another region and into another way of saying.'[18] The metaphor is not accidental: Heidegger habitually recurs to it. With regards to the gulf between the sciences and thinking, for instance, he says 'There is no bridge here – only the leap'.[19] Heidegger's metaphor takes us back not just to Kierkegaard but, even further and more decisively, to Kant. In the *Critique of judgement* we are offered the following explanation why our theoretical cognition cannot advance towards the supersensible:

16 Heidegger, *Le principe de raison*, p. 144.
17 Heidegger, *Le principe de raison*, p. 135.
18 Heidegger, *Le principe de raison*, p. 134.
19 Heidegger, *What is called thinking?*, p. 8.

> Albeit, then, between the realm of the natural concept, as the sensible, and the realm of the concept of freedom, as the supersensible, there is a great gulf fixed, so that it is not possible to pass from the former to the latter (by means of the theoretical employment of reason), just as if they were so many separate worlds, the first of which is powerless to exercise influence on the second: still the latter is *meant* to influence the former . . . There must, therefore, be a ground of the *unity* of the supersensible that lies at the basis of nature . . .[20]

A little further on Kant fills out the metaphor in more detail. Speaking of this same gulf, he remarks, 'The concept of freedom determines nothing in respect of the theoretical cognition of nature; and the concept of nature likewise nothing in respect of the practical laws of freedom. To that extent, then, *it is not possible to throw a bridge from the one realm to the other.*'[21] Kant's aim is to preclude any possibility of theoretical reason passing from the sensible to the supersensible for moral and religious reasons. We know these reasons, and we also know Kant's solution to the problem by appeal to the *a priori* principle to be found in reflective judgement. But let us put these issues to one side and discuss the relation between Kant and Heidegger more generally.

There can be no bridge, Kant tells us, from pure reason to its desired supersensible objects; but there must be, nonetheless, a ground of the unity of the supersensible at the very basis of nature. It is by this means – the limiting of pure reason – that, while according a definite privilege to *knowledge*, Kant also secures a position of honour for *thought*. Knowledge therefore keeps (or, strictly speaking, should keep) thought under scrutiny: reason's desire to construct a bridge must be abandoned in order to secure a solid ground for its legitimate operation. There is no question, for Kant, of a Kierkegaardian 'leap of faith' because his architectonic guarantees that there is no absolute discontinuity between faith and morality. Still keeping religious questions aside, Heidegger agrees with Kierkegaard rather than with Kant. For although Heidegger repeats Kant's metaphor it is evident that his account of the principle of reason is a positive revision of the Kantian model. There *is* a gulf between knowledge and thought, and the gulf is precisely the notion of *ground*.

20 Kant, *Critique of judgement*, p. 14.
21 Kant, *Critique of judgement*, p. 37. My emphasis. Cf. *Vom einen neuerdings erhobenen vornehmen Ton*, p. 486.

But is Heidegger committed to a complete rift between (1) and (2) in the same way that Kierkegaard is committed to ruptures between the aesthetic, the ethical and the religious? Like Kierkegaard, Heidegger gives some credence to a preparation for the leap. After all, he arrives at the thought of the leap only by following detours along the path of thought: 'But these paths and detours have brought us to the leap. The detours evidently could not replace the leap, still less accomplish it; but in a certain way they prepare us for the leap.'[22] Kierkegaard and Heidegger mainly differ in that the former understands the leap in terms of a gulf between philosophical and religious categories while the latter takes religious thought as a preparation for a leap from philosophy to thought. This comparison only takes us so far, however, and we can draw out the differences between the two more readily if we recur to Heidegger's earlier remarks on the leap in *An introduction to metaphysics*. We come into the discussion with Heidegger questioning the ground of the fundamental question of philosophy: 'Why?'

At first glance, he tells us, we are liable to think that the question 'Why the why?' is merely playing with words:

> But if we decline to be taken in by surface appearances we shall see that the question 'why', this question as to the essent as such in its entirety, goes beyond any mere playing with words, provided we possess sufficient intellectual energy to make the question actually recoil into its 'why' – for it will not do so of its own accord. In so doing we find out that this privileged question 'why' has its ground in a leap through which man thrusts away all the previous security, whether real or imagined, of his life. The question is asked only in this leap; it *is* the leap; without it there is no asking . . . Here it may suffice to say that the leap in this questioning arrives at its own ground. We call such a leap, which opens up its own source, the original source or origin [*Ur-sprung*], the finding of one's own ground.[23]

No doubt there are elements of existential pathos in this passage which recall Kierkegaard's opposition of speculative philosophy and life, but Heidegger is quick to distinguish his critique of philosophy's privileged question from the early Christian's rejection of philosophy as 'foolishness'. However, while the

22 Heidegger, *Le principe de raison*, p. 134.
23 Heidegger, *An introduction to metaphysics*, p. 5.

problem of the difference between beings and Being is in place here, it is only in *Der Satz vom Grund* that we find a deft formulation. First of all, there is no doubt in the later text that the leap is not a matter of existential choice, as it was for Kierkegaard, but a consequence of listening to the voice of Being. And in the second place, Heidegger draws a succinct distinction between asking the question 'Why?', which involves eliciting the ground of something else, and offering the explanation 'Because' in which one's own ground is adduced. In other words, Heidegger draws a firm line between standing *before* a ground and standing *in one's own* ground.

It is common, all too common, to picture Kierkegaard and Heidegger, in their different ways, as opposed to Hegel. Interestingly enough, though, it is Hegel who first formulates a notion of the leap; and it is Hegel who can help us specify what it is to stand in one's own ground. In the preface to the *Phenomenology* the Spirit's development through history is compared to the growth of a child who makes 'a qualitative leap' in its maturity.[24] This leap is, of course, a necessary part of the dialectic's forward motion; and Hegel's metaphor places a stress upon another important point: for the dialectic is not an *unfolding* of consciousness, it is an aleatory process of *growing*. There is no question of the dialectic being a deduction from clear and distinct *archai*; on the contrary, the dialectic must stand in its own *archai*. Donald Verene grasps the importance of this for the Hegelian dialectic: 'What consciousness requires to have the new object is a new *arche*, a new first principle. *Archai* come from nowhere. They come when needed and they come from nowhere. They are drawn forth from consciousness suddenly and without method, that is, without some set procedure. Consciousness turns to itself and suddenly has in its hands something of itself that it did not know was there in any explicit sense.'[25]

The difference between Hegel and Heidegger is that while for Hegel there are many leaps, for Heidegger there is only one. We may have distinguished Heidegger's leap from Kierkegaard's, but for those who remain uneasy about 'the voice of Being',

24 Walter Kaufman, trans. and ed., *Hegel* (New York: Anchor Books, 1966), p. 20.
25 Donald P. Verene, *Hegel's recollection*, SUNY Series in Hegelian Studies. (Albany: State University of New York Press, 1985), p. 24.

there is a need to contest the text of philosophy on its own grounds. This is, I think, the abiding difference between Heidegger and Derrida; but the difference can be uncovered more swiftly by reference to a well-known passage by Paul de Man. After discussing the apparently unbridgeable gulf between contemporary semiology and rhetorical criticism, de Man turns to an example, the closing lines of Yeats's 'Among school children'. We need concern ourselves only with the poem's final line: 'How can we know the dancer from the dance?' De Man has just blocked out the main lines of the traditional reading of the poem, the one which prizes the poem's rhetoric over its grammar:

> A more extended reading, always assuming that the final line is to be read as a rhetorical question, reveals that the thematic and rhetorical grammar of the poem yields a consistent reading that extends from the first line to the last and that can account for all the details in the text. It is equally possible, however, to read the last line literally rather than figuratively.[26]

So we have two ways of hearing the one line (and, by implication, the entire poem). More particularly, we must respond to two possible tones: the rhetorical reading (1') in which the question provides its own answer, that we *cannot* know the dancer from the dance; and the grammatical reading (2') in which the line is read as asking, with real concern, how *can* we know the dancer from the dance? Now if we adopt (2') the urgency of the tone will reverberate back throughout the entire poem, de Man assures us, so that what we normally interpret rhetorically can be interpreted grammatically. De Man nowhere mentions Heidegger in this context, but so far we have a perfectly orthodox extension of Heidegger's reading of the text of philosophy to a literary text. We may not anticipate a leap from philosophy to non-philosophy but it seems likely that de Man will ask us to make a leap from a traditional reading of the poem to a non-traditional reading. In point of fact, though, his conclusion is far more disturbing – for Heidegger as well as for literary criticism. After making out a plausible case for each reading, de Man remarks as follows:

> This . . . should suffice to suggest that two entirely coherent but entirely incompatible readings can be made to hinge on one line, whose grammatical structure is devoid of ambiguity,

26 Paul de Man, *Allegories of reading*, p. 11.

but whose rhetorical mode turns the mood as well as the mode of the poem upside down. Neither can we say ... that the poem simply has two meanings that exist side by side. The two meanings have to engage each other in direct confrontation, for the one reading is precisely the error denounced by the other and has to be undone by it. Nor can we in any way make a valid decision as to which of the readings can be given priority over the other; none can exist in the other's absence.[27]

The genealogy of this move is not hard to trace. When Kant identified the antinomies of pure reason – what he called, in a letter to Christian Garve, 'the scandal of ostensible contradiction of reason with itself'[28] – he was led to limit the scope of pure reason by critique. Hegel agreed with this identification and characterisation; but rather than claiming, with Kant, that the antinomies expose the illusions of pure reason, he maintained that *both* sides of the antinomies offer true perspectives on the nature of reality. It is true, Heidegger tells us, that there is a contradiction in reason. Indeed, it is to be found in the principle of sufficient reason itself: we may discover it by attending closely to the voice of Being, and respond by leaping from reason's domain into the realm of thought. Derrida – followed here by de Man – offers a fourth variation on this theme. Heidegger is right, he claims, to say that the antinomies are not found at the level of concepts but at the level of interpretation, and to claim that this is symptomatic of philosophy as such; but he is wrong to make a leap from reason to thought. We cannot decide between either interpretation on purely formal grounds, not for sceptical reasons but by virtue of the very systematicity of the text of philosophy. There is no need to make a leap out of philosophy because any philosophical text will generate at least one statement which escapes its jurisdiction and which will trouble philosophy from within.

The philosophical parricide has been a powerful figure from when Plato gave voice to the Eleatic Stranger in the *Sophist* 241d to the present day. To be sure, there are many contenders for the title of the thinker who ends philosophy – Nietzsche, Kierkegaard and Wittgenstein amongst them – but our present discussion provides us with a definite tradition. Kant wishes to end

27 De Man, *Allegories of reading*, p. 12.
28 Arnulf Zweig, ed. and trans., *Kant*, p. 252.

dogmatic metaphysics; in elaborating a dialectic which thrives upon its contestation, Hegel folds all future thought into his system and so places his seal on all philosophy; and Heidegger attempts to overcome philosophy as onto-theology. Finally, Derrida tropes what has become, paradoxically enough, a philosophical tradition of ending philosophy by distinguishing between 'closure' and 'end' then by situating both philosophy and the attempts to end it with respect to what cannot be named by philosophy. Yet just as philosophy survives the deconstruction of philosophy as onto-theology (by becoming grammatology, for example), so too theology may survive the deconstruction of theology as onto-theology. Derrida undoubtedly provides us with the most rigorous mode of critique of philosophy; but this needs to be supplemented by the Heideggerian reflection upon the relation between philosophy and theology.

2   God and Being

Let us retrace our steps a little. In chapter 3 I distinguished between thinking of God as a particular kind of being, and therefore a metaphysical entity, and the possibility that it is metaphysics which compels us to imagine God as a particular kind of being. I argued there that the only kind of non-metaphysical theology which would survive the strictures laid down by Derrida would be a negative theology which deconstructs the metaphysics at work within positive theology. It may be the case that God is not a being; but there is still a problem to consider: is God to be identified with Being?

Towards the end of the second volume of *Nietzsche*, Heidegger focuses upon a short untitled text of Leibniz's which he dubs 'The twenty-four statements'. These short remarks provide us with a concise account of Leibniz's view of the principle of ground. The first draws out an important consequence of the principle of sufficient reason: 'There is a *ground* in nature why something exists rather than nothing. This is a consequence of the great principle that nothing exists without a ground, just as there also must be a ground why this exists rather than something else.'[29] That this ground could be solely a formal cause is

29 Heidegger, *The end of philosophy*, (London: Souvenir Press, 1975), p. 49. This text does not appear in the English translation of *Nietzsche*.

then eliminated: 'This ground ought to be in some real being or cause. For a *cause* is nothing else than a real ground, and the truths of possibilities and *necessities* . . . would not produce anything unless the possibilities were grounded in an actually existing thing.'[30] Rightly or wrongly, Leibniz stresses the principle's ontological import.

Whether this is a clarification or a mystification is something I have touched upon earlier. Of chief importance, here and now, is the theological use to which Leibniz puts the principle. This is Leibniz's third statement:

> But this being must be necessary; otherwise, a ground would again have to be sought why it exists rather than not – contrary to our hypothesis. That being is, of course, the ultimate ground of things and is usually designated by the one word GOD.[31]

'Nothing is without ground' is not only the text of philosophy, then, it is also the text of theology. This invites the obvious question, what sort of theology are we committed to if we hear the principle of sufficient reason as (2)? The major shift we have to accomplish is not to think of God as a being – the *ens originarium, ens summum* and *ens entium* – but rather as Being: not Being as a ground for something but as standing in its own ground. In the displaced philosophical vocabulary in which Heidegger is forced to express (2), all that can be said is 'Being and ground: the same'. So it would seem likely that we should write the theological correlative of (2) as 'Being and God: the same'.

This identification of Being and God is a very common move with respect to certain grafts of Heidegger's later thought on to theology. In re-thinking Christian theology along Heideggerian lines, John Macquarrie aims to show that 'the understanding of God as being rather than as *a* being will bring new intelligibility and relevance to many traditional doctrines'.[32] One response to

---

30 Heidegger, *The end of philosophy*, p. 50.
31 Heidegger, *The end of philosophy*, p. 50. Elsewhere, Heidegger shows how the Leibnizian model of intuitive knowledge of the *archai* is that of the *visio Dei*, God's intuitive cognition. See *The metaphysical foundations of logic*, trans. Michael Heim (Bloomington: Indiana University Press, 1984), pp. 63–65 and p. x.
32 John Macquarrie, *Principles of Christian theology* (London: SCM Press, 1966), p. 107.

this claim is to cite Heidegger's various denials of it. At the 1960 meeting of 'old Marburgers', he suggested that 'philosophical thinking is to being as theological thinking is to the self-revealing God', which makes it quite clear that, in his mind, Being and God are not to be identified.[33] And elsewhere he is still more insistent, telling us that Being 'is not God' and that the word 'Being' has no place in a theology.[34] The difficulty with this response, however, is that Heidegger offers very little by way of explanation of his statements and they are by no means self-evident.

Uncertainty over Heidegger's statements concerning God and Being arise partly from his vocabulary, partly from the parallels he draws between thought and mysticism. Macquarrie offers a defence of his interpretation of Being as God in observing that 'being seems to have all the characteristics of God, even grace'.[35] True, Heidegger's later vocabulary has an unmistakable Christian resonance: the notion of *Seinsgeschick* is in some respects not unlike the Catholic belief in the progressive revelation of doctrine; and the consolation of religion is surely suggested by such words and phrases as 'Shepherd of Being', 'Openness', 'Lighting', 'Call of Being' and 'Being as gift'. Even so, Macquarrie's reasoning here is not entirely persuasive. Heidegger is loath to identify Being and God, Macquarrie argues, because 'Heidegger thinks that the God of Christianity has been conceived as an entity'.[36] To be sure, Heidegger does think that Christian theology, especially scholasticism, has apprehended God as a being; it is for this very reason that he distinguishes between the *god* of onto-theology and the divine *God* of the early Christians and the mystics. Furthermore, Heidegger agrees with Hölderlin that we live in the time of the 'default of God'.[37] Metaphysics has impaired our openness to the divine God, and all we can do, at present, is content ourselves with interpreting the traces of the withdrawn God. In any event, the metaphysical concept of God

---

33 J. M. Robinson and J. B. Cobb Jr., eds., *The later Heidegger and theology*. New Frontiers in Theology, Vol. 1. (New York: Harper and Row, 1963), pp. 43, 190.
34 Heidegger, 'Letter on humanism', in *Basic writings*, p. 210; and *The piety of thinking*, p. 184.
35 Macquarrie, *Twentieth-century religious thought* Revised edition (London: SCM, 1971), p. 355.
36 Macquarrie, *Twentieth-century religious thought*, p. 355.
37 Heidegger, 'What are poets for?', in *Poetry, language, thought*, p. 91.

must be displaced, and one way in which this can be done is by talk of the 'holy' and the 'gods' which, unlike talk of 'God', is free from metaphysical associations. But Macquarrie is not entirely in the wrong, either, for in *Der Satz vom Grund* Heidegger draws parallels between the thinker's leap out of metaphysics and the mystic's radical denial of God as a ground for beings. And this implies that there is some sort of relation between Being and God.

Yet even if Heidegger's dismissals were self-evident, there would still be difficulties. For in its valued equivocity the statement 'Being and God: the same' covers quite different formulations: Aquinas's *deus est suum esse* and Eckhart's *esse est deus*. We have seen that metaphysics articulates itself in the space between Being and beings; but there is another distinction which is of importance here, between *essentia* and *existentia*. Within metaphysics, Being is fashioned as the essence of all that exists. Now when Aquinas claims that God is His own act of being, we have an unequivocal statement of God's uniqueness: He is the one being whose existence coincides exactly with His essence. In characterising God this way, Aquinas identifies the onticoontological distinction with that between *essentia* and *existentia* and thus propounds one of the strongest possible statements of theology as onto-theology. The only way out of this situation, Heidegger insists, is to think the ground of the onticoontological distinction itself, that is, to think Being otherwise than as the Being of beings. One finds this in Eckhart's insistence, *contra* Aquinas, that the act of being is God (or, less archly phrased, that Being properly belongs only to God).

Aquinas may distinguish between God's essence and His existence in epistemological terms, but Eckhart distinguishes between them by way of ontology. To say that Being is God is to maintain that God is pure essence which refuses the possibility of any existential predicate. God, here, is not the essence of beings and therefore an absolute ground: He is essence without determinate existence. Heidegger's remarks on this are worth attention:

> When Meister Eckhart says 'God' he means Godhead, not deus but deitas, not ens but essentia, not nature but what is above nature, the essence – the essence to which, as it were, every existential determination must still be refused, from which every additio existentiæ must be kept at a distance.

255

> Hence he also says: 'Spräche man von Gott er ist, das wäre hinzugelegt'. 'If it were said of God that he is, that would be added on'. Meister Eckhart's expression 'das wäre hinzugelegt' is the German translation, using Thomas' phrase, of: it would be an additio entis . . . Thus God is for himself his 'not'; that is to say, he is the most universal being, the purest indeterminate possibility of everything possible, pure nothing. He is the nothing over against the concept of every creature, over against every determinate possible and actualized being.[38]

Heidegger is right to draw the contrast between Aquinas and Eckhart: but it can be pushed even further. Whereas for Aquinas negative theology is a correction to positive theology, for Eckhart negative theology precedes all positive theology.

Appropriately enough, Derrida selects Meister Eckhart as an exemplary practitioner of negative theology; yet, despite Eckhart's refusals to ascribe existential predicates to the Godhead, Derrida nonetheless concludes that 'This negative theology is still a theology'.[39] The evidence he cites is, at first glance, impressive; from the sermon 'Quasi stella matutina' we have the remark, 'When I said that God was not a Being and was above Being, I did not thereby contest his Being, but on the contrary attributed to him a more elevated Being'.[40] If one reads this in the context of Eckhart's entire sermon, Eckhart says that God (or Being) is to be thought in a distinct manner from beings. For Eckhart, God lives without a 'why', without a ground; and we can only be one with God when we have overcome all desire to ground our belief in God.[41] Indeed, as Heidegger implicitly shows, this very discourse regards onto-theology as an addition, a supplement, to what conditions onto-theology as such. We must remember, too, that Eckhart's account of God does not come in isolation; it is plainly framed with his brother Dominican's account in mind. Although the *form* of Eckhart's account of

---

38 Heidegger, *The basic problems of phenomenology*, trans. and introd. Albert Hofstadter (Bloomington: Indiana University Press, 1982), pp. 90–91.
39 Derrida, *Writing*, p. 146.
40 Derrida, *Writing*, p.146. Cf. 'Thus when I say that God is not being and that he is above being, I have denied him being but, rather, I have dignified and exalted being in him.' R.M. Blakney, trans. *Meister Eckhart* (New York: Harper and Row, 1941), p. 219.
41 E. College and B. McGinn, trans. *Meister Eckhart*. Pref. H. Smith. The Classics of Western Spirituality (New York: Paulist Press, 1981), p. 60.

God and Being is a reversal of Aquinas's, it is nevertheless situated with respect to a general economy. In strict terms, then, Eckhart's definition of God deconstructs Aquinas's definition.[42]

But we are getting ahead of ourselves. Eckhart's account of the relation between Being and God suggests, as Heidegger admits, 'an extreme precision and depth of thought' but we should take it as *clarifying* Heidegger's thought, not converging with it.[43] Where Heidegger departs from Eckhart is in pressing for an absolute distinction between philosophical and theological discourse: not because they are such distinct areas of enquiry but because what was possible for Eckhart is no longer possible. If comparisons between Heidegger and theologians must be made, it is perhaps more accurate to compare Heidegger's later thought with that of Karl Barth. S.U. Zuidema contends that 'with Barth God is being; and with Heidegger Being is divine', but this misses the point entirely.[44] As we have seen, Heidegger proposes an *analogia proportionalitatis* between thinking and theology. Just as thought is a response to the voice of Being, so theology is a response to faith in God's self-revelation. And as the analogy is between proportions, not elements, Heidegger in no way links God and Being. The point of the analogy, furthermore, is to show that revelation does not answer to epistemological or ontological conditions. Despite all the surface disagreements, which Heinrich Ott has patiently put into perspective,[45] Barth and Heidegger agree to reject the *analogia entis*. That is, they agree that God reveals Himself in the realm of the sacred though not in the realm of Being as defined by the ontico-ontological distinction.

If this is so, philosophy and theology are, while not wholly incommensurate, quite different in orientation. It is not just that we cannot identify God with Being; we cannot even identify God with Being's essential *origin:* talk of *Ereignis* or the *Austrag*

---

42 For Heidegger's comments on these definitions see 'A Heidegger seminar on Hegel's *Differenzschrift*', trans. William Lovitt, *Southwestern Journal of Philosophy*, 11, (1980), p. 38.

43 Heidegger, *Le principe de raison*, p. 106.

44 S.U. Zuidema, 'The idea of revelation with Karl Barth and with Martin Heidegger: the comparability of their patterns of thought', *Free University Quarterly* (Amsterdam), 4 (1955), p. 71.

45 I have in mind Ott's second book, *Denken und Sein* (1959) and I am indebted to Cornelius van Til's lucid account of Ott in his article 'The later Heidegger and theology', *Westminster Theological Journal*, 26 (1964), pp. 125–36.

belongs to a different sphere than talk of God and the holy. Heidegger insists upon this: 'nothing religious', he assures us, 'is ever destroyed by logic; it is destroyed only by the God's withdrawal'.[46] More generally, Heidegger claims that theology should derive its categories and criteria from faith, not from philosophy. Thus theology has a stake in the overcoming of philosophy as onto-theology – something I have explored in the third chapter. But now I propose to pursue the same issue from a slightly different angle, with the hope of reaching further.

There has been a good deal of work on the role of interpretation in Heidegger's thought. From time to time we have had to distinguish the Heideggerian project of *Destruktion* from the Derridean programme of deconstruction, even while admitting a filiation between them. We need to focus more intently upon them, and the best way to begin is by reminding ourselves how Heidegger introduces the notion of *Destruktion*. We must therefore turn to the beginning of *Being and time*:

> If the question of Being is to have its own history made transparent, then this hardened tradition must be loosened up, and the concealments which it has brought about must be dissolved. We understand this task as one in which by taking *the question of Being as our clue*, we are to *destroy* the traditional content of ancient ontology until we arrive at those primordial experiences in which we achieved our first ways of determining the nature of Being – the ways which have guided us ever since.[47]

So *Destruktion* does not signify a nihilist destruction but a de-structuring, a loosening up, of the history of ontology. It is a quest for the origins of the formulation of the question of Being: what is it in western philosophy which requires that Being be taken as the ground of beings?

To this question we respond with a question of our own: what is Heidegger's *attitude* to these origins? His specification of the project of *Destruktion* provides us with an answer:

> In thus demonstrating the origin of our basic ontological concepts by an investigation in which their 'birth certificate' is displayed, we have nothing to do with a vicious relativising of ontological standpoints. But this destruction is just as far from

46 Heidegger, *What is called thinking?*, p. 10.
47 Heidegger, *Being and time*, trans. J. Macquarrie and E. Robinson (Oxford: Basil Blackwell, 1973), p. 44.

having the *negative* sense of shaking off the ontological tradition. We must, on the contrary, stake out the positive possibilities of that tradition, and this always means keeping it
within its *limits* . . . On its negative side, this destruction does
not relate itself towards the past; its criticism is aimed at
'today'.[48]

Like Kantian 'critique', Heideggerian '*Destruktion*' is concerned
to set the limits within which metaphysics properly operates.
Unlike Kant, however, Heidegger understands Being as tempo-
rality and, consequently, metaphysics to be properly conditioned by historical rather than by *a priori* categories. For Kant
there can be no reason other than a lack of perspicacity on the
part of Leibniz, Hume and others why the substance of the
Critique of pure reason could not have been formulated earlier than
it actually was. Heidegger, however, seems to believe that his
critique of metaphysics depends upon a *kairos*, a particular
moment when it is appropriate to act. This brings us to a second
point. 'Destruction means – to open our ears', Heidegger tells
us, 'to make ourselves free for what speaks to us in tradition as
the Being of beings'.[49] The *Destruktion* of philosophy as metaphysics involves recovering what has remained *unheard* in a
philosophical text during the history of philosophy and putting
it to use in the project of overcoming metaphysics.

Whatever else it is, *Destruktion* is a mode of textual interpretation. But it soon becomes evident that this is a hermeneutic with
very definite presuppositions about language. 'In its essence,
language is neither expression nor an activity of man', Heidegger contends, 'Language speaks'.[50] And elsewhere we are
told, 'Language is the house of Being'.[51] Heidegger suggests that
we hear the voice of Being in language. When we read a text,
whether Aristotle's *Physics* or Trakl's 'A winter evening', we hear
the author's expression and, if we are attentive, the voice of
Being which may well run counter to what is literally said in the
text. There is a good deal of muddled exposition of Heidegger on
this point. 'In calling language the *arrival of being*', Paul Meier
argues, 'Heidegger wants to indicate the occurrence of being in a
form wherein it clears a space for itself in the human world as a

48 Heidegger, *Being and time*, p. 44.
49 Heidegger, *What is philosophy?* p. 73. Also see, *On the way to language*, p. 20.
50 Heidegger, 'Language', in *Poetry, language, thought*, p. 197.
51 Heidegger, 'The nature of Language', in *On the way to language*, p. 63.

bridge between man and the being of the world with him'.[52] What is wrong here is just this metaphor of the bridge. Meier is quick to point out that the bridge metaphor 'does not mean a subsequent connection of two independent entities, human language and being, because it is in the transition of being into language that the thingness of the world of historical existence is constituted';[53] but this still misses the point, since Heidegger insists that there can be no construction, no bridge, from language as expression to language as the revelation of Being.[54] To pass from one to the other one must negotiate a leap, 'a sudden leap of insight'.[55]

It is because of this leap from reason to thought that Heidegger prefers the word 'illumination' to 'interpretation' as a description of his 'exegetical' essays, especially those on literary texts. It is Being which illumines beings, and although Heidegger's illuminations are in some sense answerable to their texts there is no method by which one can pass from text to illumination. The New Criticism could hardly be described as a *method* of literary interpretation, but even here there are traits to locate – paradox, irony, ambiguity, and so forth – if one is to pass from text to interpretation. By contrast, Heidegger claims that 'Language speaks by saying, this is, by showing', and far from being an accidental property of language this saying as showing is essential to language.[56] Still more importantly, 'The same word, however, the word for Saying, is also the word for Being ... Saying and Being, word and thing, belong to each other in a veiled way'.[57] If we put Heidegger's etymological argument to one side we have the claim that Being is disclosed in the essence of language. Or as he elsewhere remarks, 'Being speaks always and everywhere throughout language'.[58]

Assuming for the moment that one does hear the voice of Being in a text, the interpretation – or illumination, if you will –

52 P. J. Meier, 'Fundamental ontology and positive theology: Martin Heidegger's way of thinking', *Journal of Religious Thought* (Washington), 17 (1960), p. 113.
53 Meier, 'Fundamental ontology and positive theology', p. 113.
54 Heidegger, 'The way to language', in *On the way to language*, p. 124.
55 Heidegger, 'Language in the poem', in *On the way to language*, p. 161.
56 Heidegger, 'The way to language', pp. 124, 123.
57 Heidegger, 'Words', in *On the way to language*, p. 155. Cf. p. 135.
58 Heidegger, 'The Anaximander fragment', in *Early Greek thinking*, trans. D.F. Krell and F.A. Capuzzi (New York: Harper and Row, 1975), p. 52.

which would result would be unheard in that text to the extent to which one remains within the epoch of onto-theology. There would therefore be two interpretations of the text: that which accords with metaphysics and that which leaps out of metaphysics. Heidegger does not reject the metaphysical interpretation out of hand – it has, after all, served its purpose in the history of Being – but he does claim that it is the non-metaphysical interpretation, the illumination, which is true: not because it corresponds to a certain state of affairs but because it illuminates such a state. 'There is a dialogue between *thinking* and *poetry*', Heidegger tells us;[59] but there is also a dialogue between thinking and theology which, similarly, takes its bearings from hermeneutic questions.

Which brings us to Rudolf Bultmann, the theologian with whom Heidegger's name is most often linked. In rough outline, Bultmann's project is to release the *Kerygma* of the Gospel from the detritus of mythology which, to the contemporary reader, seems to bind it to a pre-scientific world-view. To this end, Bultmann distinguishes between historical modes: *Historie*, the order of recordable factual events, and *Geschichte*, 'the stream of historical happening' as Macquarrie nicely phrases it.[60] Upon Bultmann's understanding, the Gospel is encountered in *Geschichte* not in *Historie*; and with this distinction we have a direct heir of Lessing's recognition of the unbridgeable gulf between the accidental truths of history and the necessary truths of reason.

The influence of Heidegger here is variously apparent, but I want to accent only one aspect: '*de-mythologizing*', Bultmann explains, '*is an hermeneutic method*, that is, a method of interpretation, of exegesis'.[61] Rather than hearing the voice of Being in a text, Bultmann enjoins us to listen for the voice of God in the gospels; and we can do that, it seems, only if we can hear Jesus's eschatological preaching without mythological additions. For our purposes, just two points need detain us. As Ott showed as far back as 1955, the distinction between *Historie* and *Geschichte*, between the past as past and the past as presently encountered,

---

59 Heidegger, 'Language in the poem', p. 160.
60 Macquarrie, *An existentialist theology* (Harmondsworth: Penguin, 1973), p. 151.
61 Rudolf Bultmann, *Jesus Christ and mythology* (New York: Charles Scribner's Sons, 1958), p. 45.

commits Bultmann to viewing the present as 'a point without extension [*ausdehnungsloser Punkt*] between the realm of genuine and of secondary history'.[62] Ott objects that Bultmann leaves no room for the 'great deeds of God', creation and apocalypse, and one could also point to the metaphysics harboured in Bultmann's view of time and to the allegorical character of demythologising. Although Bultmann wishes to follow Heidegger in the *Destruktion* of metaphysics, his theology keeps reintroducing what it tries to bypass.

But there is another way in which Heidegger's thought is associated with non-metaphysical theology. Here there is no question of using Heidegger's thought to construct a non-metaphysical theology but rather to spell out what it means for a theology to be non-metaphysical. The theology in question is Karl Barth's. I do not propose to see if this theology is non-metaphysical – that would take far too long – only to assess one part of the case, developed by Ott, for claiming that it is. Heidegger and Barth agree in rejecting the *analogia entis:* whereas the one thinks Being as an event of disclosure, as that which lets beings be, the other takes God to have no ontological relation with man, and as thinkable only in a relationship of faith. There is further apparent agreement in that Heidegger characterises the relationship between Being and beings by way of a double movement of revealing [*ent-bergend*] and concealing [*bergend*] – 'As it reveals itself in beings, Being withdraws', as we are told elsewhere[63] – while Barth's fundamental tenet is that God is at once wholly revealed and wholly hidden: 'He unveils Himself as the One He is by veiling Himself in a form which He Himself is not'.[64]

We must be careful not to forget that, in drawing comparisons between Heidegger and Barth, we are dealing with an analogy of proportionality, not of proportion. Accordingly, the path out of metaphysics does not consist in identifying Being and God but in attending to the ways in which Being and God reveal themselves. As I showed in part II, the metaphysics in both philosophy and theology is shaken by a double movement of revealing and concealing; and if Heidegger and Barth *do* establish

62 Heinrich Ott, *Geschichte und Heilsgeschichte in der Theologie Rudolf Bultmanns*, p. 138. Quoted by C. Van Til, 'The later Heidegger and theology', p. 126.
63 Heidegger, 'The Anaximander fragment', p. 26.
64 Barth, *Church dogmatics*, II.i., p. 52.

non-metaphysical discourses it is owing to a respect for this double movement. More often than not, however, there is a failure amongst commentators to take this equivocal movement with sufficient seriousness. Even Ott succumbs to this in affirming that when Yahweh says 'I am that I am' He 'asserts his supremacy above every concept of man. Yet he applies the idea of being to himself. There is no metaphysics here'.[65] On the contrary, there is *both* metaphysics here *and* the resources for its deconstruction. The words which the author of Exodus attributes to Yahweh express a position which, in its very act, makes use of the metaphysical concepts which he denies are applicable to Him. And it is through a systematic negation of these concepts, such as occurs in negative theology, that this metaphysics is deconstructed.

One can go further and inquire if even Heidegger takes this equivocal movement of revealing and concealing as seriously as he needs to. Part of the problem is that the project of *Destruktion*, as Heidegger initially formulates it, does not capture the double movement of veiling and unveiling. Hermeneutical violence is integral to the activity of *Destruktion*, and this may well appear to constitute a leap out of metaphysics. Yet it quickly becomes apparent that this is not the case: 'The laying-bare of Dasein's primordial Being must . . . be *wrested* from Dasein by following the *opposite course* from that taken by the falling ontico-ontological tendency of interpretation'.[66] Just as Dasein passes from inauthenticity to authenticity in this act of hermeneutical violence, so too the *Destruktion* of a text seeks to recover, as Caputo puts it, 'its essential tendencies, tendencies which the text conceals'.[67]

If we can accuse Heidegger of a failure it is the failure to think through the consequences of the groundlessness of Being. To be sure, Heidegger wants to claim that hearing the principle of sufficient reason in a new key leads us outside metaphysics: if we hear (1) *Nothing* is *without* ground, we remain within metaphysics; yet if we hear (2) Nothing *is* without *ground*, we no longer remain within. However, (1) and (2) cannot be entirely separated, since as de Man has shown, 'The two meanings have

65 Ott, *Denken und Sein*, pp. 145-46. Paraphrased by C. van Til, p. 129.
66 Heidegger, *Being and time*, p. 359.
67 Caputo, *Heidegger and Aquinas*, p. 247. Cf. Chapter III § 3.

to engage each other in direct confrontation, for the one reading is precisely the error denounced by the other and has to be undone by it'.[68] In other words, the revelation of (2) cannot entirely escape the concealment of (1). We would be overly hasty, however, if we were to conclude that the Heideggerian hermeneutic of unconcealment remains simply within metaphysics. This is plainly seen if we compare Kant and Heidegger. Kant distinguishes between two modes of interpretation, the reasonable and the mystical: the former is unequivocal and unveiled whereas the latter is equivocal and veiled. Heidegger follows suit with the qualification that his interpretations are called the reasonable and the thoughtful. Both philosophers understand there to be a leap between the interpretations. Yet whereas Kant understands the equivocal interpretation to be bad because it conceals, Heidegger holds it to be good because it simultaneously reveals and conceals. And whereas Kant takes the second interpretation to be an unnecessary supplement to the first, Heidegger takes it to supplant the first. That is, Kant thinks the supplement only phenomenally while Heidegger thinks it only transcendentally; but the deconstructive move is to think the supplement as both addition and replacement at once.

To accept (1) is to assent to, or at least remain complicit with, the God of onto-theology, and our guiding question has been what happens, theologically, if we accept (2). The *Destruktion* of the principle of sufficient reason certainly requires us to reject of the God of onto-theology, but it does not replace this with a theology of its own. While Heidegger allows room for God in his thought, he rules out imagining God as Being. With this, our discussion seems to have reached an impasse. Because Heidegger understands religion in such a way that no positive distinction between religion and mysticism can be drawn, we have attended to his residual Kantianism in several places but not where it is perhaps most hidden yet most powerful: in his remarks on mysticism. While Heidegger breaks with Kant in not allowing *thematic* differences between religion and mysticism, perhaps he covertly reinforces Kant in admitting a *structural* difference between them. If this is so, we would be in a position to refine the Heideggerian problematic to explain what goes on

68 De Man, *Allegories of reading*, p. 12.

in non-metaphysical theology. And this is exactly the position we wish to attain.

3 Negative theology *redivivus*

Far from condemning the mystics, as Kant does, Heidegger finds himself in sympathy with them. It has become a common complaint that Heidegger's thought is itself a form of mysticism. 'Unless one is content to achieve a mystical contact with reality', W. T. Jones suggests, 'one must conclude that the phenomenological route out of the Kantian paradigm has reached a dead end in Heidegger'.[69] This complaint is often, at least in part, a response to the tone Heidegger adopts in his later work, and it takes little reflection to recognise that the complaint is itself conditioned by the Kantian idea of mysticism. But there is a sense in which Heidegger's thought may have positive links with mysticism – it may help us to understand the workings of mystical theology – and it is this sense which I wish to explore.

Whereas Kant reads mysticism as philosophy's dangerous 'other', Heidegger testifies to 'the extreme precision and depth of thought' which is to be found in 'great and authentic mysticism'.[70] At first glance, though, what Heidegger means by 'mysticism' seems to differ markedly from Kant's understanding:

> It is the characteristic quality of *medieval mysticism* that it tries to lay hold of the being ontologically rated as the properly essential being, God, in his very essence. In this attempt mysticism arrives at a peculiar speculation, peculiar because it transforms the idea of essence in general, which is an ontological ground of a being, its possibility, its essence, into what is properly actual. This remarkable alteration of essence into a being is the presupposition for the possibility of what is called mystical speculation.[71]

The mystic, accordingly, does not improperly regard Being as the ground of beings – *ens originarium, ens summum* or *ens entium* – which is the metaphysical theologian's congenital problem. Being is properly thought as constituting its own ground, as being groundless. Unlike a thinker such as Heidegger himself,

---

69 W. T. Jones, *A history of western philosophy* (New York: Harcourt Brace Jovanovich, 1975), Vol. V, p. 331.
70 Heidegger, *Le principe de raison*, p. 106.
71 Heidegger, *The basic problems of phenomenology*, p. 90.

however, the mystic makes an additional move: Being, once properly understood, is *then* taken as a being.

It may be worth looking at this more closely. We know that Kant frames mysticism twice: it is the death of all philosophy, and it is a parergon to religion properly conceived. As we have seen, Heidegger has a good deal to say about religion 'properly conceived'; for it is only when religion orients itself by reflecting upon faith and not by deducing its categories from philosophy that it is understood properly. Here mysticism cannot be a parergon to religion, since no qualitative distinction between them can be drawn. So much for the second framing – what about the first? Quite clearly, mysticism maintains a rapport with thought, for it thinks outside the confines of the ontico-ontological distinction; yet it is also outside thought in regarding essence in general as a being. Mysticism, then, is a parergon to thought: in *Der Satz vom Grund*, recall, Heidegger meditates upon Eckhart and Angelus Silesius as a necessary 'detour' *before* making the leap from being to Being.

This Kantian filiation can be traced in more detail, since what makes mysticism a parergon in Heidegger's view is its insistence upon conceiving a general essence as a personal particular. This is a variation upon the case that Kant presents when concluding 'About a recently raised superior tone in philosophy':

> only . . . the didactic proceeding is actually alone philosophical, to bring the moral law in us on to clear concepts according to logical kind of teaching, but that one [proceeding], to personify that law and to make a veiled ISIS out of the morally commanding reason . . . is an aesthetic kind of conceptualization of just the same item; of which one can well make use after, when through the former the principles have already been cleared up, in order to enliven those ideas through sensory even although only analogical representation, but always with some danger of happening into fanciful vision that is the death of all philosophy.[72]

Like Kant, Heidegger has a use for mysticism only when it is already purified by thought. And this is why mysticism must remain a supplement to thought, supplying it with, first, a means of approaching thought and, second, a concrete historical instance of how philosophy can be overcome. There can be no

72 Kant, *Vom einem neuerdings erhobenen vernehmen Ton*, pp. 494–95.

question that Heidegger is far more sympathetic to mysticism than is Kant. But upon my reading, there can also be no question that Heidegger's treatment of mysticism gets its bearings from the critical philosophy.

Does this mean that Heidegger's thought, like Kant's, is itself a negative theology? After a brief study of the Pseudo-Dionysius and St John of the Cross, Ernesto Grassi argues that Heidegger presents us with nothing less than a *reversal* of negative theology:

> The essential difference between Heidegger's philosophy of unhiddenness and negative theology as found in Dionysius and John of the Cross consists in their completely different starting points. They understand divine Being as a Being in and for itself, outside of history, so that it emerges primarily through the theophany of a mystic. Heidegger, however, claims that Being emerges through the 'clearing' of different, purely historical spaces in which particular gods, institutions, and arts appear historically. For negative theology, as well as for Heidegger, Being (God) is 'sublime', but in a fundamentally different sense. In negative theology the sublime and elevated nature of God is defined in the sense that it finally can be made visible only by relinquishing those capacities (rational knowledge, memory, and will) that make possible the 'day' of rational life.[73]

Grassi's construction of negative theology is prone to several objections. Dionysius does not think of God as a being: it is just that image which his negative theology is concerned to deconstruct. And the same holds true of St John of the Cross. Also, it is not the case that Christian mystics entirely *relinquish* rational knowledge, memory and will – that is a stark impossibility. The central point which most mystics make is that one must be *detached* from the things of the world. The mystic does not deny reason, memory or the will; he or she situates them with respect to a far wider configuration. And finally, the mystic does not claim that God is 'made visible' by a revelation: the complicating feature of most mystical discourse is the insistence upon a double movement of revealing and concealing.

Consider St John of the Cross, the bulk of whose theological

73 Ernesto Grassi, *Heidegger and the question of Renaissance humanism* (Binghamton, N.Y.: Center for Medieval and Early Renaissance Studies, 1983), pp. 90–91.

work is cast as commentary upon several of his poems. Explicating the line 'By the secret ladder, disguised' St John writes, 'Not only does a man feel unwilling to give expression to this wisdom, but he finds no adequate means of similitude to signify so sublime an understanding and delicate a spiritual feeling'.[74] The wisdom of God's love is, as he says, 'so secret that it is ineffable'.[75] Now St John may demur at the thought of being able to express his experience of God's grace, but this very scruple occurs in a commentary on a poem which is, as we are repeatedly told, about mystical experience. The poem unveils the experience, yet simultaneously veils it to the extent that it requires a commentary which itself needs to be further unveiled. We must be careful to distinguish between the poem's and commentary's *thematic* point that mystical experience is a matter of both veiling and unveiling, and the *structural* relation of veiling and unveiling which applies generally to all texts. Indeed, it is this very distinction which will help us in coming to a final statement of the difference between grafting the Heideggerian and the Derridean problematics onto the question of non-metaphysical theology.

To go back just one step: Grassi's case that Heidegger's thought reverses negative theology is far from persuasive. The counter argument is more forceful. While Heidegger allows room for God in his thought, he denies any identification of God as Being. If this is so, however, Heidegger seems committed to a negative theology: that God is otherwise than Being. The weak link in the argument is the formulation 'allows room for God in his thought'. For we can say that Heidegger's thought is a negative theology only if he affirms God in the first place. There is no difficulty in establishing Kant's belief in God, and in his case the argument goes through. But Heidegger is somewhat more difficult to pin down. For despite the existential pathos of *Being and time*, Heidegger nearly always speaks as 'thinker', not as man, and as he never fails to remind us the thinker *qua* thinker does not speak of God. Heidegger's personal views, though, are very much beside the point. The important issue is what happens if we add our refinement of the later Heidegger's

74 St John of the Cross, 'The dark night', in *The collected works of St. John of the Cross*, trans. Kiernan Kavanaugh and Otilio Rodriguez (Washington: ICS Publications, 1979), pp. 368–69.
75 St John of the Cross, 'The dark night', p. 368.

thought on to the question of theology. And as we are dealing with an unequivocal affirmation of God, there is no doubt that the theology which follows is a negative theology.

We need only ask now if this Heideggerian negative theology is of a restricted or a general kind. A general negative theology contests metaphysics as such; but, as we have seen, Heidegger's *Destruktion* of metaphysics remains complicit with metaphysics to the extent that it betrays, as Derrida puts it, 'a nostalgic desire to recover the proper name, the unique name of Being'.[76] This suggests that the Heideggerian thematic is ultimately answerable to metaphysics; and this may well be so. Yet where Derrida breaks decisively with Heidegger is in his recognition that metaphysics is structurally encrypted within discourse. It is only through the twin strategies of erasure and palæonymy that metaphysics can be isolated; and the mode of 'isolation' is to situate metaphysics with respect to the general economy of *différance*. Heideggerian theology therefore remains, like its Kantian precursor, a restricted negative theology. However, if we add the Derridean problematic to theology what results is a general negative theology, one which places the value of the proper name in question, and thus provides us with an account of the only possible way in which a theology can resist the illusions of metaphysics.

76 Derrida, 'Deconstruction and the other', p. 110.

Bibliography

Alexander, H. G. ed. *The Leibniz-Clarke correspondence: together with extracts from Newton's Principia and Optiks*. Manchester: Manchester University Press, 1956.

Allen, Judson Boyce. *The ethical poetic of the later middle ages: a decorum of convenient distinction*. Toronto: University of Toronto Press, 1982.

Altieri, Charles. 'Wittgenstein on consciousness and language: a challenge to Derridean literary theory'. *Modern Language Notes*, 91 (1976), pp. 1397–423.

Altizer, Thomas J. J. *et al. Deconstruction and theology*. New York: Crossroad Publishing Co., 1982.

Anderson, James F. *An introduction to the metaphysics of St Thomas Aquinas*. Chicago: Henry Regency, 1969.

Angeles, Peter, ed. *Critiques of God*. Buffalo, NY: Prometheus Books, 1976.

Aquinas, St Thomas. *Summa theologiæ*. London: Eyre and Spottiswoode. Vol. 3. Trans. Herbert McCabe OP (1964). Vol 45. Trans. Roland Potter OP (1970).

Aristotle. *The works of Aristotle*. Ed. W. D. Ross. London: Oxford University Press, 1928. Vols. I, VIII, IX.

Attridge, Derek and Daniel Ferrer, eds. *Post-structuralist Joyce: essays from the French*. Cambridge: Cambridge University Press, 1984.

Augustine, Saint. *The city of God*. Trans. Marcus Dods. Introd. Thomas Merton. New York: Modern Library, 1950.

On Christian doctrine. Trans. D. W. Robertson Jr. New York: Library of Liberal Arts, 1958.

Confessions. Trans. R. S. Pine-Coffin. Harmondsworth: Penguin, 1961.

Bakan, David. *Sigmund Freud and the Jewish mystical tradition*, 1958; rpt. Boston: Beacon Press, 1975.

Barth, Karl. *Church dogmatics*. Ed. G. W. Bromiley and T. F. Torrance. Edinburgh: T. and T. Clarke. Vol. II.i (1957), III.ii (1960).

Barthes, Roland. *Image, music, text*. Trans. Stephen Heath. New York: Hill and Wang, 1977.

The grain of the voice: interviews 1962–1980. Trans. Linda Coverdale. New York: Hill and Wang, 1985.

Bataille, Georges. *Death and sensuality: a study of eroticism and the taboo*. New York: Walker and Co., 1962.

270

Oeuvres complètes. Paris: Gallimard, 1973. Vol. V.
Visions of excess: selected writings, 1927–1939. Ed. and introd. Allan Stoekl. Trans. Allan Stoekl, with Carl R. Lovitt and Donald M. Leslie, Jr. Theory and History of Literature Series, 14. Minneapolis: University of Minnesota Press, 1985.
Benjamin, Walter. *The origins of German tragic drama*. Trans. John Osborne. London: NLB, 1977.
Bernstein, R. J. *Beyond objectivism and relativism: science, hermeneutics, and praxis*. Oxford: Blackwell, 1983.
Blakney, Raymond Bernard, trans. *Meister Eckhart: a modern translation*. New York: Harper and Row, 1941.
Bloom, Harold. *Kabbalah and criticism*. New York: Seabury Press, 1975.
A map of misreading. New York: Oxford University Press, 1975.
Bloom, Harold, et al. *Deconstruction and criticism*. London: Routledge and Kegan Paul, 1979.
Bloomfield, Morton W., ed. *Allegory, myth, and symbol*. Harvard English Studies 9. Cambridge, MA: Harvard University Press, 1981.
Bogel, Fredric V. 'Deconstructive criticism: the logic of Derrida's différance'. *Centrum: working papers of the Minnesota Center For Advanced Studies in Language, Style, and Literary Theory*, 6 (1978), pp. 50–60.
Booth, Wayne C. *A rhetoric of irony*. Chicago: University of Chicago Press, 1974.
Critical understanding: the powers and limits of pluralism. Chicago: University of Chicago Press, 1979.
Bultmann, Rudolf. *Jesus Christ and mythology*. New York: Charles Scribner's Sons, 1958.
Caputo, John D. *The mystical element in Heidegger's thought*. Athens, Ohio: University of Ohio Press, 1978.
Heidegger and Aquinas: an essay on overcoming metaphysics. New York: Fordham University Press, 1982.
Cassirer, Ernst. *Kant's life and thought*. Trans. James Haden. Introd. Stephan Körner. New Haven: Yale University Press, 1981.
Colson, F. H. and G. H. Whitaker, eds. *Philo*. 10 Vols. Loeb Classical Library. London: Heinemann, 1929–71.
Condillac, Etienne Bonnot de. *An essay on the origin of human knowledge: being a supplement to Mr. Locke's Essay on the human understanding*. Facsimile of translation by Thomas Nugent. Introd. Robert G. Weyant. Gainesville, FL. Scholars' Facsimiles and Reprints, 1971.
Croce, B. *What is living and what is dead of the philosophy of Hegel*. Trans. D. Ainslie. London: Macmillan, 1915.
Crossan, John Dominic. *Cliffs of fall: paradox and polyvalence in the parables of Jesus*. New York: Seabury Press, 1980.
Culler, Jonathan. *On deconstruction: theory and criticism after structuralism*. Ithaca: Cornell University Press, 1982.
Curtius, E.R. *European literature and the Latin middle ages*. Trans. W. R. Trask. London: Routledge and Kegan Paul, 1953.
Daniélou, Jean. *From shadows to reality: studies in the biblical typology of the Fathers*. London: Burns and Oates, 1960.

271

'The conception of history in the Christian tradition'. *Journal of Religion*, 30 (1950), pp. 171–79.

'The problem of symbolism'. *Thought* (New York), 25 (1950), pp. 423–40.

'The Fathers and the Scriptures'. *Theology: A Monthly Review*, 57 (1954), pp. 83–89.

Dante. *Paradiso*. The Temple Classics. 1899; rpt. London: J. M. Dent and Sons, 1965.

Dean, William. 'Deconstruction and process theology'. *The Journal of Religion*, 64 (1984), pp. 1–19.

De Lange, N. R. M. *Origen and the Jews: studies in Jewish–Christian relations in third-century Palestine*. Cambridge: Cambridge University Press, 1976.

De Man, Paul. *Allegories of reading: figural language in Rousseau, Nietzsche, Rilke, and Proust*. New Haven: Yale University Press, 1979.

Blindness and insight: essays in the rhetoric of contemporary criticism. 2nd ed., revised. Introd. Wlad Godzich. London: Methuen, 1983.

Derrida, Jacques. *Speech and phenomena: and other essays on Husserl's theory of signs*. Trans. and introd. David B. Allison. Preface Newton Garver. Evanston: Northwestern University Press, 1973.

Of grammatology. Trans. and preface Gayatri Chakravorty Spivak. Baltimore: Johns Hopkins University Press, 1976.

Writing and difference. Trans. and introd. Alan Bass. London: Routledge and Kegan Paul, 1978.

Edmund Husserl's The origin of geometry: an introduction. Trans. and introd. John P. Leavey, Jr. Ed. David B. Allison. Stony Brook, NY: Nicholas Hays, 1978.

Spurs: Nietzsche's styles/Eperons: les styles de Nietzsche. Introd. Stefano Agosti. Trans. Barbara Harlow. Chicago: University of Chicago Press, 1979.

The archeology of the frivolous: reading Condillac. Trans. and introd. John P. Leavey, Jr. Pittsburgh: Duquesne University Press, 1980.

Dissemination. Trans. and introd. Barbara Johnson. London: Athlone Press, 1981.

Positions. Trans. Alan Bass. Chicago: University of Chicago Press, 1981.

Margins of philosophy. Trans. Alan Bass. Chicago: University of Chicago Press, 1982.

Signéponge/Signsponge. Trans. Richard Rand. New York: Columbia University Press, 1984.

Mémoires: for Paul de Man. The Wellek Library Lectures at University of California, Irvine. Trans. Cecile Lindsay, Jonathan Culler and Eduardo Cadava. New York: Columbia University Press, 1986.

Glas. Trans. John P. Leavey, Jr. and Richard Rand. Lincoln: University of Nebraska Press, 1986.

The post card: from Socrates to Freud and beyond. Trans. Alan Bass. Chicago: University of Chicago Press, 1987.

The truth in painting. Trans. Geoff Bennington and Ian McLeod. Chicago: University of Chicago Press, 1987.

De l'esprit: Heidegger et la question. Paris: Galilée, 1987.

Psyché: inventions de l'autre. Paris: Galilée, 1987.

'Limited inc: a b c . . .' Trans. Samuel Weber. *Glyph: Textual Studies*, 2 (1977), pp. 162–254.

'The law of genre'. Trans. Avital Ronell. *Glyph: Textual Studies*, 7 (1980), pp. 202–32.

'The principle of reason: the university in the eyes of its pupils'. Trans. Catherine Porter and Edward P. Morris. *Diacritics*, 13 (1983), pp. 3–20.

Derrida, Jacques, *et al*. *The ear of the other: otobiography, transference, translation*. Ed. Christie V. McDonald. Trans. Peggy Kamuf and Avital Ronell. New York: Schocken Books, 1985.

Descombes, Vincent. *Modern French philosophy*. Trans. L. Scott-Fox and J. M. Harding. Cambridge: Cambridge University Press, 1980.

Detweiler, Robert, ed. *Derrida and biblical studies*. *Semeia* 23. Chico, CA.: Scholars Press, 1982.

Dionysius Areopagita, Pseudo-. *The works of Dionysius the Areopagite*. Trans. Rev. John Parker. 1897–99; rpt. Merrick, NY: Richwood Publishing Co., 1976.

The divine names and mystical theology. Ed. and introd. John D. Jones. Milwaukee: Marquette University Press, 1980.

The divine names and the mystical theology. Trans. C. E. Rolt. London: SPCK, 1940.

Dockrill, D. W. and R. Mortley, eds. *The via negativa*. Papers on the history and significance of negative theology from the Via Negativa Conference held at St Paul's College, University of Sydney, 22–24 May 1981. *Prudentia*, Supplementary Number 1981.

Donoghue, Denis. *Ferocious alphabets*. London: Faber and Faber, 1981.

Dufrenne, Mikel. *Le poétique: précédé de 'Pour une philosophie non théologique'*. Paris: Presses Universitaires de France, 1973.

Eckhart, Meister. *Meister Eckhart: The Essential Sermons, Commentaries, Treatises, and Defense*. Eds. Edmund Colledge and Bernard McGinn. Pref. Huston Smith. The Classics of Western Spirituality. New York: Paulist Press, 1981.

Eco, Umberto. *Semiotics and the philosophy of language*. London: Macmillan Press, 1984.

England, F. E. *Kant's conception of God: a critical exposition of its metaphysical development together with a translation of the Nova dilucidatio*. 1929; rpt. New York: Humanities Press, 1968.

Fackenheim, Emil L. *The religious dimension in Hegel's thought*. Bloomington: Indiana University Press, 1967.

Ferguson, Margaret W. 'Saint Augustine's region of unlikeness: the crossing of exile and language', *Georgia Review*, 29 (1975), pp. 824–64.

Fichte, J.G. *Science of knowledge: with the first and second introductions*. Ed. and trans. Peter Heath and John Lachs. Cambridge: Cambridge University Press, 1982.

Flew, Anthony and Alasdair MacIntyre, eds. *New essays in philosophical theology*. London: SCM Press, 1955.

Foucault, Michel. *The order of things: an archæology of the human sciences.* London: Tavistock, 1970.

The birth of the clinic: an archaeology of medical perception. Trans. A. M. Sheridan Smith. New York: Vintage Books, 1975.

Fraser, Nancy. 'The French Derrideans: politicizing deconstruction or deconstructing the political?' *New German Critique*, 33 (1984), pp. 127–54.

Freud, Sigmund. *Jokes and their relation to the unconscious.* Trans. and ed. James Strachey. Ed. for Penguin by Angela Richards. The Pelican Freud Library, Vol. 6. Harmondsworth: Penguin, 1976.

Gadamer, Hans-Georg. *Truth and method.* Trans. and ed. Garrett Barden and John Cumming. London: Sheed and Ward, 1975.

Hegel's dialectic: five hermeneutical studies. Trans. P. Christopher Smith. New Haven: Yale University Press, 1976.

Geffré, Claude. 'Silence et promesses de la théologie catholique française'. *Revue de théologie et de philosophie*, 114 (1982), pp. 227–245.

Gellrich, Jesse M. *The idea of the book in the middle ages: language theory, mythology, and fiction.* Ithaca: Cornell University Press, 1985.

Gilson, Etienne. *History of Christian philosophy in the middle ages.* London: Sheed and Ward, 1955.

God and philosophy. New Haven: Yale University Press, 1941.

Goodenough, Erwin R. *An introduction to Philo Judaeus.* Second edition. Oxford: Blackwell, 1962.

By light, light: the mystic gospel of Hellenistic Judaism. 1935; rpt. Amsterdam: Philo Press, 1969.

Goodheart, Eugene. *The skeptic disposition in contemporary criticism.* Princeton: Princeton University Press, 1984.

Gould, Eric. 'Deconstruction and its discontents', *Denver Quarterly*, 15 (1980), pp. 90–106.

Graff, Gerald. *Literature against itself.* Chicago: University of Chicago Press, 1979.

Graham, Joseph F., ed. *Difference in translation.* Ithaca: Cornell University Press, 1985.

Grassi, Ernesto. *Heidegger and the question of Renaissance humanism: four studies.* Medieval and Renaissance texts and studies. Binghamton, NY: Center for Medieval and Early Renaissance Studies, 1983.

Greenblatt, Stephen J., ed. *Allegory and representation: selected papers from the English Institute, 1979–80.* New Series, 5. Baltimore: Johns Hopkins University Press, 1981.

Greer, R. A., trans. and introd., *An exhortation to martyrdom, prayer and selected works.* The Classics of Western Spirituality: Origen. London: SPCK, 1979.

Grissoni, Dominique. *Politiques de la philosophie.* Paris: Bernard Granet, 1976.

Guttmann, Julius. *Philosophies of Judaism: the history of Jewish philosophy from biblical times to Franz Rosenzweig.* Introd. R. J. Zuri Werblowsky. Trans. David W. Silverman. New York: Holt, Rinehart and Winston, 1964.

Handelman, Susan. *The slayers of Moses: the emergence of Rabbinic interpre-*

tation in modern literary theory. Albany: State University of New York Press, 1982.

Hans, James S. 'Derrida and freeplay'. *Modern Language Notes*, 94 (1979), pp. 809–26.

'Hermeneutics, play, deconstruction'. *Philosophy Today*, 24 (1980), pp. 299–317.

Hartley, David. *Observations on man, his frame, his duty, and his expectations*. 1749; rpt. Gainsville, FL: Scholars' Facsimiles and Reprints, 1966.

Hartman, Geoffrey H. *Saving the text: literature/Derrida/philosophy*. Baltimore: Johns Hopkins University Press, 1981.

Hebblethwaite, Brian and Stewart Sutherland, eds. *The philosophical frontiers of Christian theology: essays presented to D. M. MacKinnon*. Cambridge: Cambridge University Press, 1982.

Hegel, G.W.F. *Lectures on the history of philosophy*. Trans. E. S. Haldane and Frances H. Simson. Vols. I–III. 1892; rpt. London: Routledge and Kegan Paul, 1955.

Encyclopedia of philosophy. Trans. Gustav Emil Mueller. 1817; rpt. New York: Philosophical Library, 1959.

Lectures on the philosophy of religion: together with a work on the proofs of the existence of God. Trans. E. B. Speirs and J. Burdon Sanderson. Vols. I–III. 1895; rpt. Atlantic Highlands, NJ: Humanities Press, 1974.

The phenomenology of mind. Trans. and introd. J. B. Baillie. 1931; rpt. New York: Harper and Row, 1967.

Philosophy of mind: being part three of the encyclopædia of the philosophical sciences. Trans. William Wallace. Together with the *Zusätze* in Boumann's Text (1845) translated by A. V. Miller. Oxford: Clarendon Press, 1971.

Logic: being part one of the encyclopædia of the philosophical sciences. Trans. William Wallace with foreward by J. N. Findlay. 1830; rpt. Oxford: Clarendon Press, 1975.

Science of logic. Trans. A. V. Miller. Foreword J. N. Findlay. London: George Allen and Unwin, 1969.

The difference between Fichte's and Schelling's system of philosophy. Trans. H. S. Harris and Walter Cerf. Albany: State University of New York Press, 1977.

Lectures on the philosophy of religion. Ed. Peter C. Hodgson. Berkeley: University of California Press, 1984.

Heidegger, Martin. *What is philosophy?* Trans. and introd. William Kluback and Jean T. Wilde. New York: Twayne Publishers, 1962.

The question of Being. Trans. and introd. W. Kluback and Jean T. Wilde. London: Vision Press, 1959.

Kant and the problem of metaphysics. Trans. James S. Churchill. Bloomington: Indiana University Press, 1962.

Le principe de raison. Trans. André Préau. Pref. Jean Beaufret. Paris: Gallimard, 1962.

What is a thing? Trans. W. B. Barton Jr and Vera Deutsch with an analysis by Eugene T. Gendlin. Chicago: Henry Regnery, 1967.

What is called thinking? Trans. J. Glenn Gray. New York: Harper and Row, 1968.
An introduction to metaphysics. Trans. Ralph Manheim. New Haven: Yale University Press, 1968.
Identity and difference. Trans. Joan Stambaugh. New York: Harper and Row, 1969.
The essence of reasons: a bilingual edition, incorporating the German text of Vom Wesen des Grundes. Northwestern University Studies in Phenomenology and Existential Philosophy. Evanston: Northwestern University Press, 1969.
On the way to language. Trans. Peter D. Hertz. New York: Harper and Row, 1971.
On time and Being. Trans. Joan Stambaugh. New York: Harper and Row, 1972.
Being and time. Trans. John Macquarrie and Edward Robinson. Oxford: Blackwell, 1973.
Early Greek thinking. Trans. David Farrell Krell and Frank A. Capuzzi. New York: Harper and Row, 1975.
The end of philosophy. Trans. Joan Stambaugh. London: Souvenir Press, 1975.
Poetry, language, thought. Trans. and introd. Albert Hofstadter. New York: Harper Colophon, 1975.
The piety of thinking. Trans., ed., notes and commentary by James G. Hart and John C. Maraldo. Bloomington: Indiana University Press, 1976.
The question concerning technology and other essays. Trans. and introd. William Lovitt. New York: Harper and Row, 1977.
Basic writings: from Being and time (1927) to The task of thinking (1964). Ed. and introd. David Farrell Krell. London: Routledge and Kegan Paul, 1978.
Nietzsche, Vol. IV: *Nihilism.* Trans. Frank A. Capuzzi. Ed. David Farrell Krell. San Francisco: Harper and Row, 1982.
The basic problems of phenomenology. Trans. and introd. Albert Hofstadter. Bloomington: Indiana University Press, 1982.
The metaphysical foundations of logic. Trans. Michael Heim. Bloomington: Indiana University Press, 1984.
Schelling's treatise on the essence of human freedom. Trans. Joan Stambaugh. Athens, Ohio: Ohio University Press, 1985.
History of the concept of time: prolegomena. Trans. Theodore Kisiel. Bloomington: Indiana University Press, 1985.
'The principle of ground'. Trans. Keith Hoeller. *Man and World,* 7 (1974), pp. 207–22.
'A Heidegger seminar on Hegel's *Differenzschrift'.* Trans. William Lovitt. *Southwestern Journal of Philosophy,* 11 (1980), pp. 9–45.
Heijenoort, J. van, ed. *From Frege to Gödel: a source book in mathematical logic, 1879–1931.* Cambridge, MA: Harvard University Press, 1977.
Hirsch, E. D. 'Derrida's axioms'. Rev. *On deconstruction: theory and criticism after structuralism* by J. Culler. *London Review of Books,* 21 July–3 August 1983, pp. 17–18.

Hoy, David Couzens. *The critical circle: literature, history, and philosophical hermeneutics.* Berkeley: University of California Press, 1978.

Hume, David. *A treatise of human nature.* Ed. L. A. Selby-Bigge. Second edition. Revised P.H. Nidditch. Oxford: Clarendon Press, 1978.

Husserl, Edmund. *The crisis of European sciences and transcendental phenomenology: an introduction to phenomenological philosophy.* Trans. and introd. David Carr. Evanston: Northwestern University Press, 1970.

Cartesian meditations: an introduction to phenomenology. Trans. Dorian Cairns. The Hague: Martinus Nijhoff, 1977.

Logical investigations. Trans. J. N. Findlay. London: Routledge and Kegan Paul, 1970.

Inge, W. R. *Christian mysticism: considered in eight lectures delivered before the University of Oxford.* 1899; rpt. London: Methuen, 1948.

Inwood, M. J. *Hegel.* The Arguments of the Philosophers. London: Routledge and Kegan Paul, 1983.

John of the Cross, St. *The collected works of St John of the Cross.* Trans. Kieran Kavanaugh and Otilo Rodriguez. Washington, DC: ICS Publications, 1979.

Johnston, William. *The mysticism of The cloud of unknowing.* Foreword by Thomas Merton. The Religious Experience Series, 8. 1978; rpt. Wheathampstead, Herts.: Anthony Clarke, 1980.

Jones, Rufus M. *Studies in mystical religion.* London: Macmillan and Co., 1923.

Jones, W. T. *A history of western philosophy.* Second edition, revised. Vol. V. New York: Harcourt Brace Jovanovich, 1975.

Kant, Immanuel. *Werke.* Ed. E. Cassirer *et al.* Berlin: Bruno Cassirer, 1912–22.

Critique of pure reason. Trans. Norman Kemp Smith. London: Macmillan, 1933.

Critique of practical reason and other writings in moral philosophy. Trans. and ed. Lewis White Beck. Chicago: University of Chicago Press, 1949.

The critique of judgement. Trans. James Creed Meredith. 1928; rpt. Oxford: Clarendon Press, 1952.

Critique of practical reason. Trans. Lewis White Beck. Indianapolis: Bobbs-Merrill Educational Publishing, 1956.

Religion within the limits of reason alone. Trans., introd. and notes by Theodore M. Greene and Hoyt H. Hudson. 1934; rpt. New York: Harper and Row, 1960.

Lectures on philosophical theology. Trans. Allen W. Wood and Gertrude M. Clarke. Introd. Allen W. Wood. Ithaca: Cornell University Press, 1978.

'The conflict of the faculties'. Trans. Bernard Bartl. Unpublished partial translation, 1986. Typescript held in the Boyce Gibson Library, University of Melbourne.

'About a recently raised superior tone in philosophy'. Trans. Bernard Bartl. Unpublished translation, 1986. Typescript held in the Boyce Gibson Library, University of Melbourne.

Katz, Nathan. '*Prasanga* and deconstruction: Tibetan hermeneutics and the Yana Controversy'. *Philosophy East and West: A Quarterly of Asian and Comparative Thought*, 34 (1984), pp. 185–204.

Kaufman, Walter, ed. and trans. *Hegel: texts and commentary: Hegel's preface to his system in a new translation with commentary on facing pages and 'Who thinks abstractly?'* New York: Anchor Books, 1966.

ed. *Existentialism from Dostoevsky to Sartre*. Rev. and expanded edition. New York: New America Library, 1975.

Kearney, Richard, ed. *Dialogues with contemporary continental thinkers: the phenomenological heritage*. Manchester: Manchester University Press, 1984.

Kearns, James and Ken Newton. 'An interview with Jacques Derrida'. *Literary Review* (Edinburgh), 14 (1980), pp. 21–22.

Kemp, Peter. 'L'éthique au lendemain des victoires des athéismes: réflexions sur la philosophie de Jacques Derrida', *Revue de théologie et de philosophie*, 111 (1979), pp. 105–21.

Kierkegaard, Søren. *Concluding unscientific postscript*. Trans. David F. Swenson and Walter Lowrie. Princeton: Princeton University Press, 1941.

The concept of irony: with constant reference to Socrates. Trans. Lee M. Capel. London: Collins, 1966.

Knowles, David. *What is mysticism?* London: Burns and Oates, 1967.

Knox, Norman. *The word IRONY and its context, 1500–1755*. Durham, North Carolina: Duke University Press, 1961.

Krupnick, Mark, ed. *Displacement: Derrida and after*. Bloomington: Indiana University Press, 1983.

Lacoue-Labarthe, Philippe and Jean-Luc Nancy, eds. *Les fins de l'homme: à partir du travail de Jacques Derrida*. Paris: Éditions Galilée, 1981.

Lampe, G. W. H. and Woollcombe, K. J. *Essays on typology*. Studies in Biblical Theology, 22. London: SCM Press, 1957.

Lauer, Quentin. 'Hegel's negative theology'. *Journal of Dharma: An International Quarterly of World Religions*, 6 (1981), pp. 46–58.

Leibniz, G. W. *Theodicy*. Trans. L.M. Huggard. New Haven: Yale University Press, 1952.

Léon-Dufour, Xavier, ed. *Exégèse et herméneutique*. Paris: Seuil, 1971.

Lessing, Gotthold. *Lessing's theological writings: selections in translation with an introductory essay*. Ed. and trans. Henry Chadwick. Stanford: Stanford University Press, 1957.

Levinas, Emmanuel. *Totality and infinity: an essay on exteriority*. Trans. Alphonso Lingis. The Hague: Martinus Nijhoff, 1979.

Otherwise than Being or beyond essence. Trans. Alphonso Lingis. The Hague: Martinus Nijhoff, 1981.

Longxi, Zhang. 'The *Tao* and the *Logos:* notes on Derrida's critique of logocentrism'. *Critical Inquiry*, 11 (1985), pp. 385–98.

Lossky, Vladimir. *The mystical theology of the eastern church*. London: James Clarke and Co., 1957.

Louth, Andrew. *The origins of the Christian mystical tradition: from Plato to Denys*. Oxford: Clarendon Press, 1981.

McKenna, Andrew J. 'Biblioclasm: joycing Jesus and Borges'. *Diacritics*, 8 (1978), pp. 15–29.

Mackey, Louis. 'Slouching toward Bethlehem: deconstructive strategies in theology'. *Anglican Theological Review*, 65 (1983), pp. 255–72.

MacKinnon, D. M. *The problem of metaphysics.* Cambridge: Cambridge University Press, 1974.

'Kant's philosophy of religion'. *Philosophy*, 50 (1975), pp. 131–44.

Macksey, Richard and Eugenio Donato, eds. *The structuralist controversy: the languages of criticism and the sciences of man.* Proceedings of The Languages of Criticism and the Sciences of Man symposium. 18–21 October, 1966. Baltimore: Johns Hopkins University Press, 1972.

MacLeod, C. W. 'Allegory and mysticism in Origen and Gregory of Nyssa'. *Journal of Theological Studies*, ns 22 (1971), pp. 362–79.

Macquarrie, John. *Principles of Christian theology.* London: SCM Press, 1966.

Twentieth-century religious thought: the frontiers of philosophy and theology, 1900–1970. Rev. ed. London: SCM Press, 1971.

An existentialist theology: a comparison of Heidegger and Bultmann. Harmondsworth: Penguin, 1973.

Magliola, Robert. *Derrida on the mend.* West Lafayette, IN: Purdue University Press, 1984.

Mallarmé, Stéphane. *The poems.* Trans. and introd. Keith Bosley. Harmondsworth: Penguin, 1977.

Marion, Jean-Luc. *Dieu sans l'être.* Paris: Fayard, 1982.

Marshall, David. 'Scepticism and deconstruction'. Unpublished paper read at the Department of English, Yale University, n.d.

Mauss, Marcel. *The gift: forms and functions of exchange in archaic societies.* Trans. I. Cunnison. New York: Norton, 1967.

Megill, Allan. *Prophets of extremity: Nietzsche, Heidegger, Foucault, Derrida.* Berkeley: University of California Press, 1985.

Meier, Paul J. 'Fundamental ontology and positive theology: Martin Heidegger's way of thinking'. *Journal of Religious Thought* (Washington) , 17 (1960), pp. 101–115.

Merleau-Ponty, Maurice. *In praise of philosophy.* Trans. John Wild and James M. Edie. Evanston: Northwestern University Press, 1963.

Merrell, Floyd. *Deconstruction reframed.* West Lafayette, IN: Purdue University Press, 1985.

Meschonnic, Henri. *Le signe et le poème.* Paris: Gallimard, 1975.

Migne, Jacques Paul, ed. *Patrologiæ cursus completus: series Græca.* 1882; rpt. Westmead, Hants.: Gregg Press, 1965. Vol. 37.

Mitchell, Solace and Michael Rosen, eds. *The need for interpretation: contemporary conceptions of the philosopher's task.* London: Athlone Press, 1983.

Montefiore, Alan, ed. *Philosophy in France today.* Cambridge: Cambridge University Press, 1983.

Moore, G. E. *Some main problems of philosophy.* London: George Allen and Unwin, 1953.

Moran, John H. and Alexander Gode, trans. *On the origin of language: Jean-Jacques Rousseau, Essay on the origin of languages; Johann Gottfried*

Herder, Essay on the origin of language. New York: Frederick Ungar, 1966.

Newman, John Henry. *An essay on the development of Christian doctrine*. Ed. and introd. J. M. Camberon. 1845; rpt. Harmondsworth: Penguin, 1974.

Nietzsche, Friedrich. *Philosophy in the tragic age of the Greeks*. Trans. and introd. Marianne Cowan. South Bend, IN: Gateway Editions, 1962.

The will to power. Trans. Walter Kaufmann and R. J. Hollingdale. Ed. Walter Kaufmann. New York: Vintage Books, 1968.

The gay science: with a prelude in rhymes and an appendix of songs. Trans. Walter Kaufmann. New York: Vintage Books, 1974.

Beyond good and evil: prelude to a philosophy of the future. Trans. and introd. R. J. Hollingdale. Harmondsworth: Penguin, 1977.

Daybreak: thoughts on the prejudices of morality. Trans. R. J. Hollingdale. Introd. Michael Tanner. Cambridge: Cambridge University Press, 1982.

Twilight of the idols and the anti-Christ. Trans. and ed. R. J. Hollingdale. Harmondsworth: Penguin, 1968.

Untimely meditations. Trans. R. J. Hollingdale. Introd. J. P. Stern. Cambridge: Cambridge University Press, 1983.

Norris, Christopher. *Deconstruction: theory and practice*. New Accents. London: Methuen, 1982.

The contest of faculties: philosophy and theory after deconstruction. London: Methuen, 1985.

'Transcendental vanities'. Rev. of *Reading deconstruction/deconstructive reading*, by G. Douglas Atkins. *Times Literary Supplement*, 27 April 1984, p. 470.

Nygren, Anders. *Agape and eros*. Trans. Philip S. Watson. London: SPCK, 1953.

O'Leary, Joseph S. *Questioning back: the overcoming of metaphysics in Christian tradition*. Minneapolis: Winston Press, 1985.

Orsini, G. N. G. *Coleridge and German idealism: a study in the history of philosophy with unpublished materials from Coleridge's manuscripts*. Carbondale: Southern Illinois University Press, 1969.

Otto, Rudolf. *The idea of the holy: an inquiry into the non-rational factor in the idea of the divine and its relation to the rational*. Trans. John W. Harvey. 2nd edition. 1923; rpt. Oxford: Oxford University Press, 1958.

Palmer, Richard E. 'Allegorical, philological and philosophical hermeneutics: three modes in a complex heritage', *University of Ottawa Quarterly*, 50 (1980), pp. 338–60.

Paz, Octavio. *Alternating current*. Trans. Helen R. Lane. London: Wildwood House, 1974.

Plato. *The collected dialogues of Plato: including the letters*. Ed. Edith Hamilton and Huntington Cairns. Princeton: Princeton University Press, 1963.

Price, John Valdimir. *The ironic Hume*. Austin: University of Texas Press, 1965.

Quintillian. *Institutio oratoria*. Trans. H. E. Butler. Loeb Classical Library. Cambridge, MA: Harvard University Press, 1976. Vol. III.

Raschke, Carl A. *Moral action, God, and history in the thought of Immanuel Kant*. American Academy of Religion Dissertation Series, 5. Missoula, MT: Scholars Press in conjunction with AAR, 1975.

Ricœur, Paul. *Husserl: an analysis of his phenomenology*. Trans. Edward G. Ballard and Lester E. Embree. Northwestern University Studies in Phenomenology and Existential Philosophy. Evanston: Northwestern University Press, 1967.

Freud and philosophy: an essay on interpretation. Trans. Denis Savage. New Haven: Yale University Press, 1970.

The conflict of interpretations: essays in hermeneutics. Ed. Don Ihde. Northwestern Studies in Phenomenology and Existential Philosophy. Evanston: Northwestern University Press, 1974.

The rule of metaphor: multi-disciplinary studies of the creation of meaning in language. Trans. Robert Czerny with Kathleen McLaughlin and John Costello, SJ. Toronto: University of Toronto Press, 1978.

'A response'. *Biblical Research*, 24/25 (1979–80), pp. 70–80.

Robinson, James M. and John B. Cobb Jr. eds. *The later Heidegger and theology*. New Frontiers in Theology, 1. New York: Harper and Row, 1963.

Rorty, Richard. *Consequences of pragmatism (essays: 1972–80)*. Brighton: Harvester Press, 1982.

'Derrida on language, Being, and abnormal philosophy'. *The Journal of Philosophy*, 74 (1977), pp. 673–81.

'Deconstruction and circumvention'. *Critical Inquiry*, 11 (1984), pp. 1–23.

Rosenzweig, Franz. *The star of redemption*. Trans. William W. Hallo. New York: Holt, Rinehart and Winston, 1971.

Rousseau, Jean-Jacques. *The social contract and discourses*. Trans. and introd. G. D. H. Cole. Rev. and augmented by J.H. Brumfitt and John C. Hall. London: J. M. Dent and Sons, 1973.

Russell, Bertrand. *Logic and knowledge: essays 1901–1950*. Ed. Robert Charles Marsh. London: George Allen and Unwin, 1956.

Ryan, Michael. *Marxism and deconstruction: a critical articulation*. Baltimore: Johns Hopkins University Press, 1982.

Salusinszky, Imre. *Criticism in society: interviews with Jacques Derrida et al*. London: Methuen, 1987.

Schelling, F. W. J. *The unconditional in human knowledge: four early essays*. Trans. and commentary Fritz Marti. Lewisburg: Bucknell University Press, 1980.

Schleiermacher, Friedrich. *The Christian faith*. Ed. H. R. Mackintosh and J. S. Stewart. Introd. Richard R. Niebuhr. New York: Harper and Row, 1963. Vol. 2.

'The aphorisms on hermeneutics from 1805, and 1809/10'. Trans. Roland Haas and Jan Wojcik. *Cultural Hermeneutics*, 4 (1977), pp. 367–90.

Scholem, Gershom G. *The messianic idea in Judaism and other essays on Jewish spirituality*. New York: Schocken Books, 1971.

Scott, W. ed. and trans. *Hermetica: the ancient Greek and Latin writings which contain religious or philosophic teachings ascribed to Hermes Trismegistus*. Oxford: Oxford University Press, 1936.

Seldon, Raman. *Criticism and objectivity*. London: George Allen and Unwin, 1984.

Seung, T. K. *Structuralism and hermeneutics*. New York: Columbia University Press, 1982.

Skinner, Quentin, ed. *The return of grand theory in the human sciences*. Cambridge: Cambridge University Press, 1985.

Smith, Margaret. *An introduction to the history of mysticism*. 1930; rpt. Amsterdam: Philo Press, 1973.

Smith, Ronald Gregor. *J. G. Hamann 1730–1788: a study in Christian existence with selections from his writings*. London: Collins, 1960.

Sowers, S. G. *The hermeneutics of Philo and Hebrews: a comparison of the interpretation of the Old Testament in Philo Judæus and the Epistle to the Hebrews*. Basel Studies of Theology, 1. Richmond, VA: John Knox Press, 1965.

Spinoza, Benedict de. *Ethics: preceded by On the improvement of the understanding*. Ed. and introd. James Gutmann. New York: Hafner Publishing Co., 1949.

Stace, W. T. *The teaching of the mystics*. New York: Mentor, 1960.

Stam, James H. *Inquiries into the origin of language: the fate of a question*. New York: Harper and Row, 1976.

Steinkraus, Warren E., ed. *New studies in Hegel's philosophy*. New York: Holt, Rinehart and Winston, 1971.

Strong, Tracy B. *Friedrich Nietzsche and the politics of transfiguration*. Berkeley: University of California Press, 1975.

Taylor, Mark C. *Deconstructing theology*. Foreword by Thomas J. J. Altizer. New York: Crossroad Publishing Co.; Chico, CA.: Scholars Press, 1982.

    Erring: a postmodern a/theology. Chicago: University of Chicago Press, 1984.

    'Deconstruction: what's the difference?' *Soundings: An Interdisciplinary Journal*, 66 (1983), pp. 387–403.

Teresa, St. *The complete works of St Teresa of Jesus*. Trans. E. Allison Peers. London: Sheed and Ward, 1978.

Tertullian. *The writings of Tertullian*. Ante-Nicene Christian Library. Edinburgh: T. and T. Clark, 1870. Vol. 2.

    Adversus Marcionem. Ed. and trans. Ernest Evens. 2 Vols. Oxford: Clarendon Press, 1972.

Ulmer, Gregory L. 'Jacques Derrida and Paul de Man on/in Rousseau's faults'. *The Eighteenth Century*, 20 (1979), pp. 164–81.

Underhill, Evelyn. *Mysticism: a study in the nature and development of man's spiritual consciousness*. 1911; rpt. New York: E. P. Dutton, 1961.

Van Til, Cornelius. 'The later Heidegger and theology'. *Westminster Theological Journal*, 26 (1964), pp. 121–61.

Verene, Donald Philip. *Hegel's recollection: a study of the images in the Phenomenology of spirit*. SUNY Series in Hegelian Studies. Albany: State University of New York Press, 1985.

Weber, Samuel. 'Closure and exclusion'. *Diacritics*, 10 (1980), pp. 35–46.

Winquist, Charles E., ed. *The archeology of the imagination. Journal of the American Academy of Religion Studies*, 48 (1981).

Wittgenstein, Ludwig. *Culture and value.* Ed. G. H. Von Wright and N. Nyman. Second edition. Oxford: Blackwell, 1980.

Wolfson, Harry Austryn. *Philo: foundations of religious philosophy in Judaism, Christianity, and Islam.* Vols. 1 and 2. Cambridge, MA: Harvard University Press, 1948.

'Philo Judæus', *The encyclopedia of philosophy,* 1967 edition.

Wolosky, Shira. 'Derrida, Jabès, Levinas: sign-theory as ethical discourse'. *Prooftexts: A Journal of Jewish Literary History,* 2 (1982), pp. 283–302.

Wood, David and Robert Bernasconi, eds. *Derrida and difference.* Warwick: Parousia Press, 1985.

Worcester, David. *The art of satire.* New York: Russell and Russell, 1960.

Yeh, Michelle. 'The deconstructive way: a comparative study of Derrida and Chuang Tzu'. *Journal of Chinese Philosophy,* 10 (1983), pp. 95–126.

Zuidema, S.U. 'The idea of revelation with Karl Barth and with Martin Heidegger: the comparability of their patterns of thought'. *Free University Quarterly* (Amsterdam), 4 (1955), pp. 71–84.

Zweig, Arnulf, ed. and trans. *Kant: philosophical correspondence 1759–99.* Chicago: University of Chicago Press, 1967.

Index of people

285

Index of people

Rosenzweig, F., 183, 223 n. 32
Rousseau, J.-J., 16, 49, 61, 113; and Nietzsche, 117–27, 141–50
Russell, B., xi, 33, 83, 112, 207
Ryan, M., 232

Sartre, J.-P., 27
Saussure, F. de, 12, 15, 20, 22, 44, 166, 228–9
Scarpetta, G., 165
Schelling, F. W. J. von, 192, 221–2, 244
Schlegel, F., 158
Schleiermacher, F. D. E., 48–9, 175, 228
Schneidau, H., 22
Scholem, G., 240 n. 5
Schopenhauer, A., 147
Seldon, R., 143 n. 6
Seung, T. K., 115, 144
Smith, M., 204
Socrates, 158, 160–1
Sollers, P., x, 139
Sowers, S. G., 53
Spinoza, B., 57
Spivak, G. C., 43–5, 66, 112, 183, 232
Stace, W., 180
Stam, J. H., 63 n. 46
Swedenborg, E., 208, 210, 224
Swift, J., 158

Tarski, A., 112
Taylor, M. C., 23, 46, 64, 119, 161, 186
Teresa of Avila, 101–2, 189–90, 208, 210, 214, 225
Tertullian, 97–101, 169
Thales, 98
Theodoret, 180
Theophilus of Antioch, 180
Todorov, T., 228
Trakl, G., 259

Ulmer, G., 120

Valéry, P., 144, 151
Verene, D., 249

Warburton, W., 33
Weber, S., 146 n. 14
Williamson, R., 192 n. 45
Wittgenstein, L., 99–101, 207, 251
Wolfson, H., 55
Wolosky, S., 63 n. 49, 66 n. 56
Woollcombe, K. J., 203
Worcester, D., 158
Wordsworth, W., 181

Yea, M., 65
Yeats, W. B., 250

Zola, E., 151
Zuidema, S. U., 257

Index of topics

289